C0-DAD-537

Staffelstein
Kulmbach
Ebrach
Bayreuth
Würzburg
Bamberg
Wiesentheid
Pommersfelden
Lindenhardt
Iphofen
Forchheim
Ochsenfurt
...eim
Erlangen
Aub
Creglingen
Nuremberg
Rothenburg ob der Tauber
Heilsbronn
Amberg
Ansbach

...isch Hall
Dinkelsbühl
Weissenburg
BAVARIA
Donaustauf
Walhalla
...sch-Gmünd
Nördlingen
Eichstätt
Kelheim
Regensburg
Neresheim
Pappenheim
Harburg
Weltenburg
Straubing
Donauwörth
Rohr
Osterhoven
...lm
Ingolstadt
Altenmarkt
Landshut
Passau
...ngen
Freising
Augsburg
Schleissheim
Altötting
Neuötting
MUNICH
Burghausen
Landsberg am Lech
Berg am Laim
Ebenhausen-Schäftlarn
Wasserburg
Diessen am Ammersee
Andechs
Rott am Inn
Ottobeuren
Wessobrunn
Laufen
Peissenberg
Frauenchiemsee
Steingaden
Rottenbuch
Herrenchiemsee
Wies
Oberammergau
Schliersee
Neuschwanstein
Benediktbeuern
Füssen
Ettal
Berchtesgaden
Linderhof
Mittenwald

CZECHOSLOVAKIA
AUSTRIA
ITALY

Art Treasures in southern Germany

0		20		40		60 M
0	20	40	60	80		K

4/50

Art Treasures in 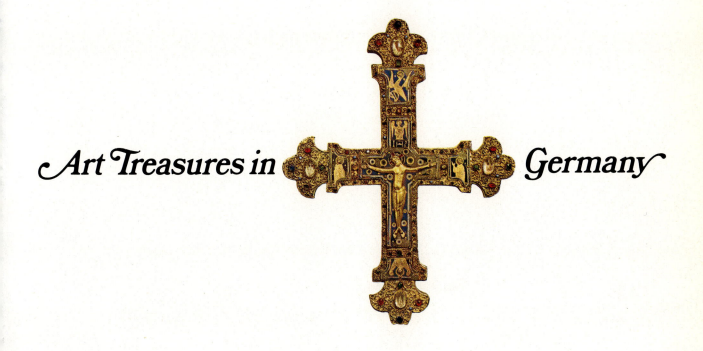 *Germany*

Art Treasures in Germany

Monuments, Masterpieces, Commissions and Collections

Introduction by Stephan Waetzoldt
Director General of the Staatliche Museen, West Berlin

McGraw-Hill Book Company

New York Toronto

General Editors
Bernard S. Myers
New York
Trewin Copplestone
London

half title illustration
Portrait medallion of a
Knight of the Golden Fleece,
c. 1450; Residenzmuseum,
Munich
frontispiece
View of Schloss Nymphenburg
from the Park, 1761, by Bernardo
Bellotto; Residenz, Munich
opposite
Winter by Balthasar
Permoser; Grünes Gewölbe,
Dresden

Library of Congress Catalog Card Number 73-76759
44229
Published jointly by
McGraw-Hill Book Company, New York and Toronto
and The Hamlyn Publishing Group Limited, London and Sydney
Hamlyn House, The Centre, Feltham, Middlesex, England
© The Hamlyn Publishing Group Limited 1970. All rights reserved.
Printed in Italy by Officine Grafiche Arnoldo Mondadori, Verona
Photoset by B.A.S. Printers Limited, Hampshire, England

Contents

Introduction

The art treasures to be seen in Germany show, even more clearly than the events of political history, that this country forms the geographical centre of Europe. The development of the visual arts there has been so determined by influences from neighbouring countries that it has seemed necessary to speak of specifically German phenomena as *Sonderleistungen* (special achievements) of German art. And it is surely significant that only one museum – the Germanische Nationalmuseum – restricts its collection entirely to German art.

The traditions of antiquity, transmitted by way of Italy and Byzantium, fertilised the art of the Carolingians, which had grown up on German and French soil. It was from France that German architecture of the 13th to 15th centuries took over a type of structure which is basic to even such individualistic architectural inventions as the late Gothic hall church and

the north German brick-built cathedral. Early German painting, particularly that of Nuremberg and Cologne, is modelled on French manuscript illumination and on Italian panel painting, this last entering Germany by way of Bohemia. Without the influence of Italy, neither the paintings of Albrecht Dürer nor the architecture of the southern German late Baroque could have emerged.

It is against the background of such diverse stimuli that the particular qualities of German art first became clear, as, for instance, the supremacy of the graphic arts. This is shown by early medieval illuminated manuscripts as well as by the incomparable drawings of Schongauer, Dürer, Grünewald, Holbein, Carstens, Schwindt, Rethel and the masters of Expressionism. German prints are of an equally high standard. Not a few artists — from Dürer and Burgkmair to the artists of the Brücke — proved themselves more successful as engravers than as painters, for at all times the Germans have expressed themselves better in line than in colour.

Another quality of the best German art is intimacy, and many fine works have been produced by artists giving expression to personal experience and emotions. Thus, among the most popular subjects for paintings are landscape (Konrad Witz, the Danube School, Elsheimer, C. D. Friedrich, Blechen, Koch, Böcklin, Thoma and Nolde) and portraiture (Cranach, Dürer, Holbein, the Renaissance miniaturists, Sandrart, Graff, Leibl and Lenbach). This same intimacy also occurs in sculpture, particularly in devotional works of a particular stamp, such as *Pietà* groups, carved figures of Christ together with St John, and the so-called *schöne Madonnen* (beautiful Madonnas).

The medieval German town, the imperial cathedrals of the Salians, the hall church, the single-tower façade of the Gothic cathedral, the characteristic German town hall, the brick buildings of the north and the abbeys and pilgrimage churches of the south . . . these are all high points in the history of European architecture. And the picture of German art would be incomplete without its applied art, whose beauty and historical importance is still too little regarded. The ecclesiastical treasures of the Middle Ages, the art of the Augsburg and Nuremberg goldsmiths during the Renaissance, the 18th-century porcelain from Meissen and Nymphenburg and the industrial designs of the Bauhaus are among the finest products of European art.

The German museums (of which there are more than six hundred) contain masterpieces of the art of all nations from prehistory to the present, for German collectors have always been internationally-minded. The large museums owe the nucleus of their collections either to a princely need for show (Berlin, Munich, Darmstadt, Kassel, Karlsruhe, Stuttgart, Dresden) or to the collecting zeal of well-to-do merchant-citizens (Frankfurt, Hamburg, Cologne). In the first case, dynastic connections had, from the outset, precluded the restriction of the collections to purely German art, while, in the second, the outlook of the middle-class merchants had been broadened by international contacts.

It was in the 19th and 20th centuries, however, when they came under professional direction, that the museums acquired their own particular stamp. As important institutions for education and research, they followed a policy of acquisition which aimed at providing, through examples of the highest quality, a complete picture of the history of art. Thus, in the museums of Germany, the masterpieces of German art are displayed as a part of the European artistic heritage within a general art-historical context. Many of the finest of these masterpieces are described and illustrated in this book.   Stephan Waetzoldt

MAXIMILIAN LEARNING
THE ARTS OF
DRAWING AND PAINTING
c. 1518
Hans Burgkmair 1473 – 1531
woodcut

Maximilian I took his title of Holy Roman Emperor very seriously, and was resolved to revive the glories of the original Roman empire in his German lands. He was a patron of the type so prevalent in Renaissance Italy, and counted among his personal friends scholars such as Willibald Pirckheimer and artists such as Dürer and Burgkmair. This woodcut is one of Burgkmair's several hundred illustrations for *Der Weisskunig*, a romance of the achievements of Maximilian's reign, believed to be largely the emperor's own work.

Celtic Europe was a vast barbarian empire, stretching from the Black Sea in the east to Ireland in the west and composed of many nations all speaking the same language, following the same customs and worshipping the same gods. Around the shores of the Mediterranean sea lay the city states of the Greeks, Etruscans, Romans and Carthaginians which together comprised classical civilisation, while in the north and north-east lived the ancestors of the German people with an economy based on hunting and primitive agriculture. Between these very different societies was situated the tribal world of the Celts.

From their formation in the 8th century BC, the Celtic tribes were influenced by the advanced techniques and art styles of the south. Indeed when the Romans seized control of the fertile lands of central Europe in the first century BC, the Celts found themselves incorporated into a civilised world that was not altogether new to them. They abandoned their tribal ways in favour of a settled life in and around cities, but their identity as a people was not destroyed.

Throughout their long history, the Celts were constantly harrassed by their Germanic neighbours, who coveted their rich land and gradually drove them westwards towards the Rhine. The Germans eventually prevailed over the Celts by sheer weight of numbers as they were later to do over the Roman army, but, fortunately, they were all the time exposed to the influences of Celtic Rhineland culture. When the Rhine frontier, which was one of the key defences of the Roman empire, was at last overwhelmed by the Franks and other Germanic peoples, the conquerors were intent on preserving the culture of the society that they found. Without the Romano-Celts of the Rhineland, the 5th and 6th centuries AD – the beginning of the so-called Dark Ages – would have been even darker.

The character of Celtic art
The rivers Rhône, Danube, Po and Rhine all rise in the Alps whence they flow north, south, east and west like the spokes of a wheel. They provided a route for the transport of goods and ideas from early times, as the references in the works of ancient writers confirm. In his *Argonautica*, written in the middle of the 3rd century BC, Apollonius of Rhodes tells how the good ship *Argo* on her voyage home from the Black Sea sailed up the Po to a lake in the Alps, around which the Daughters of the Sun sat weeping tears of amber. Amber was, in fact, brought from the Baltic by Celtic traders and sold to the Greeks and Etruscans, who greatly valued it. Other exports from central Europe to southern markets included skins, salt, metal and slaves.

Archaeology is the main source for evidence of Greek and Etruscan imports into the Celtic world. In the period from the mid-6th to the mid-5th century BC the middle Rhine region was an important centre of Celtic civilisation, richly represented by the so-called Chieftains' Graves, in which were found a very fine series of bronze and pottery vessels of Greek origin as well as objects of local Celtic workmanship. The Greeks and Etruscans regarded such articles as virtual necessities, for even the poorest households would own drinking cups and one or two bronze vessels. In the Celtic world, however, such everyday objects were priceless treasures invested with princely significance, and they are found in the strongholds and graves of mighty warriors. Indeed in one Chieftain's Grave at Klein Aspergle, Württemberg, two ordinary Greek cups were beautified by the addition of gold leaf.

Celtic craftsmen gradually adapted the artistic motifs they had seen in imported objects (for example the palmette and the face-mask) to produce a highly individualistic abstract style which was particularly well adapted

Celts and Romans on the Rhine

c. 550 BC – AD 500

I

HEAD OF A SATYR
1st century BC, if not a later copy bronze; eyes inlaid with silver
5·5 × 4·25 × 4 in (14 × 10·8 × 10·5 cm)
Historisches Museum der Pfalz, Speyer

This head from Schwarzenacker, with its enigmatic expression, matted hair and pointed animal ears, probably depicts Silenus, the wise old satyr with whom Socrates was often compared. Undoubtedly the work of a Greek craftsman, it may have been made as early as the 1st century BC and cherished thereafter as an heirloom, but it more probably belongs to the full imperial period. By the import of such objects, the artistic heritage of Greece was able to reach new areas.

for the decoration of curved surfaces. Celtic ornament is, in fact, confined almost exclusively to weapons, drinking vessels and jewellery.

Celtic art is intensely personal; no two pieces are ever alike. The warrior attempted at all times to draw attention to himself by his proud speech and deeds of valour and by what he wore. He can be compared with the medieval knight, for to both military prowess and honour were more important than life, but, unlike his more recent counterpart, he fought completely naked except for his bronze helmet and armlets and his torcs of flashing gold. These were an essential part of his equipment, for the neck torc in particular was associated with power, but he would have scorned to wear armour because he believed that glory came from victory in duels between highborn adversaries, not in the mêlée and carnage of total war. Two men engaged in such a conflict could trust in their long slashing swords with hilts finely inlaid in gold or enamel, for society accepted certain conventions which forbade anyone not engaged in the duel from taking advantage of an unguarded flank. In this lay the military weakness of the Celts in face of the land-hungry Germans or the professional Roman armies, for whom the end justified the means.

The life of a Celtic chieftain was short, for if he survived the sword-blows of his adversaries he would probably fall victim to disease in the unsanitary and flimsy habitations of his hilltop stronghold. Yet while it lasted existence was pleasant, and so it seemed natural to the sorrowing relatives of the dead man that life should continue after his death. Weapons, drinking vessels and jewellery were placed in the tomb for the use of the dead person, and, in many cases, remained there until their rediscovery in recent times by archaeologists. In France and Britain many of the best examples of Celtic art have been found in streams and bogs dedicated to the deities of the countryside, but almost all the finest pieces of Iron Age craftsmanship in Germany come from tombs.

The Klein Aspergle tomb contained drinking horns and a flagon of Celtic workmanship, as well as the adapted Greek cups mentioned above, while the site of Waldalgesheim in the Rhineland gave its name to the magnificent Celtic art style which flourished over a large part of central and eastern Europe in the 4th century BC. The Waldalgesheim style is characterised by a harmonious stylisation of classical motifs, particularly the leaf and tendril motif, and is well represented on the embossed gold torcs which formed part of the finds in the Waldalgesheim tomb. In ancient Germany as in the very early Greek society described by Homer there was equality between the sexes, at least at the feast. The tomb of a princess at Rheinheim near Saarbrücken contained a fine collection of torcs and bracelets, some of them decorated with strange masks that bear human features.

Celtic sculpture and architecture

Although the Celtic peoples of Germany valued the art of the smith above all others and accorded him a favoured position in their society, sculpture was also an important art form. Sculptors adapted techniques learned in northern Italy to the commemorative and religious art of their homeland on the upper Danube and the Rhine. At Hirschlanden near Stuttgart a sandstone figure of a warrior surmounted a 6th-century tomb. In accordance with tradition, he is shown naked except for a belt, in which he wears a short sword. On his head is a helmet and around his neck a torc. The modelling of the figure shows distinctly Greek characteristics, probably introduced from Etruria—the legs, for example, resemble those of standing archaic youths. A cruder statue from Holzgerlingen, Württemberg, has two heads; the upper part of the body is here indicated with some

2

TORC FROM WALDALGESHEIM
late 4th century BC
gold
internal diameter 7·3 in (18·5 cm)
Rheinisches Landesmuseum, Bonn

Apart from this fine torc, the rich contents of the Waldalgesheim grave included a pair of gold bracelets and two wine vessels—a flagon adapted from an Etruscan prototype and a large bucket of Italian manufacture, used as a mixing bowl. The accomplished style of the torc and the bracelets marks the final synthesis of classical and native elements in early Celtic art. An effect of great beauty is achieved with remarkable understanding of how to work within the very restricted areas provided by such items of jewellery.

3

RITUAL OBJECT FROM SCHIFFERSTADT

c. 900 BC
beaten gold with repoussée decoration
h. 11·25 in (28·3 cm)
Historisches Museum der Pfalz, Speyer

A geometric style of decoration such as that on the 'golden hat' from Schifferstadt was prevalent in central Europe from the end of the second millennium until the 6th century BC. This long period saw the emergence of Celtic-speaking communities, whose goldsmiths eventually rebelled against such monotony of form and introduced exciting new artistic concepts based on the flowing line. Despite its name the enigmatic 'golden hat' is more likely to have been used as a vessel for religious offerings than as part of a ceremonial head-dress.

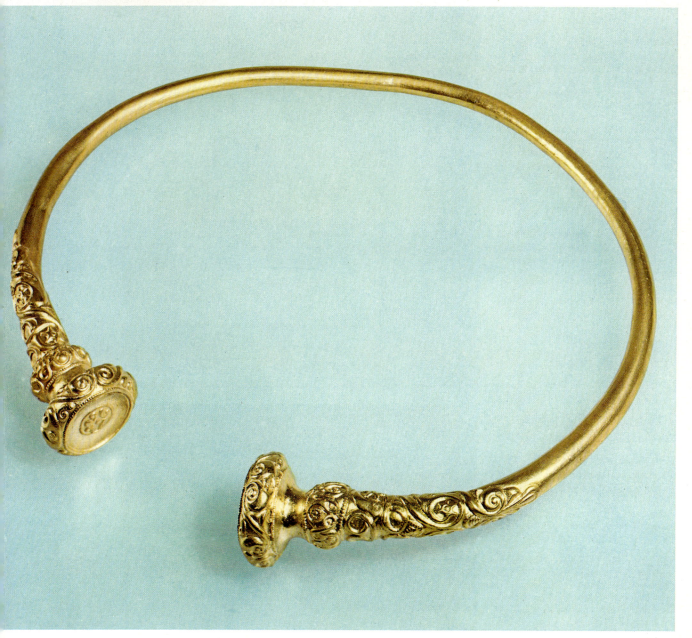

4

RITUAL SCULPTURE FROM PFALZFELD

late 5th century BC or later
coarse-grained limestone
h. 58·5 in (148 cm)
Rheinisches Landesmuseum, Bonn

Celtic sculpture was ultimately derived from the Mediterranean area, but it would be difficult to imagine an object more different in intention and effect from the familiar works of classical humanism than the Pfalzfeld pillar. Repellent human masks, surrounded by small ornament in the Waldalgesheim style, adorn its four sides, and the pillar was probably originally surmounted by a carved head. The Celts invested the head with an independent existence distinct from that of the body, an idea which recurs in their religion and legends.

5 *centre*

THE JUPITER COLUMN PLINTH

c. AD 66
limestone
Samus and Severus
Zentralmuseum, Mainz

The Jupiter Column (**6**), honouring both Jupiter and the emperor Nero, has been reconstructed from over 2,000 fragments and now consists of a column surmounted by a Corinthian capital that once supported a statue of Jupiter. Despite its early date there is no trace of any native cult surviving in the deities represented. Indeed gods such as Hercules and Apollo (portrayed upon the plinth), and the many other deities shown, were chosen for their importance in the official state religion.

6 *far right bottom*

THE JUPITER COLUMN *detail*

This section of the Jupiter Column proper shows the earth goddess Tellus, crowned with ears of corn.

7

A MOSELLE WINE BARGE

first quarter of 3rd century AD
sandstone
60 × 120 in (153 × 305 cm)
Rheinisches Landesmuseum, Trier

In Roman times, as now, wine was one of the mainstays of the economy of the Moselle region. Barges such as this one, shown on a tomb from Neumagen, must have been a common sight, although doubtless few had such elaborate prows and sternposts. Unlike Spanish wine, which was packed in amphoras, Moselle wine travelled in wooden casks, and there is evidence that it was enjoyed throughout a considerable area of western Europe, including Britain.

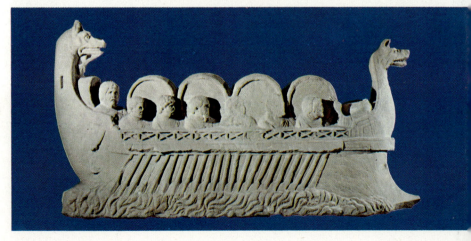

8 *above*

THE PHILOSOPHER MOSAIC
detail

early 3rd century AD
diameter of panel 38·5 in (98 cm)
Römisch-Germanisches Museum, Cologne

The mosaic floor uncovered in the garden
of the Bürgerhospital in 1844 is composed
of decorative panels and of *emblemata*
depicting Greek philosophers – Kleobulos,
Socrates, Cheilon, Diogenes – and the
dramatist Sophocles. The portrait of
Diogenes reclining in his barrel
occupies the central position on the
pavement. Themes of this nature are
known from many other places in the
empire and doubtless formed a distinct
category in mosaicists' pattern books.

competence, but the figure finishes at the waist and the lower part of the statue is uncarved. This may also be the result of southern influence, as simple fertility images called herms, in which a head surmounted a pilaster instead of a body, often stood in Greek shrines.

In the 5th and 6th centuries, artisans broke away from this alien approach to representation, and employed the Celtic style of intricate curving scrolls. The Pfalzfeld Pillar, sadly defective as it is in lacking the upper part, is one of the most striking examples of Celtic art in existence. It is in the form of an elongated pyramid, originally surmounted by a human head, and its surface is covered with masks and curvilinear relief as on the gold torcs. Very few pre-Roman sculptures survive in Germany, partly because, as focuses of pagan worship and superstition in the countryside, such sculptures were destroyed when Christianity was established. Some of those that survive (for example the pillar at Irlich near Koblenz and the monument from Pfalzfeld itself) apparently proved too powerful for the Christian evangelists, who merely had them moved or built churches alongside them, so that in the course of time the worship of idols would merge into the veneration of saints.

In architecture, the main advances made by the Celts were in the sphere of defensive building. Their settlements were fortified with timber and earth banks which were effective against all but the most determined assaults. The defences of the hill-fort of the Heuneburg in Württemberg were unusual in incorporating Mediterranean architectural ideas which demonstrate the capacity of individual chieftains to experiment. Here in the 6th century BC, a wall of mud bricks was erected on stone foundations forming a series of closely-spaced rectangular bastions in the Greek style. It was undoubtedly designed with the help of an architect from the Mediterranean and must—when approached from below—have given the appearance of a strong southern city; indeed the structure, which only surrounds one flank of the hill, was built for prestige rather than for strategic reasons. The effect of a non-Mediterranean climate on the unbaked clay bricks, however, brought this princely folly to the ground within a few seasons.

Roman Germany

The days of the Celtic Rhineland seemed to be numbered when, in the middle of the 1st century BC, Ariovistus, chieftain of the Suebi, led a mixed force of Germans westwards against the Celtic tribes, and founded German settlements on the left bank of the Rhine. Probably few of the leaders of the beleaguered Celts had seen the growing power of Rome as their salvation; even when Julius Caesar, who defeated Ariovistus in 58 BC, crossed the Rhine in 55 to assert Roman control over the Rhine frontier and thus brought Gaul and the people of western Germany under Roman rule, the conquest was by no means welcome. A few chieftains, more clear-sighted than the rest, could see the true reality—that under the protectorate of Rome their illiterate and poor subjects would move forward to literacy, wealth and the comforts of civilisation.

Julius Caesar, who created the province of Gaul in 51 BC, with the Rhine as its eastern boundary, did not attempt to extend the domination of Rome beyond the river. During the reign of Augustus, however, the frontier was, in 9 BC, pushed as far east as the river Elbe by the general Drusus (brother of the future emperor Tiberius), but he was unable to consolidate his gains. Tiberius, who replaced Drusus in the Rhineland, affirmed Rome's domination over the east bank of the Rhine in 8–7 BC.

Roman ambitions in Germany received a severe setback in AD 9, when the general Quintus Varus was ambushed in the Teutoburg Forest and his

9

THE DIONYSUS MOSAIC *detail*
2nd century AD
mosaic
diam. of octagon within border 38·5 in (98 cm)
Cologne, in situ

A splendid mosaic, measuring 10·57 by 7 metres, covers the floor of the principal room in a luxurious dwelling house in Cologne. It celebrates the pleasure of wine – a fitting theme in a place set aside for conviviality and entertainment. The mosaic is divided into fifteen main sections which show Bacchus (Dionysus) the god of wine, Pan, a cupid, satyrs and maenads, a panther and baskets of fruit. In the scene depicted here, with considerable vitality, a dark-skinned satyr is beginning to dance with a maenad.

10
DECORATIVE CARRIAGE
FITTING
2nd century AD
bronze
h. 5·5 in (14 cm)
Historisches Museum der Pfalz, Speyer

The vehicles in which Roman aristocrats travelled along the well-built roads of the empire were sometimes elaborately decorated. This attachment of unknown use, found at Eisenberg in the Palatinate, was probably from a carriage. It consists of an eagle's head confronted by that of a basilisk. The piece recalls certain Celtic chariot fittings and there is almost certainly some influence from Sarmatian art. Nevertheless, these non-classical elements have been subordinated and refined in the interests of order and simplicity.

army of three legions massacred by the Cherusci tribe under their chieftain Arminius. There are few traces of this great disaster, which soured the last days of the emperor Augustus. However, one of the finest military tombstones to survive from this time is the cenotaph of a Roman centurion, Marcus Caelius, who was killed in 'Varus's War'. He is shown with his two servants, killed with him, on a monument erected by his brother Publius outside the fortress of the eighteenth legion at Xanten.

Following the loss of Varus's three legions, Augustus abandoned any further attempt to extend Roman domination east of the Rhine. The disaster had an important long-term result in that the Rhineland was turned into a frontier district in which the army was always in evidence. The area occupied by the legions in the 1st and 2nd centuries is now crossed by the borders of Germany, France and Holland. Important roles in the Roman history of western Europe were played by the legions in their encampments at Xanten, Bonn, Mainz and Strasbourg, by the auxiliary forces in smaller forts along the river line and by the civilians who supplied the troops with necessities and luxuries. This army was a peculiar institution in that it was both a ruthless and efficient fighting force and also a medium for the education of provincials. To be enrolled in a legion, the aspiring recruit had to be a Roman citizen; provincials who had not been granted the rights of citizenship had to be content with service in an auxiliary regiment which carried a grant of citizenship on discharge. In both types of unit the Latin language was spoken, and the dress and customs of Rome were imposed on areas which regarded the toga with awe and the bath with astonishment. If common soldiers lived in such fine style, how much more did the descendants of chieftains, ambitious to mix with the Roman officers and administrators, thirst for Roman culture? Crude huts were no longer enough when it was possible to live in a house built of brick, and the old abstract art did not have the flexibility and interest of the new Roman narrative sculpture.

A typical chieftain was Julius Indus of the Treveri, who helped the Roman authorities to suppress a revolt, and married his daughter Julia Pacata to the chief financial officer of Roman Britain. As her name appears on an inscription at Trier this high-born lady seems to have maintained an interest in her home province. Friendship towards Rome was widespread, and it is not surprising to find large-scale classical sculpture being erected in honour of the Roman emperor by native Celts. Mainz boasts the remains of two fine monuments: a column and an arch. The former was dedicated **5, 6** by two merchants, Quintus Julius Priscus and Quintus Julius Auctus, to the Roman god Jupiter for the wellbeing of the emperor Nero. Its sculptors, whose names were Samus and Severus and who possibly came from the south of France, produced a very competent rendering of formal Roman relief sculpture. The lavishly-decorated arch (of which fragments survive) was set up for Jupiter and the imperial family by the heirs of Dativius Victor, a magistrate of the local settlement of the Taunenses, in accordance with the terms of his will.

One of the most important results of the Roman military presence was the growth of towns. Sometimes a colony of Roman citizens was established, as at Cologne, where the name is still a reminder of the fact. The cities became focal points for romanisation, and Mainz, Cologne and, above all, Trier flourished. Every fort, even the smallest, had a civil settlement of traders, many of whom were foreigners from distant provinces, with the result that, as time passed, the old tribal existence gave way before the attractions and opportunities of urban life. An interesting passage in Tacitus's account of the rebellion of some disgruntled Treveri

11
ALTAR DEDICATED TO JUPPITER CONSERVATOR

AD 232, limestone
43·5 in (110 cm)
Rheinisches Landesmuseum, Bonn

This altar was found early in the 17th century at Xanten (Vetera), the fortress of the 30th Legion, raised by Trajan in AD 100 and named after him. It was dedicated to Jupiter the Preserver by Tertinius Vitalis, a clerk attached to the commander of the unit, on behalf of himself and his family. It depicts Jupiter holding a thunderbolt and with his eagle at his feet standing in a niche between two richly decorated pilasters. The style is strongly classicising and the piece is of truly remarkable quality amongst the productions of military workshops.

in AD 70 indicates that, barely a hundred years after the Romans had arrived in Germany, the distinction between the conquerors and the natives was beginning to become blurred. The citizens of Cologne pointed out to the rebels that, since they had intermarried with Romans, to join the revolt was as good as to kill their parents, brothers and children.

Sepulchral art

The soldiers and civilians of Roman Germany came to share a common attitude to life and death, which is exemplified in the great quantity of sculpture and inscriptions on tombstones and in the religious dedications which have been found. Military gravestones are usually simple, consisting of a relief showing the deceased in his uniform, together with a brief inscription giving his age, length of service and the name of the person who erected the monument. The stereotyped form of the carving suggests that the masons were unofficially attached to the camp and achieved a vast output through mass-production. The facial features, however, are individualised, for the graveslab served both as a monument to the dead man and as a substitute for the portrait-bust that gave him a measure of reality in the land of shadows.

The tombstones of legionary soldiers are easily distinguished from those of men in auxiliary regiments by the inscription giving the formal Roman name of the dead man and by the distinctive legionary armour and weapons shown on the relief. Auxiliary soldiers, on the other hand, are often depicted holding the traditional weapons of their people; sometimes they are shown on horseback, either stationary or riding down a barbarian foe.

Mortality was high in the Roman army, and many men died, either in battle or of disease, before they reached middle age. The afterlife was conceived as a banquet. A number of military tombstones at Mainz, Cologne and elsewhere show the dead man lying on a couch and being served with wine. Although this theme was widespread throughout the empire, in Germany it recalled the sentiments of earlier days. It is found both on the gravestones of retired soldiers who had entered civil life and on civilian tombstones. The best illustration of the theme is a worn relief from Neumagen near Trier, with the feast depicted as a realistic family party.

The important series of tomb reliefs from Neumagen, dating from the 1st to 3rd centuries AD, were carved on the splendid monuments erected for members of the Celtic aristocracy of the lands of the Treveri, who flourished by agriculture, the wine trade and cloth production. The tombs, which were dismantled in the 3rd century, and used to build town walls as a protection against barbarian invaders, were carved with scenes taken from daily life which, in their naturalism and attention to detail, stand comparison with the best pieces from Italy.

One relief shows a great lady sitting in a basket chair while four maids assist her with her toilet. An even more engaging piece represents a schoolmaster seated between two pupils. The naturalism of the scene is such that for a moment we are transported into a Roman school, where the education based on grammar was almost identical to that provided in English schools until comparatively recent times. The world of commerce is
13 represented on a relief that depicts peasants paying taxes to the imperial tax collectors. On the table is a basket and a pile of waxed tablets for accounts. One of the officials seems to be questioning the validity of a coin, a reminder that, despite savage penalties on detection, forgery was widespread in the Roman empire. Commercial activity is also shown in a
7 famous representation of a Rhine boat carrying casks of wine, perhaps destined for the market in Britain.

Other sites have also produced fine tomb sculptures. From Hirzweiler

12

THE IGEL MONUMENT
mid-3rd century AD
red sandstone
h. 75 ft (23 m)
Igel, near Trier

This is the only large mausoleum to survive complete in the neighbourhood of Trier. The scenes shown here combine details of the daily life of the Secundinii, a family of cloth merchants, with mythological happenings. Themes include Hercules being translated to Olympus, a team of mules loaded with bales of cloth and a man standing between two griffons, which represent the all-devouring power of death.

TOMB RELIEF
OF TAX COLLECTION

early 3rd century AD
sandstone, 23 × 55 in (60 × 141 cm)
Rheinisches Landesmuseum, Trier

This relief from Neumagen depicts tax collectors taking a collection from a group of peasants. The social distinction between clerical and labouring occupations is strongly marked, both by physical differences – the tax collectors are unbearded and wear different garments from the countrymen – and also by a certain superiority of manner on the part of the officials. On the table there is a pile of waxed tablets used for taking accounts and a basket on which some of the tax has already been deposited.

14

MERCURY

late 1st century AD
bronze, h. 8·5 in (21·4 cm)
Historisches Museum der Pfalz, Speyer

The veneration of Mercury was particularly fervent in the western provinces of the empire, where he was identified with very powerful native gods. Many representations, both in bronze and stone, have been found in Germany. This fine statuette found at Odenbach is ultimately derived from a work by the 5th-century artist Polykleitos. It demonstrates how the Greco-Roman conception of deity overlaid the somewhat amorphous Celtic one, which lacked a strong visual basis. The god is shown carrying a purse which signifies his patronage of commerce.

there is a representation of a shop selling fabrics: two assistants hold out a rug with a long fringe which they are about to sell. The cloth industry is the theme of the memorial to a family of merchants – the Secundinii – which still stands at Igel near Trier. Although some of the scenes are rather worn, we can still see details of the manufacture of cloth and of the management of a large estate. Not all tombs were of this type. On the one hand, at Weyden, near Cologne, an underground vault was discovered many years ago containing stone representations of furniture and portrait busts which date to the 2nd century AD, and a sculptured sarcophagus from a later period. At the other extreme is a touching little memorial from Bonn, its Greek inscription commemorating a pet dog.

12

Religious art

Religion played a large part in the lives of both soldiers and civilians in Roman Germany. The gods and goddesses most frequently worshipped were those indigenous to the country, but they were equated with the Roman deities – thus in Trier, Mars Lenus was worshipped, while in Aachen Apollo Grannus was invoked. Even the column dedicated to Jupiter at Mainz may owe something to pre-Roman totemism, as may other pillars supporting statues of giants holding up horsemen, of which a number of examples are known in Germany. The most popular cult was, however, that of the three mother goddesses who went under such outlandish names as Vesuniahenae, Axsinginehae or Aufaniae. A magnificent relief from Bonn – one of several dedicated to the Aufaniae – shows the three goddesses sitting on a couch; two of them wear the elaborate hairstyles fashionable in the 2nd century. These native deities were worshipped in temples of distinctive design consisting of a central shrine surrounded by a colonnade. At Trier a temple quarter has been excavated, which proves the continuation of fervent religious devotion even in the largest of Roman cities.

5, 6

15

In the course of time foreign traders brought their own gods, and as the military situation became increasingly uncertain more and more people turned to the worship of Asian deities such as Cybele and Atys or the great Egyptian goddess Isis, who offered salvation to those who believed in them. Germany has provided more evidence for the cult of the Persian Mithras – the 'Unconquered God' – than almost any other part of the empire, and much fine Mithraic relief sculpture has been found there.

16

Mithras was usually worshipped in a small basilica with a nave and aisles, rather like a church except that it was often partly underground and that the aisles were filled with benches on which the worshippers reclined for the ritual meal. At one end of the building was a great relief showing Mithras slaying the bull in a cave. In the mithraeum at Neuenheim, near

ALTAR DEDICATED TO THE AUFANIAE

AD 164
limestone
h. 51 in (130 cm)
Rheinisches Landesmuseum, Bonn

This altar, found at Bonn, is dedicated to three Celtic mother goddesses (*matres*). It was erected by Quintus Vettius Severus, a local government official from Cologne, and the workmanship is fully in the classical tradition. The *matres* are conceived as three society ladies. The two older women have very elaborate coiffures, whilst the girl shown between them has long flowing hair. All are dressed in heavy mantles and hold baskets of fruit in their laps. Behind them are three figures, possibly intended as portraits of Severus and two members of his family.

16
MITHRAIC CULT RELIEF

late 2nd century AD
sandstone
35.5 × 33.5 in (90 × 85 cm)
Kreis- und Stadtmuseum, Dieburg

This cult relief erected in the mithraeum at Dieburg is one of the most unusual in the empire. One face (not shown) depicts Mithras enthroned as a sun god, and the other presents him involved in a variety of legendary scenes. The central area shows Mithras out hunting and the two *dadophori* who symbolise day and night. The often enigmatic events evoked in the border panels include the birth of Mithras from a rock, his struggles with the bull and his communion with the sun god.

Heidelberg, scenes depicted around the central relief tell the whole story of how the young god was born and a new age of the world began; he is shown mastering the bull, which breaks away at one point but is finally dragged to the cave and killed. There is a similar and even finer relief from Heddernheim, near Frankfurt am Main, while from Dieburg, near Darmstadt, comes an unusual representation of Mithras enthroned as a sun god. The fine quality of Mithraic art shows that the religion was confined to the wealthy few, especially army officers and, amongst the provincials, rich merchants. Women never had any part in the rites.

Domestic art

Unlike the pre-Roman Celts, who had few belongings other than their weapons and jewellery, the Romans lived in an acquisitive society which was based on the family group. The rooms in a wealthy man's house would have had wall paintings and mosaics and a system of underfloor heating. Although furniture merely consisted of a few tables and chairs and a low couch, the family would certainly own an assortment of pottery and glass vessels and probably a service of silver plate for use on special occasions, as well as bronze cutlery, writing materials and statuettes. Large country houses, such as the villa at Welschbillig near Trier, might contain a considerable quantity of stone sculpture. Much of the pottery and glass was made locally, particularly in the 3rd and 4th centuries, Cologne glass being especially famed because the very fine local sands allowed the immigrant Syrian glass-workers to practise their best skills. Vessels of every form and colour were made, some moulded and engraved with figure scenes, while others show a consummate handling of form. The best

17

23 pieces are the variegated cut glass *dietreta* (vases covered by a filigree-like network of pierced glass) which must have been extremely expensive to buy. Very few specimens survive complete.

There is little good surviving silver from Germany apart from the remarkable Hildesheim treasure, which was found outside the imperial frontier near Hannover, and was probably looted from the province at some time in the 2nd century. Besides fine drinking cups, saucepans, ladles and dishes, the hoard contained a silver tripod with elegantly worked feet, designed to take a large vessel. Not all the pieces were functional, some being designed purely for show, such as the bowl whose
18 centre is occupied by a medallion in high relief showing the infant Hercules strangling two snakes, or another which represents a seated Minerva. Silverware of this quality was made in the eastern Mediterranean by Greek artists and was naturally scarce. The Hildesheim treasure must have belonged to a very wealthy individual, possibly a provincial governor or a general.

The Roman art most admired today is that of the mosaicist, whose work consists of tiny cubes of coloured stone, fitted together to form either a geometric pattern or a scene showing events from classical mythology or the routine of daily life. The best examples in Germany came from Cologne and Trier.

A large house in Cologne, built in the Italian style around a courtyard, had a magnificent mosaic in one of its main rooms, consisting of a complicated geometric pattern in which were set little scenes celebrating the pleasures of wine. In the central panel Bacchus himself leans drunkenly on
9 the shoulders of a satyr, while the other large panels show the satyrs and maenads who comprise his following. Around the border are various birds, a little dog and – rather incongruously – some oysters. Near Trier, at Nennig, are the remains of a country house laid out in fine style and still conserving a good mosaic showing gladiators in the amphitheatre. Such scenes of cruelty and bloodshed were popular throughout the western empire; another mosaic with the same subject is to be found at Cologne.

Not all provincials had the same tastes and it is pleasant to record that
8 the great philosophers (including Socrates and Diogenes) are the theme of a fine mosaic in Cologne, while a mosaic at Trier, signed by Monnus, depicts the Muses and some of the more famous Greek and Roman poets. Also at Trier there is an unusual mosaic which must be connected with an otherwise unknown mystery cult – one of those strange, new religions which were brought from the East. It shows members of a religious community and depicts a ritual concerned with the birth from an egg of Castor and Pollux, the two heavenly guardians of Rome.

Cologne and Trier

With the major exception of one city, Trier, few sites in Roman Germany conserve the remains of important public buildings. In Cologne, the capital of the province of Lower Germany, the groundplan of the governor's palace has been revealed by excavation. The palace, which has few parallels in the empire, was built in the 1st century AD and later extended, a great suite of state rooms being added in the 4th century to give it more dignity. There are also very well-preserved public baths at Badenweiler, which reminds us that the Romans well appreciated the value of taking the waters at a spa.

19 However, Trier contains the ruins of palaces and baths far more splendid than these, both in conception and in their present state of preservation. Other remains include a bridge over the Moselle and a famous gateway,
21 the Porta Nigra. In the 2nd century, the city was important enough to

17

HERM FROM WELSCHBILLIG
detail

probably 4th century AD
limestone
total height of herm 51 in (130 cm)
Rheinisches Landesmuseum, Trier

More than a hundred herms (pillars of rectangular section each surmounted by a head), connected by a trellis, formed an ornamental surround to a large pool belonging to a luxurious villa near Trier. Over forty heads survive and they depict a remarkable variety of physical types, ranging from Greek philosophers to Germanic tribesmen. While some of them could be as early as the 2nd century, others exhibit later features. Certainly the youth shown here, with his long hair and neck torc, resembles Barbarians depicted on some 4th-century works.

18

ORNAMENTAL BOWL

1st century BC
silver plate, partly gilded
diameter 8·5 in (21·2 cm)
Staatliche Museen, West Berlin

Silver plate, such as that found in the Hildesheim hoard, was avidly collected by wealthy Romans. This piece is perhaps a century earlier in date than most of the other items in the hoard and was evidently a treasured family heirloom. The central relief (*emblema*) depicts the baby Hercules crushing two snakes sent to strangle him by Juno, queen of the gods. Despite the undoubted skill exhibited by the Greek artist responsible, this particular *emblema* is somewhat over-elaborate and academic.

have magnificent public baths (the Barbara Baths) and a fine amphitheatre of which remains can still be seen. In the following century German raids across the river were frequent, and in 257 they assumed the nature of an invasion which the central government was powerless to quell. The so-called Gallic empire was established by the Rhine army with strong local support as a measure of self-defence, and Trier naturally assumed the position of an imperial capital. One of the most effective of the 'Gallic emperors' was originally tribune of the guards there, and his name—Marcus Piavonius Victorinus—appears on a mosaic from what was presumably his house. After the 'Gallic empire' had again been merged into the rest of the Roman world under Aurelian, Trier continued to be an important centre, and finally, under the emperors Constantius Chlorus and his son Constantine at the end of the 3rd century, it again became the effective capital of the West.

It was at this time, if not earlier, that the great walls, which have a circumference of three and a half miles and enclose an area of over 700 acres, were built. The great north gateway, the Porta Nigra—now, as its name **21** implies, somewhat blackened with age—is an imposing monument with two passageways set between flanking towers. It was regarded as a symbol of the might of the empire.

Of the luxurious imperial palace, built at the time of Constantine, the great brick audience chamber (Aula Magna) survives, although the wall paintings and mosaics that dazzled contemporaries have now, sadly, disappeared. Fragments of wall plaster were found in the excavation of another part of the palace, and some panels from the roof have been reconstructed to show Fausta, the wife, and Helena, the mother, of Constantine resplendent in gold and jewels. These paintings may have been produced to celebrate the marriage of Constantine's son Crispus in AD 321. Soon afterwards Constantine, believing that Fausta and Crispus were guilty of adultery, had them both executed. Filled with remorse, he later pulled down part of the palace and built a great double basilica which is the origin of the present cathedral and its neighbour the Liebfrauenkirche. This great church was even larger than the basilica built by Constantine at the Vatican (Old St Peter's).

Trier also has its great bath suite, the Constantinian Baths, whose **19** apsidal caldarium (hot room) still confronts the visitor with the great sweep of its windows. The symmetrically arranged rooms were never completed as planned, and in the later 4th century this fine building was converted into yet another palace.

Christianity was the religion of the emperors from the time of Constantine onwards (with the sole exception of Julian, AD 361–63), and the excavation of Roman churches such as St Gereon and St Severin in Cologne and the cathedral at Trier suggests that in the German towns most of the leading citizens quickly embraced the new faith, although paganism probably remained dominant in the countryside. The Christian Church had the strength which the empire lacked as a military force. When the Germanic tribes took control of the Rhineland in the 5th century, they brought with them fine gold or silver-gilt jewellery of a new and strange type which owed its inspiration in part to the nomadic people of the Russian steppe and in part to Rome. They also brought their own customs and language, but the forces which proved strongest of all in the end were those of Christianity and of Rome. Under new masters, Roman Germany merged imperceptibly into the Christian empire of the Middle Ages.

Martin Henig

19

CALDARIUM OF THE IMPERIAL BATHS

early 4th century AD, limestone and brick, Trier

The ruins of the so-called Imperial Baths at Trier are among the most extensive in the empire. The baths were planned on a truly ambitious scale but the project was severely modified when the emperor Constantine decided to move his capital in AD 316. At some period during the reign of Valentinian I or Gratian, the bathing establishment was converted into a palace, and the caldarium appears to have served as a second audience chamber. It was probably here that Valentinian I was seized with his fatal heart attack in AD 375 while addressing an embassy from the German tribe known as the Quadi.

20

PARADE MASK FROM STRAUBING

probably 2nd century AD
thin bronze, h. 11 in (27·9 cm), Straubing Museum

Examples of face masks worn for manoeuvres conducted by the *auxilia* of the imperial army are known from Britain, Holland and Germany. At the fort of Straubing in Bavaria no less than five were discovered, three of which had idealised 'Grecian' features, whereas two others, including this one, are decidedly oriental in appearance.

21

THE PORTA NIGRA

probably early 4th century AD, sandstone blocks, Trier

The sole surviving gateway of Roman Trier is conceived on a truly grand scale. Evidently it was intended to impress the traveller with the fact that he was approaching a city which contained the 'sacred palace' of the emperor. However, it was never finished – the pilaster-capitals, for example, remain uncarved – perhaps because Constantine decided to move his residence to Byzantium.

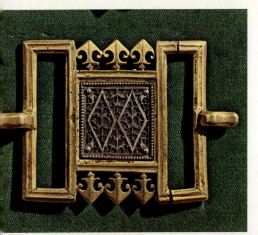

22

ROMAN BUCKLE

late 3rd century AD
silver-gilt, length 3·75 in (9·5 cm)
Römisch-Germanisches Museum, Cologne

During the period of the early empire
dress and personal ornament were
comparatively restrained. However, from
the 3rd century onwards a taste for
elaboration began to manifest itself in
objects such as this buckle from Cologne,
which were partially inspired by the art of
barbarian peoples. The belt fitting has a
central panel worked in *opus interrasile*
(a technique whereby a perforated plate
is set against a solid metal backing). Such
work foreshadows the achievements of
Teutonic smiths in the succeeding age.

23

A DIATRETON

first half of 4th century AD
cut glass, h. 4.75 in (12·1 cm)
Römisch-Germanisches Museum, Cologne

Diatreta (cage cups) were the finest and
most expensive products of the late Roman
glass industry. Their manufacture
involved the cutting of a perforated outer
network of coloured glass around an
apparently plain goblet. In view of the
great skill required for this kind of work it
is not surprising that the *diatretarii* were
honoured members of the artisan
community and even exempt from
taxation by imperial edict. This
magnificent example includes a Greek
inscription: 'Drink, live happily always.'

Throughout the centuries when Celts and Romans flourished in central Europe, the Germanic peoples had gradually been spreading from their original homeland in the north until, by the 1st century AD, they were established over an area stretching from the Rhine in the west to the Vistula in the east. The movements of these peoples, unrecorded at first, became a powerful historical force in the 3rd century AD, when the period of the *Völkerwanderungen* (migrations) began. Large parts of Europe were overrun by the so-called barbarians, and the weakened Roman empire eventually gave way before the vigorous warrior tribes.

By the 6th century, the end of the period of migrations, kingdoms had been established by the Ostrogoths in Italy, the Visigoths in Spain and the Vandals in Corsica, Sardinia and north-east Africa. No such unity existed in the area covered by present-day Germany, where five main tribal groupings—the Franks, Saxons, Swabians, Thuringians and Bavarians—were established.

Out of the chaos of intertribal feuding which followed the final withdrawal of the Romans east of the Rhine, the Franks on the middle and lower Rhine emerged as dominant. The Merovingian dynasty rose to preeminence over all the Franks, both west and east of the Rhine, in the 6th century, and these kings also tried to extend their domination to other German tribes, but with only partial success. It was to be under another dynasty, that of the 'Mayors of the Palace', who for about a century wielded the power held nominally by the Merovingian kings, that the tribes were to be unified.

Early Frankish art

The culture of the Merovingian era was naturally Germanic. Instead of the classically-oriented art productions of the Roman era, a type of art flourished which shows a mingling of influences from the east, the Latin peoples of the west and the Scandinavians of the north. Its most characteristic feature is a use of animal decoration, often reduced to almost abstract form. In its irrationality and abstraction and the rare representation of the human form, Germanic art shares some of the features of the pre-Roman Celtic art.

Merovingian art in Germany achieved its finest expression in jewellery, of which a number of magnificent pieces survive. Such jewellery is largely found in Frankish graves of the 6th and 7th centuries, since, despite the court's adoption of Christianity, the pagan custom of burying possessions with their owners persisted. One of the finest pieces is a 7th-century silver-gilt fibula set with garnets from Wittislingen in Bavaria, apparently dedicated by a wife to her husband. Eastern influence is apparent in the Byzantine techniques adopted in such jewellery, although the decorative motifs are largely Germanic. Coptic and Early Christian Syrian elements have also been discerned in Merovingian art, and indeed actual Coptic imports of the period have been unearthed in Germany. Oriental inspiration is also in evidence in pre-Carolingian manuscript illumination with its gay disorder and its animal motifs which bear no relation to the text. Examples of such manuscripts are, however, much rarer in Germany than in France.

Charlemagne's court

With Charlemagne, a new life and direction was brought to western Europe at the end of the 8th century, following the unification of the five great tribes of northern Europe and the consolidation of the Christian faith with special reference to Rome. From his father Pepin the Short (last of the Mayors of the Palace and first king of the new dynasty) Charlemagne inherited a kingdom stretching from western France to the borders

The Merovingians, Charlemagne and the Ottonians

c. 500 – 1024

24

LORSCH ABBEY GATEWAY

c. 800

Although the gateway at Lorsch could never be mistaken for an Italian building, the underlying principle is based on the design of a similar entrance at Old St Peter's in Rome. The building reflects Charlemagne's desire to revive the heritage of Rome, as can be seen in such features as the three arches flanked by engaged columns, and the fluted pilasters above them.

39

25
THE PALATINE CHAPEL
late 8th century
Aachen

The octagon of the Palatine chapel is perhaps the finest surviving example of Carolingian architecture. Built under the emperor's personal supervision, this was the most splendid of the many churches and abbeys founded under Charlemagne. For political reasons, Charlemagne took a great interest in strengthening the Church. His work in this direction was based on that of St Boniface, who largely re-organised the church in Germany during the 8th century following its near-collapse towards the end of the Merovingian era.

26
THE FOUR EVANGELISTS
early 9th century
manuscript
Cathedral Treasury, Aachen

The gospel book from which this page is taken is an example of the work of the New Palace School of the Carolingian court. The style of this school of illumination is closely related to that of Hellenistic painting. In strong contrast with the slightly earlier Ada group of manuscripts (**38**), also from the palatine scriptorium, both the colours and the composition are subdued. The figures of the Evangelists, mainly in white with touches of red, are set against a simple bluish-grey background.

of Saxony, and during his own lifetime the emperor's territory was extended to include the Spanish Marches, Saxony and the major part of the Italian peninsula. Although he travelled much throughout the empire, Charlemagne always regarded his capital, Aachen (Aix-la-Chapelle), as his home, and stayed there often during his later years.

Charlemagne had the highest regard for the Byzantine emperors, and it is fitting that the Palatine Chapel at Aachen should have been modelled **25** on the church of San Vitale at Ravenna, a 6th-century building that represents the great architectural achievement of a majestic Byzantine ruler, Justinian. The Palatine Chapel was built for Charlemagne by Bishop Odo of Metz, and dedicated to the Virgin by Pope Leo III in 805, just five years after Charlemagne's celebrated coronation as Holy Roman Emperor in Rome. In comparison with the complex interlocking subtleties of design at San Vitale, this northern chapel may at first appear to be over-simple, but the architect had clearly absorbed the principle of an octagon with a projecting apse. Later, the apse was replaced by a soaring 14th-century choir, but the impact of this sturdy Carolingian building is by no means destroyed. The two tiers of arcading are ornamented with marble columns especially imported from Ravenna and Rome, and both levels are lit by a single window on each face of the octagon. Originally the chapel formed only part of the great plan of a palace with first-floor galleries leading away on the north side to the residential quarters. A better idea of the exterior of the church may be gained from the later so-called Karlsschrein, **44** on which the chapel is depicted being dedicated to the Virgin by Charlemagne. Charlemagne richly endowed the chapel with religious relics and sacred vessels. The throne from which the emperor followed the services and which was used as a coronation chair throughout the Middle Ages is still in the gallery facing the altar.

At Aachen, Charlemagne gathered numerous scholars and advisers about him, including Peter of Pisa and Alcuin of York. The academy of learning founded under the guidance of these scholars was based on classical lines, and there was a conscious desire to revive the standards of Roman literacy. Many of the Roman classics are known to us only as a result of the Carolingian copies made there. At the same time, there was a return to the correct use of Latin and a development of a clear, legible script, known as the Carolingian miniscule. The illuminations of the gospel books made at Aachen are grouped together under the heading of the Palace School and, like the Palatine Chapel, they reflect Charlemagne's **26** devotion to the Byzantine culture. Much of the text was written on vellum dyed to a deep purple colour and the illustrations are of a sensitivity that suggests the actual presence of artists from Byzantium. One of these remarkably beautiful gospel books remains in the cathedral treasury at Aachen.

Other treasures of Carolingian art
The copying of manuscripts was not restricted to the court at Aachen. Many churches and abbeys were founded as part of Charlemagne's political-educational programme for his empire, and, in connection with these foundations, scriptoriums and art workshops were also established and subsidised by the emperor.

A fine Carolingian manuscript, known as the Ada Gospels, is in the cathedral treasury at Trier in the Moselle valley. This contains a poem referring to 'mother Ada, servant of God,' and is traditionally supposed to have been commissioned by a sister of Charlemagne. Full-page illustra- **38** tions of the Evangelists at their desks preface each of the gospels. By comparison with the Aachen Gospels the illustrations may seem more prosaic, and yet with their firm outlines, the sense of figural composition and the controlled colouring the illuminations are technically far in advance of anything else made at that date.

Manuscripts contain the most representative examples of painting from these early days, simply because they have been protected within the confines of cathedral and municipal libraries, away from strong sunlight and damp weather. By contrast, very little fresco painting of the Carolingian age has survived and the preservation of the few figures from the walls of the crypt of St Maximin at Trier is a characteristic accident of history. In 882, marauding Norsemen destroyed the church and the crypt was afterwards walled up, thus protecting the paintings, which probably date from the late 9th century, until modern times. On the back wall of the crypt is a painting of the Crucifixion and also a Procession of Holy Martyrs arranged beneath a painted colonnade.

Charlemagne, like his father Pepin, readily appreciated the value of strengthening the church for the good of the state and he sent many of his theologians to reform and develop monastic foundations. Remains of Carolingian monastic architecture are rare, however. At Lorsch there remains a three-arched gateway that once formed the entrance to an important 8th-century abbey church, traditionally the burial place of Louis the German and other royal personages. The rest of the monastic buildings there were destroyed during the Thirty Years War, but the gateway, with rounded arcading at ground level and fluted pilasters decorating the upper storey, is one of the most characteristic examples of architecture of the Carolingian era. The ruler's admiration of Roman architecture can be discerned in the use of attached colonnettes and classical capitals as at Aachen, but the diapering (small repeated patterns) and other decorative effects are the invention of 8th-century architects.

For the evolution of medieval architecture, the most important contribution of the Carolingians was the development of the westwork, the massive block-like façade that dominates so many churches in Germany and other areas north of the Alps. The idea seems to have originated in the north of France at St Riquier and Corbie, but quickly spread to Germany where it was used in the Benedictine abbey of Corvey on the Weser, founded in 822 by monks from Corbie. The towering west end of the late 9th-century church has retained its original form. With its twin towers and projecting entrance porch, the building behind must have been effectively masked by the façade.

Apart from such isolated examples little remains of Carolingian architecture in Germany, partly because these early monastic foundations, as they grew in importance, modernised their buildings in order to keep abreast of structural and technical achievement, and partly because the choice of stone and brick as building materials was by no means universal and many wooden churches must have since perished.

The other medium in which Carolingian artists excelled was in the so-called 'minor' arts of metalwork and ivory carving. The lavish manuscripts were bound between wonderfully wrought covers, decorated in gold relief and studded with precious gems. Also, the liturgy called for ceremonial objects such as ivory stoups and pyxes, and precious relics were contained in elaborate caskets. A splendid example of intricate metalwork still forms the cover to the 9th-century Codex Aureus of St Emmeram of Regensburg, now in the Staatsbibliothek, Munich. The outside border of the cover has pearls and green and blue gemstones set in golden filigree. In the centre part is a relief figure of Christ in Glory, surrounded by the Evangelists and scenes from the Saviour's life. Here, the figures are

27

COVER OF THE CODEX AUREUS

c. 870
gold set with pearls and gems
Bayerische Staatsbibliothek,
Munich (clm. 14000)

The binding of the Codex Aureus of St Emmeram of Regensburg is a magnificent example of Carolingian metalwork. The lavish use of gold filigree and precious stones is here combined with delicately chased religious images. In detail each scene is a masterpiece, the slender figures being handled with a great feeling for movement and vitality. The central panel, which is raised above the other reliefs, shows Christ in Majesty. The codex was produced for the emperor Charles the Bald, probably at Rheims or St Denis.

28

CORVEY ABBEY CHURCH

873–885

A rare example of a Carolingian westwork is preserved in the church of the Benedictine abbey of Corvey. Such massive west ends, which had their beginnings in Carolingian architecture, were to become one of the most characteristic features of Romanesque churches. This view of the interior shows how the thick walls are carried on solid piers of masonry. Above, the weight of the wall is lightened by the introduction of arcaded openings.

delicate and full of movement reflecting the manuscript illuminations made at Rheims at that date. The whole book appears to have been made in France, and the illuminations are the greatest masterpiece of the court school of Charles the Bald, grandson of Charlemagne. It was presented by Charles to the Benedictine convent founded over the tomb of the 7th-century martyred bishop of Poitiers, St Emmeram.

Just as Charlemagne succeeded in uniting the greater part of Europe under a single ruler, the arts too surpassed the narrow confines of small nations to develop into an international style such as was not to be seen again until the International Gothic style of the 15th century emerged.

Art centres under the Ottonians

The Carolingian empire was too dependent on the powerful personality of Charlemagne to be held together by his successors. In the division of lands between his three grandsons at the Treaty of Verdun in 843, the countries of Europe as they are today began to emerge, the area to the east of the Rhine being apportioned to Louis the German. The ensuing century was a period of political unrest in the German lands, during which the minor duchies fought to acquire lands and political supremacy. Political power became stabilised in 936, however, when both Franks and Saxons agreed that the Saxon duke Otto should be king; significantly, this Saxon was crowned at Charlemagne's old capital of Aachen. Crowned Holy Roman Emperor in 961, Otto I became the first in a dynastic line of rulers which played a highly important role in Europe throughout the 10th and early 11th centuries. As art patrons, he and his successors endowed many religious foundations with treasures and elaborate manuscripts.

The art of the Ottonian period was, as opposed to the more international Carolingian art, a product of the German genius. Combining Carolingian elements with influences from the Eastern empire (particularly following the marriage of Otto II with the Byzantine princess Theophano), a new style arose which achieved its finest expression in manuscript illumination. Here, the Ottonian stamp is seen in dramatic gestures and noble faces and in the expression of spiritual depth.

The most important centre for illuminated manuscripts was at Reichenau, a monastery situated on an island at the western end of Lake Constance and therefore on the direct route taken by the emperors to Rome. It seems likely that the monks of Reichenau had books of the late classical period in their possession, for one of the early manuscripts made there, the Codex Egberti (Stadtbibliothek, Trier), contains obvious borrowings. This book was made about 985 for Archbishop Egbert of Trier, who was the emperor's chaplain and chancellor of the empire, and it seems that its principal artist may have soon moved to Trier, for the style, characteristic of manuscripts from Trier, did not persist at Reichenau. Most typical of the Reichenau manuscripts are the gospel book and apocalypse prepared for Emperor Henry II and his wife as a gift for the Cathedral of Bamberg between 1002 and 1014. Classical artists of earlier centuries had tried to indicate depth in a painted scene by use of subtle gradations of colours fading towards the skyline, and the artists of Reichenau took up this idea without understanding its prime function. Thus, scenes in the Gospel Book of Henry II (Staatsbibliothek, Munich) are set against bands of solid colour that deny any impression of depth. The figures themselves are painted with immense strength and the faces have a visionary quality. This manner of treating the human figure is particularly apt for the dramatic events shown in the Bamberg Apocalypse, a manuscript which still remains in the city after which it is named. The energetic tension of such scenes as the Angel with the Millstone seems to be an innate charac-

29

29

THE FIRST RIDER

c. 1007
manuscript
Staatliche Bibliothek,
Bamberg (cod. A II 42)

In 1007 Henry II founded the church of St Stephan at Bamberg and it seems likely that the manuscript known as the Bamberg Apocalypse, which was ordered from Reichenau as a gift for that foundation, was made at the same time. The subject of the Apocalypse was obviously ideally suited to the dramatic visionary style that was so successfully expounded by the artists of Reichenau.

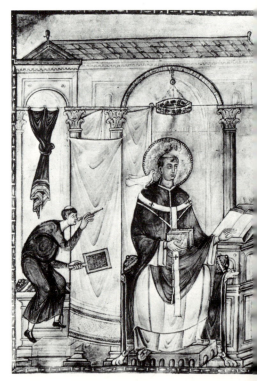

30

STORM IN THE SEA OF GALILEE

999–1021
manuscript
11·4 × 5·6 in (29 × 22 cm)
Landesbibliothek, Darmstadt (MS 1640)

The gospel book made for Abbess Hitda of Meschede is illustrated with a series of delightful scenes handled in a free painterly manner that contrasts with the stark dramatic outlines of Reichenau paintings (**29**). The Ottonian scriptorium at Cologne, of which this is a product, was based on the New Palace School of Charlemagne. Its earliest important works, including the Hitda Codex, show Greek influence in the iconography, the backgrounds and the use of colours.

31

ST GREGORY IN HIS STUDY

c. 983
Master of the Registrum Gregorii
manuscript
Stadtbibliothek, Trier

This is one of the two surviving miniatures from the Codex of the Registrum Gregorii, which was produced for Archbishop Egbert and presented by him to the cathedral in Trier in the late 10th century. Several other important works of illumination have been attributed to the same artist, whose style has a serene classicism which suggests that he may have travelled to Rome.

teristic of German art, Dürer's apocalyptic scenes having the same fervour.

By contrast, the manuscripts prepared at Trier under the auspices of Archbishop Egbert are much more serene. No artist of this time is known by name, but one – the so-called Master of the Registrum Gregorii – was obviously a highly gifted and original man. Only two pages of the Registrum Gregorii survive; one of these, in the Stadtbibliothek at Trier, **31** shows St Gregory in his study. The scene is handled with simple outlines and a realistic sense of colour that gives an entirely different impression from the bold, expressive forms of Reichenau illuminations. St Gregory is set within a small building of the classical type and is separated from his deacon Petrus by means of a draped curtain; some attempt has been made to set the figures in space and the draperies have an adequate sense of volume. The Master of the Registrum Gregorii seems to have set the style for the whole scriptorium at Trier, for all the manuscripts made there during the Ottonian period to some extent reflect his art.

Under Archbishop Egbert a school of ivory carvers and goldsmiths also flourished at Trier. The cover of the Codex Epternacensis (now at Nuremberg) has enamels and semi-precious stones set in filigree around a central ivory panel of the Crucifixion. The portable altar of St Andrew in the cathedral treasury at Trier is a magnificent example of the goldsmith's art. The altar, surmounted by a reliquary in the shape of a foot to contain St Andrew's sandal, is richly decorated with jewels and enamel set in gold and ivory. The whole is supported by four seated lions.

The presence of a single Carolingian manuscript in a monastery library often became an important factor in the development of the style of the scriptorium, as can be seen at Regensburg. The Sacramentary of Henry II, (Staatsbibliothek, Munich), produced at the monastery of St Emmeram in the beginning of the 11th century, clearly reflects the earlier Codex Aureus of Charles the Bald, a longstanding possession of the monastery.

At Cologne, where Gero was archbishop from 969–76, yet another style of illumination was developed. Gero himself commissioned a gospel book for the cathedral from Reichenau (Landesbibliothek, Darmstadt), but at Cologne the style of painting was inclined to be more delicate and sensitive, as seen in the Hitda Gospel Book (also in the library of **30** Darmstadt). This manuscript was made for Abbess Hitda of Meschede (978–1042), during the episcopate of Heribert (999–1021). At about the same time, the goldsmiths of Cologne made the famous Golden **41** Madonna of Essen at the request of Abbess Matilda of Holy Trinity, a grand-daughter of Otto I. One of the earliest free-standing statuettes of the Virgin, it is made of wood heavily overlaid with beaten gold.

Just as Archbishop Egbert was responsible for the major artistic achievement at Trier, so Bernward stands out as a remarkable patron at Hildesheim, a town situated to the north-west of the Harz mountains. Before succeeding to the bishopric in 993, Bernward had been the tutor and advisor to the young Otto III and chaplain at the imperial court. On several occasions he accompanied his young pupil to Italy and the art of Early Christian Rome is reflected in all his commissions. The bronze doors, which are now in the cathedral at Hildesheim, are the earliest **42** medieval examples of such doors to have been cast in one piece. Each is divided into panels, one door showing scenes from the Book of Genesis and the other scenes from the Life of Christ. The design and handling of the figures is highly sophisticated and compares most favourably with the much later Mosan metalwork of Renier de Huy. Bernward's fascination with both pagan and Christian Rome is even more evident in the bronze Paschal Candlestick, which is an imitation of the column erected in Rome **43** by the emperor Trajan to celebrate his campaigns. In just the same way as Trajan's campaigns are shown on the column, the Life of Christ is depicted in a continuous band of narrative that spirals around the candlestick. Both the doors and the candlestick were made for Bernward's Church of St Michael, which has recently been restored after war damage, **40** so that one may now have a good idea of the original appearance of the church. Under construction throughout the episcopacy of Bernward, the church, completed by 1033, had eastern and western transepts with towers over the crossings. The nave arcade is a simple elevation of the alternating type and decoration is restricted to a superb series of carved **61** capitals. The fine painted roof dates from the time of a rebuilding which began at the end of the 12th century.

Imperial-sponsored architecture

Many of the churches in Cologne also suffered extensive damage during the Second World War, but surviving parts of the Benedictine foundation of St Pantaleon date from the Ottonian era. The arcaded gallery and twin towers on the façade of this church, built in the time of Archbishop Bruno, a brother of Otto I, are typical of the early German westwork.

By far the most impressive Ottonian church to have survived is the **33** Convent of St Cyriakus at Gernrode. It was founded by a Saxon margrave in 961, and the emperor Otto II later took a personal interest in its construction. The basic design is that of an Early Christian basilica with an aisled nave and semi-circular apse, but the nave arcade has an alternating system of pier and pillar supports and a gallery runs over the aisles in the manner of many later Romanesque buildings. As at St Pantaleon, Cologne, St Cyriakus has a raised block-like façade flanked by tall circular towers. Another purely Romanesque feature is the use of pilaster strips and blind arcading for the exterior decoration of the fabric.

In 1024, Conrad II, first of the Rhine Frankish Salian house, succeeded Henry II as emperor and moved his court to the Rhineland. Among other building enterprises, Conrad set about rebuilding the old Cathedral of Speyer, which he planned to make the dynastic burial place of the Salians. Little of the existing church above ground can be safely attributed to Conrad and yet it was he who determined the immense size and scale of the cathedral – at that time, only St Peter's in Rome and Mayeul's abbey church at Cluny in France were larger. Conrad's church appears to have been complete by 1061. The impressive crypt with its stout columns, crowned by cushion capitals and supporting groin vaulting, seems to be part of Conrad's enterprise. It supports the whole of the transept and the apsidal sanctuary of the upper church.

Apart from Speyer Cathedral, Conrad II also founded the Benedictine monastery of Limburg an der Hardt, which was completed by 1042. Today, Limburg is merely an imposing ruin, and yet the influence of Cluny's abbey church is discernible in the monumental proportions of its design. In plan, the aisled church terminated in three projecting apses; the crossing was crowned by a central tower. It is difficult to define the precise moment when medieval architecture may be termed Romanesque. From the purely technical point of view, Romanesque architects were intrigued with the possibilities of spanning a wide space with some kind of stone vaulting and to this end walls became thicker and more articulated. Limburg is by no means as adventurous as the second building campaign at Speyer in the late 11th century, and yet the interest in piers with attached pilasters and the general conception marks a turning point in German architecture and heralds the great achievements at Speyer, Mainz and Worms.

Sabrina Mitchell

32

FIRST CROSS OF MATILDA
973–982
gold set with enamel, pearls and gems
Cathedral Treasury, Essen
h. 17·75 in (45 cm)
The crucifix of Matilda, abbess of the convent of the Holy Trinity at Essen, was made in Cologne at a time when that city was renowned for its fine metalwork, and it is the earliest extant work from that workshop. A small enamel plaque portraying the abbess and her brother, Duke Otto of Bavaria and Swabia, is inlaid beneath the figure of Christ.

33

ABBEY CHURCH OF ST CYRIAKUS

961–970s
Gernrode

The abbey of St Cyriakus was founded by Gero, margrave of the Eastern March, in 961. The church, built under the auspices of the emperor Otto II, is one of the best preserved examples of Ottonian architecture. In this view, from the gallery, the interior is given the appearance of a complexity which it does not in fact possess, for the main space of the church is a simple rectangle in three storeys – an arcade, a gallery and a clearstory.

34

THE CHURCH OF ST MICHAEL

791–822
Fulda

St Michael's in Fulda is one of the oldest churches in Germany. The crypt and the rotunda above it date from around 822, when the church was consecrated, although the rest of the building belongs to the 11th century. It was restored in the mid–19th century. The rotunda, shown here, was largely modelled on Old St Peter's in Rome, and is thus yet another instance of the Carolingian reverence for the Eternal City.

35

CROOK OF A BISHOP'S STAFF

c. 1008
Cathedral Treasury, Hildesheim

The crozier at Hildesheim is yet another
witness to the remarkable patronage of
Bishop Bernward. The works of art
commissioned by him are a curious
mixture of inspiration from the past and a
feeling for something completely new.
The crook, with its figures arranged
among foliate interlace, was made soon
after the year 1000, and yet it would not
have seemed out of fashion a century later.

36

THE TRANSFIGURATION

c. 1000
manuscript
Bayerische Staatsbibliothek,
Munich (cod. Lat. 4453)

The Gospel Book of Otto III is a
supreme example of the Reichenau
school of manuscript illumination. The
monastery at Reichenau was an imperial
abbey under the Ottonians, its abbot being
directly responsible to the emperor. It may
at one time have been the principal centre
of imperial art. In this *Transfiguration*,
Christ and the two men dominate the
scene, set against a plain background. The
stylised handling of the Mount of Olives
only enhances the emotional impact.

37

CHRIST IN MAJESTY

10th century
ivory
7·5 × 5·1 in (19·1 × 13 cm)
Staatliche Museen, West Berlin

The carved ivory cover for a gospel book
is a work of the Palace School at Aachen.
It is distinctly classical in style, and this
fact, together with the high standard of
workmanship, suggests that the artist had
good classical models on which to base
his work – probably items from the
imperial collection. Within the mandorla,
Christ is surrounded by cherubim and by
the sun and moon, while the symbols of
the Evangelists fill the four corners of the
cover

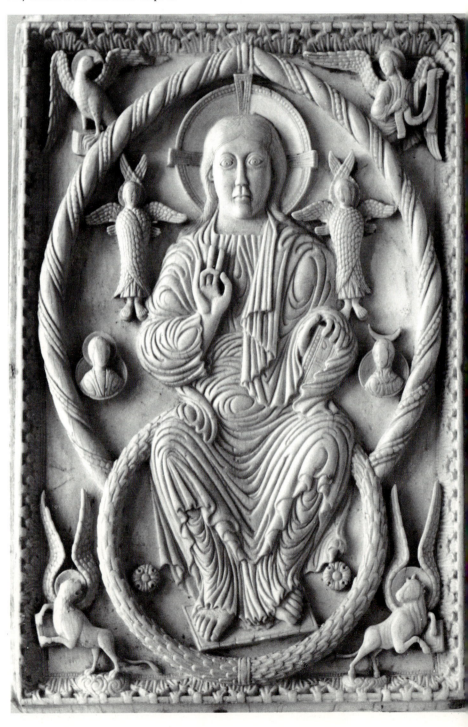

38
ST MARK

c. 800
manuscript
Cathedral Treasury, Trier

The Ada Gospels, from which this
magnificent page comes, give the name
to a stylistically related group of
manuscripts made in the court circle of
Charlemagne. In contrast to the Palace
School (**26**), the Ada manuscripts are
painted with a feeling for rich colours,
including the use of gold. The crisp
outlines contrast with the delicate
linearism of Palace School works.

39
FRANKISH JEWELLERY

7th century
silver-gilt, gold and precious stones
diameter of circular brooch 3·1 in (7·9 cm)
Bayerisches Nationalmuseum, Munich

For many years the art of the Franks was
simply dubbed 'barbaric', and yet the
filigree and inlaid precious stones on their
jewellery are worked with considerable
finesse. The jewellery illustrated was found
at Wittislingen in Bavaria, in a rock-cut
tomb, apparently the grave of a Christian
woman. The large fibula bears a Latin
inscription addressed to Uffila
(presumably the husband of the dead
woman) and swearing fidelity to him.

40

CHURCH OF ST MICHAEL

c. 1015
Hildesheim

St Michael's Church at Hildesheim was the centre of Bishop Bernward's patronage. Both the Paschal Candlestick (**43**) and the famous bronze doors (**42**) were made to adorn its fabric. The present building, though restored, recaptures some of the church's original splendour.

41

THE GOLDEN MADONNA OF ESSEN

c. 1000
wood covered in gold, filigree,
gems and enamel
h. 29 in (74 cm)
Cathedral Treasury, Essen

Free-standing statues of the Virgin became popular during the 13th century, when they were treated with a tenderness of expression typical of the current Gothic idiom (**73**). How different is this early Romanesque example, with its strict outlines, firm bulk and sense of hieratic power. The Madonna, like the crucifix in the same treasury (**32**), was made for Abbess Matilda of Essen.

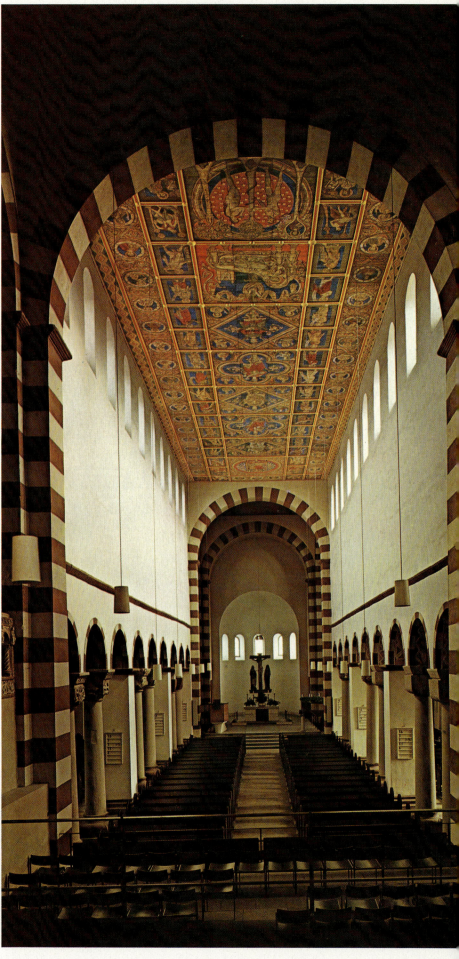

THE HILDESHEIM DOORS *detail*

c. 1015
bronze
each panel approximately 21·5 × 37·5 in
(54·6 × 95·2 cm)
Cathedral Treasury, Hildesheim

These bronze doors were commissioned
by the great patron Bishop Bernward for
the church of St Michael in Hildesheim.
As a young man, Bernward had travelled
to Rome as tutor to the young Otto III
and had become interested in its art. The
Hildesheim doors are reminiscent of the
5th-century wooden doors of Sta Sabina
in Rome, yet the design of the
individual panels harks back to
Carolingian manuscript illuminations.

43 *above*

BERNWARD'S COLUMN *detail*

c. 1020
bronze
height of column 12 ft 5 in (3·79 m)
Cathedral Treasury, Hildesheim

The tall column, intended as a monumental
Paschal candlestick, is ornamented with a
continuous narrative of the Life of Christ
in twenty-eight scenes which spiral
upwards. It is unique in northern art of the
period, and was obviously inspired by the
Column of Trajan in Rome, which
Bernward must have seen during his
travels. As Trajan's Column celebrated
triumphs of the emperor, Bernward's
column was intended to show Christ's
triumph on earth.

During the 11th and early 12th centuries Germany was dominated by the emperors of the powerful Salian dynasty, which succeeded that of the Ottonians in 1024. The visual magnificence of the cathedrals and art treasures created under the patronage of the Salians is an important symbol of their authority. Like the Ottonians before them, the Salian rulers initiated specific imperial programmes of building and commissioning, the basis of which was an appeal for recognition of the legitimacy of their rule. One of the greatest phases of imperial patronage began after 1080 with the refurbishing of Speyer Cathedral by the emperor Henry IV.

Although the new building was, like works of the Ottonian period, based on an appeal to the past, it is not a rebirth of Ottonian architecture but rather the introduction of an avant-garde style. One of the reasons for this was the medieval attitude to proof and progress. It has been stated that the most radical advances at this time were suggested as returns to sound earlier practice; thus, in the field of architecture, if a builder wished to make innovations, one of the surest methods of swinging the opinion of those who mattered was to claim that he was merely re-establishing what had been achieved by builders in former (and presumably better) times. Historical accident also played a part in the formation of the new style. To the northern emperors, whether of the 9th, 10th or 11th centuries, the great imperial past meant Italy, and naturally they did not always choose their models with antiquarian thoroughness. Unlike the Ottos, Henry turned not to Rome but to Lombardy, where the Early Christian tradition had been replaced by a massive, solid, vaulted, Lombard style. Thus the new Speyer has the first nave vault in Germany, and, in fact, one of the widest in Romanesque architecture, approaching fifteen metres. Even the side aisles would make respectable churches.

The reason for the reconstruction of the cathedral, which was not necessitated by any collapse or catastrophe, probably lies in the religious conflict in which Henry IV became involved during his reign. Lacking the piety and tact of his father, he tended to estrange the supporters of the movement for religious reform which had begun in the 10th century and which was centred on the gigantic and powerful Benedictine order at Cluny in France. He was thus opposed to the papacy, at this period in many respects an arm of Cluniac policy, and to some high churchmen in Germany. In the 1060s he quarrelled with the archbishops of Cologne and Hamburg, and 1077 saw his dramatic confrontation with Pope Gregory VII at Canossa where, threatened with deposition, Henry begged for forgiveness and absolution. The pope's openly avowed aim of making himself the material as well as spiritual lord of Christendom was quite sufficient to cause Henry to look to his imperial laurels, and he cannot be blamed for seeing the Cluniac order as something of a fifth column to be resisted as steadfastly as the recalcitrant bishops of his own empire. In the light of this conflict, the rebuilding of Speyer Cathedral takes on a clear significance, especially as the enormous third church at Cluny began to go up in the same decade.

The cathedrals of Henry IV

For Henry the reconstruction of the cathedral was very much a family affair, partly because of his immense pride and personal interest in the undertaking, and partly because nepotism was one of the few reliable methods of getting done what one wanted. In 1090 John of Kraichgau, his nephew, became bishop of Speyer, and in 1097 a personal follower named Otto was placed in charge of the workshops. One of the most interesting characters connected with Speyer was Benno, the anti-reformist bishop of Osnabrück. He was 'well versed in the art of architecture'

45

44
THE CHARLEMAGNE SHRINE
early 13th century
silver-gilt, copper-gilt, enamel,
filigree and gems
whole shrine 80·25 × 37 × 22·5 in
(204 × 94 × 57 cm)
Cathedral Treasury, Aachen

Long after his death the emperor Charlemagne was venerated as a saint in the church he had built at Aachen. His relics were translated in 1215 to the magnificent shrine known as the Karlsschrein in the presence of the emperor Frederick II. Charlemagne is here portrayed sitting between two other saints and holding the church on his outspread hand.

45
SPEYER CATHEDRAL
c. 1030–60 and c. 1080–12th century

Speyer Cathedral, founded *c.* 1030 by the emperor Conrad II, remained closely connected with the imperial Salian family until the death of its last member, Henry V. Its greatest patron was Henry IV, who initiated the rebuilding of the cathedral in the 1080s. In this view of the east end the most immediately obvious characteristics are clarity and power. The first is achieved by the careful visual separation of all the different parts of the church, and the second is expressed by the verticality of the towers and the solidity of the masses.

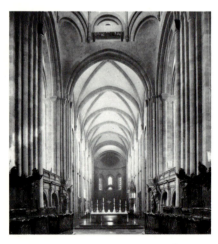

46
MAINZ CATHEDRAL
1080s–12th century

The cathedral at Mainz was one of the objects of the imperial patronage of Henry IV in the 11th century. After its destruction by fire in 1081 (one of several such disasters) the cathedral was rebuilt on a yet grander scale. The interior is marked by a contrast between the firm forcefulness of the solids and the spacious openness of the voids between them. Much of this may be due to the aesthetics of the modern restorers, but it is a happy result.

and in a very practical manner it would seem, as his chief service to the cathedral was in saving it from being undermined by the waters of the Rhine. The imperial connection of Speyer was sealed by Henry's burial there in 1106, following that of Conrad II, builder of the crypt, and of Henry III. With Henry's death, building activity slowed down, but even when the transepts were repaired in the 1160s the initial concept was retained, and Italian influences were prominent. The groin vaults of the 1090s were replaced by ribs with a square profile, which derive, ultimately at least, from Italy. Below these the walls were thickened to take niches treated in an Italianate manner.

The present Cathedral of Mainz is very like Speyer in both form and **46** history. Its arcades are cut through massive walls so that the rectangular section of the piers is clearly expressed. The main arches of the elevation are giant orders, rising above arcade level and enclosing blind areas below the clearstory windows. Both groin and rib vaults are used.

The grand Ottonian church had been partially burned down in 1081. Rebuilding, again under the auspices of Henry, proceeded until his death in 1106 when his biographer's lament at the loss to the city indicates that it was not yet finished. The cry—alas Mainz!—is an apposite one since a jinx with remarkable powers of persistence seems to have attached itself to the building in the 11th century. The cathedral of Archbishop Willigis was razed to the ground by fire on the very day of its consecration in 1009, so that the unfortunate man had to recommence work immediately. Over the next two hundred years fires were a commonplace occurrence, interspersed with an earthquake and even a hurricane. However, continual complaints about the state of the fabric and the protraction of building operations until the 13th century were due as much to a simple shortage of cash and a superabundance of riot and civil disorder as to the depredations of nature.

In sculpture, as in architecture, the predominant influence in the reign of Henry IV was from Italy, the imperial 'homeland', particularly in the field of architectural sculpture, the most important type during the Romanesque period. This again is first clearly seen at Speyer in the 1080s, where carvings on one window in the south transept very closely resemble carvings on the apse of the church of Sant' Abbondio in Como. The result is a paradoxical juxtaposition of classical acanthus capitals with anti-classical reliefs in the Lombard manner, showing triple-stranded thongs sprouting foliage inhabited by birds and exotic beasts. An even closer correspondence exists between carvings in the south-east porch of Mainz Cathedral and those on the north-east door of San Fedele in Como and on the pulpit on the Isola San Giulio in Lago d'Orta.

The minor arts in the 11th century

Surprisingly, the direct influence of patronage on stylistic changes in the minor arts (chiefly ivories, metalwork and manuscripts), is much more difficult to pinpoint than in the case of architecture and sculpture. It is clearest up to the middle of the 11th century, as most royal books have, as much for political as for artistic reasons, resplendent imperial portraits based on Byzantine prototypes. There is so much variety, however, that one cannot define a royal school, or even say that all other styles were dependent on court manuscripts. This point is illustrated by the contrast between the hieratic representations of Otto II in the Registrum Gregorii (*c.* 980) and Conrad II before Christ in the Golden Evangelistary of Speyer (*c.* 1045) on the one hand, and the much more impressionistic pictures in the Evangelistary of the abbess Hitda of Meschede (*c.* 1030) on the other.

In the field of the minor arts, the candlesticks, crozier, crucifixes and **35** bronze column and door produced in the workshops of Bishop Bernward of Hildesheim set the tone for the whole of the 11th century. In bronze doors and candlesticks the Hildesheim tradition was in fact still dominant in the middle of the 12th century, when the Magdeburg doors (now in Novgorod) and the Brunswick Candlestick (*c*. 1170) were produced.

Byzantine influences

The years around 1100 saw a reorientation of artistic production, directly or indirectly dependent on Byzantium. There is no political event such as a convenient marriage or church-state conflict to explain why this is so, nor is it certain that the first crusade was of cultural importance for Germany, which was sulking in its quarrel with the papacy and racked by internal

47
PORTABLE ALTAR OF ABDINGHOF ABBEY

c. 1100–20
probably Roger of Helmarshausen
copper-gilt
4·6 × 7·3 × 12·2 in (11·8 × 18·5 × 31 cm)
Franziskanerkirche, Paderborn

This portable altar is similar enough in style to the better-known altar by Roger of Helmarshausen, in Paderborn Cathedral, to be attributed to the same craftsman. The side illustrated here depicts the martyrdom of St Blaise; on the left he is shown being tortured, while on the right we see his beheading. The harshness of the engraver's style is well suited to the subject matter, the jerky movements stressing the violence of the episode.

trouble precipitated by the impatience of Henry IV's sons at their father's longevity. Although evidence of the influence of the Byzantine empire may be interpreted as another manifestation of Henry's interest in Italy, natural intermediary for influences from the East, there are two arguments against this. The first object in which the new style occurs, the portable altar of St Kilian and St Liborius in Paderborn Cathedral of *c*. 1100, has nothing to do with the court, and further, its chief stylistic connections are with paintings in the ambient of Cluny, namely frescoes at Berzé-la-Ville and illuminations in a Cluniac manuscript of Ildefonsus now in Parma. Whether Cluny in this case is dependent on Germany or vice versa, or whether both separately derive from Italy, this Byzantine-influenced group of works introduces a hard, architectonic style into northern Europe which remains paramount until the arrival of a further Byzantine wave in the third and fourth quarters of the 12th century as German interests spread eastwards.

The Paderborn altar, made by Roger of Helmarshausen for Bishop Heinrich von Werl, shows a versatile application of the new 'damp-fold' technique, which expresses form by surrounding large, empty, salient areas with a series of tightly-packed, near-parallel lines forming tight curves and staccato angles. The result, whether in half relief or merely engraved, is a highly stylised figure which nevertheless manifests its debt to real forms simply because the lines are ultimately derived from natural fold patterns. A refined version of this style occurs in the Annunciation page of the Gengenbach Evangelistary of around 1120. The statuesque figures of the Virgin and St Gabriel stand out boldly in front of rectangles of bright colour which make no pretence of being anything other than a background plane. This style lies at the root of one of the greatest English manuscripts of the century, the St Alban's Psalter, produced in the second quarter of the 12th century and now, fittingly enough, in Hildesheim.

The portrait of the first Hohenstaufen emperor Frederick Barbarossa **48** with his sons in the Weingarten Chronicle of the 1180s is still in this style,

48
FREDERICK BARBAROSSA AND HIS SONS

c. 1180
manuscript
Hessisches Landesbibliothek, Fulda, (MS D.11)

On this page from the Weingarten Guelph Chronicle the three figures represent the emperor Frederick I (Barbarossa) of Hohenstaufen between his two eldest sons, the future emperor Henry VI and Frederick, Duke of Swabia. Their identity is shown by the inscriptions above their heads as well as by the accompanying text. This representation of members of the Hohenstaufen family in the Weingarten Chronicle was a result of the emperor's having acquired Weingarten from its ruler Welf VI in 1179.

perhaps because Frederick, like his great predecessor in the previous century, Henry IV, preferred a traditional style (the old High Romanesque) to a more developed 'modern' one. Although old-fashioned, the portrait is a work of no mean accomplishment. Frederick's taste was not always so conservative, however, as is indicated by the portrait bust of himself which he gave to Otto of Kappenberg, probably in the 1160s. In this representation of the vigorous German emperor, who strove for thirty years to subjugate Italy and succeeded in extending imperial authority to Burgundy, Bohemia, Poland and Hungary, the face is barbaric and stylised to give an impression of cruelty. The upper eyelids are particularly extreme, sagging down across the cheek bones towards the ear, and echoed above by two ridges. The eyebrow is treated like a piece of rope and is perfectly arched. Head hair and beard consist of stylised curls. The base was made in a different shop from the head, under the orders of the recipient. The three figures of angels actually bearing the load are in a gentler style, dependent on the metalwork and manuscript ateliers of the Meuse Valley, in Belgium.

Shrines of Cologne

The Low Countries and Salzburg fostered two of the most important progressive schools of 12th-century art in the empire. Though these lie outside modern Germany, the Meuse school at least shows close connections with Cologne. Unlike the artists responsible for the Paderborn altar, the Gengenbach Evangelistary and the Weingarten Chronicle, those of the Meuse and Cologne workshops display an understanding of Byzantinising models which increases consistently throughout the century. An example of work from Cologne is the shrine of St Heribert made to receive his relics in the late 1160s. St Heribert himself, seated on one end of the shrine, relates much more gently and naturalistically to the background and the base of the panel than does the Christ on the Paderborn altar. Similarly the two saints flanking Christ in the latter work are frontal, rigid mannikins with downward-pointing toes and stiff, metallic drapery. The figures of Charity and Humility on the Cologne shrine, on the other hand, bend and turn more or less gracefully towards the saint. There are of course iconographic reasons for the frontality of the earlier work, but the stylistic change is nonetheless quite clear. The seated figures on the long sides of the reliquary are like the Paderborn Christ but slightly elongated and with all sharp edges rounded off. Their bodies are less stumpy and their demeanour more relaxed. This increasing understanding of Byzantine models is at the same time a move towards both naturalism in itself and the naturalistic sources of Byzantine art, namely Greek and Roman bronze and stone sculpture. Consequently it is not surprising to find in the last quarter of the 12th century the development of new types of drapery technique which must depend directly on antique statuettes.

The greatest exponent of this classicising style, Nicholas of Verdun, has left a perfect example of his work in the Cathedral of Cologne in the form of a shrine made to house the relics of the Three Magi. Here the figures are nearly of normal proportion, their movements are free and there are obvious bodies beneath the clothing. The drapery is able to express mass and movement because it is so unrestricted and flowing in character, being made up of a multiplicity of fine channels. This manner of handling cloth may be compared with that on the antique statue of Augustus as commander of the Roman legions or the figures carved in relief on the Ara Pacis in Rome. The head of the prophet Daniel is equally classicising and may have been modelled from a cameo.

It is worth noting that this object is a reliquary and not just a monument.

49

BUST OF
FREDERICK BARBAROSSA

between 1155 and 1171
bronze gilt with eyes inlaid
height of head 9·5 in (24 cm)
Kappenberg Church

The bust was a gift of the emperor
Frederick Barbarossa to his godfather
Otto of Kappenberg, who added the base
with its Atlas-like angels. Otto donated
the object to his local church for use,
rather inappropriately, as a container for
the relics of St John the Evangelist. The
agile character of the angels is in marked
contrast to the hieratic rigid and staring
representation of the emperor.

50

CHOIR SCREEN

1186
stucco and stone
Church of St Michael, Hildesheim

The outer face of this screen is highly
ornamented with foliage in the form of
palmettes and interlacing acanthus leaves,
as well as with a series of angels seated
frontally in the lunettes between the
arches. The architecture and decoration
are both characteristic of the mid-12th
century in Germany, with the exception
of the angels, which are much more
antique in style than earlier figures and
represent the 'transitional' phase between
Romanesque and Gothic.

These unlikely relics, the bones of the Three Wise Men who disappear
from the scene of the biblical narrative after rendering homage to the
infant Christ, are supposed to have been acquired by Milan from Con-
stantinople at some unspecified date. Their traceable history begins in
1159 at the siege of Milan by Barbarossa. As the church in which they
were kept, Sant' Eustorgio, lay outside the walls, the Milanesi abandoned
it and moved the relics into the city, but in vain, for after the success of the
siege they speedily constituted part of Frederick's loot. The shrine was
constructed for them some time after their arrival in Germany.

Late Romanesque architecture and sculpture

So successful and so impressive was the type of architecture and sculptural
decoration imported and developed in the late 11th century that it
dominated the whole of the 12th century far beyond the end of the
Salian dynasty and even retarded the acceptance of Gothic in the 13th.

For this reason the west end of Mainz Cathedral, built between 1200
and 1250, is in substantially the same style, though more complex, as the
11th-century east end. Worms Cathedral, begun in the 1170s, and completed by 1234, retains the height and the clifflike walls of the earlier
buildings, and is vaulted throughout, though the more advanced rib has
ousted the old-fashioned groin. At Worms east and west ends are equally
stressed by apses and groups of towers opposite one another. The placing
of the entrances on the north and south side and not at the west end indicates that the logic of this 'double-ended' arrangement had been accepted.
Italianisms such as arched corbel tables (ranges of stone projections running
below the eaves) still characterise the exterior, and the sculpture on the sills
of the east windows is clearly derived from that at Mainz.

12th-century German sculpture, like architecture, remains traditional,
following models laid down in the late 11th century and hence continuing
to be dependent on architectural work in Italy. This occurs both on a small
scale, as in the Augustinian abbey of Hamersleben, near Halberstadt, and
on a large scale, as in the aisle portal of Königslutter Abbey, which is a
pastiche of Italian ideas. The nightmarish and essentially anti-humanistic
nature of this type of carving is well illustrated by the south porch of St
Jakob at Regensburg. Here the main sculptural elements bulge forward
out of flat areas of wall flanking the door, bounded by attached columns
and blind arches. It is difficult to discern any iconographic programme.
The sculptor's interest is taken up by half-length lions emerging from the
base moulding, and by griffins and dragons of a gross, almost pneumatic
type, so that one of them looks more elephantine than reptilian.

The new humanism of 13th-century Gothic sculpture owes nothing to
this tradition, but it is probably connected with the large figures produced
in Ottonian times. The standing figures on the Holy Sepulchre at Gernrode are a late manifestation of this type, around 1100. Classicising forms
are again popular by 1180. Examples of these are the superb free-standing
crucifixion and the series of imposing apostles seated under arches in
the Cathedral of Our Lady in Halberstadt. The choir screen at Hildesheim **50**
of 1186 is again strongly dependent on antiquity. Whereas in France
this classicising trend manifested itself on church façades and especially
portals, in Germany and Italy it is more frequent on items of church
furniture.

13th-century French influence

French influence on German Gothic sculpture makes its appearance much
later, around 1240, in the Visitation group at Bamberg. The figures of **65**
Mary and Elizabeth stand against piers inside the church, unlike the statues
from which they are derived on the façade of Rheims Cathedral. The

style of the whole can be described as a semi-digested German version of a French view of antique sculpture, but the result is certainly individual. One of the chief motives for this turning to France was doubtless an appreciation of the chivalric and kingly ideal embodied in the person of King Louis IX. French court manners, like French architecture, were the most widely respected and copied in the 13th century. An explicit 51 example of such influence occurs in the statue known as the Bamberg Rider. The rider has his index finger hooked through his cloak-fastener in a very mannered gesture – perhaps a sign of good breeding – which also occurs on a figure of a king at Rheims.

63   The figures on the tomb of Henry the Lion (duke of Saxony and Bavaria and enemy of the imperial Hohenstaufen family) in Brunswick Cathedral, were made about 1230, some thirty years after the duke's death. The drapery has the same semi-rational quality as that of the Visitation group, mixing natural folds with stylised curves and angles, while the faces have the same odd impish expression. Also posthumous are the 54 figures of patrons carved for the piers of the choir at Naumburg Cathedral which belong to the third quarter of the 13th century; these are portraits in the sense that they represent individuals, though they are not the specific worthies whose names they bear.

13th-century sculpture always keeps something of a German quality. In architecture, on the other hand, the purity of the early Gothic style is at first mitigated by local elements and attitudes, and then around 1250 French buildings are virtually recreated in the empire.

64   The Church (now Cathedral) of St George at Limburg an der Lahn probably has the finest site in Europe. Perched on a low cliff above a sweeping bend in the river Lahn, its spiky silhouette makes it resemble a product of the imagination of a 19th-century romantic. Begun by Henry, count of Limburg, in the early 13th century, it was consecrated in 1235. Although the structural features of the building are Gothic, their nature is counteracted by a bulging Romanesque weightiness. Whether this dilution was due to Count Henry's wishes or simply to the character of his architect it is impossible to say. Whereas Limburg is a Gothic conception which has been reduced by means of Romanesque forms, the archi-56 tecture of the Cistercian order, exemplified by the abbey of Maulbronn, is Romanesque with Gothic characteristics, onto which certain new elements have been added, producing an effect not unlike that of Limburg.

66, 68   In contrast to both of these, Cologne Cathedral, built only a decade or two later, was designed on the lines of Amiens Cathedral, with a few changes which are reflections of even more advanced formulae from the Ile de France.

Painting, like sculpture, retains a distinct indigenous aspect throughout 61 the 13th century. The paintings on the ceiling of St Michael's, Hildesheim, of the early 13th century, are in the same mixed Romanesque and Gothic style as characterised the tomb effigy of Henry the Lion. The Bamberg Psalter of around 1230 is also illuminated in a semi-Gothic style, but one in which the traditions of the Byzantine empire are recognisable. Forms, especially complex drapery folds, are outlined in white, creating a strange, electric effect which has given rise to the term *Zackenstil*.

Except at the very beginning, the arts in the empire in the two centuries under discussion drew their inspiration from elsewhere, but by means of various changes, in themselves often quite small, transmuted this into something which is clearly recognisable as German, whether on building site, slab or page.

Eric Fernie

51

THE BAMBERG RIDER
c. 1230–40
Bamberg Cathedral
This lifesize figure has not been identified. Similarities with figures of kings at Rheims have led to the suggestion that it is Conrad III of Germany or Stephen of Hungary. However, the horse and rider may well have formed part of a religious tableau such as the Adoration of the Magi.

52 *above*

BAMBERG CATHEDRAL

dedicated 1237

Bamberg Cathedral was founded as early as 1004 by Henry II, but this first structure was destroyed by fire in 1185. The rebuilding was started in the first quarter of the 13th century under Bishop Egbert. As can be seen from this view from the south-west, the cathedral is double-ended, with an apse at the west as well as the east end. The main mass of the building is very Romanesque in its solidity and opacity, but the west towers, built some thirteen years later, show French Gothic influence.

53 *left*

THE ADAM PORTAL

c. 1230–40
Bamberg Cathedral

The three figures of St Peter, Adam and Eve occupy the jambs on the right-hand side of the portal known as the Adam Portal. They are closely dependent on the sculpture of Rheims, and are thus avant-garde works. Their setting, on the other hand, is old-fashioned. The figures of Adam and Eve are of particular interest in that they are monumental nudes, unusual for that time.

54 *far left*

DONOR FIGURES OF EKKEHARD AND UTA

after 1249
Master of Naumburg
Naumburg Cathedral

This pair of figures is one of several representing the founders of Naumburg Cathedral with their wives. Despite their appearance of being portraits, the representations are both posthumous – Ekkehard, who was margrave of Meissen, died in 1046. The figures are invested with a type of 'ideal particularity', and are clearly intended to give an illusion of reality, which must have been rendered complete by the painted decoration.

55

WISE VIRGINS

c. 1240–50
stone
Magdeburg Cathedral

The magnificent sculpture of Magdeburg
Cathedral, which is heavily dependent on
the slightly earlier work at Bamberg, has
been attributed to three different masters.
One of these was responsible for the figures
of the Wise and Foolish Virgins which
here, for the first time, form the
sculptural theme of a whole cathedral
portal. The maidens stand in niches
beneath a canopy, the wise ones holding
their lighted lamps and smiling happily.

56

MAULBRONN ABBEY:
CLOISTER WALK AND
CHAPTER HOUSE

c. 1220–60

This view shows two later additions to the
12th-century Cistercian abbey of
Maulbronn – the first cloister walk of *c.*
1220 and the chapter house, built around
1260. The latter is one of the earliest
examples of the full Gothic style in
Germany. The slim colonnettes and bar
tracery have a typical Gothic lightness,
and decoration is held to a minimum.
These characteristics are far removed from
the weightiness and elaborate decoration
of the late Romanesque, but have much in
common with the chief qualities of
12th-century Cistercian buildings.

57 *right*

ST MARK

1050–70, paint on parchment
12·8 × 18 in (32 × 45 cm)
Hessisches Landesbibliothek, Fulda
(codex A. a. 44)

The gospel book from which this
sumptuous page is taken was produced at
the monastery of Hersfeld, a Carolingian
foundation. The illumination shows St
Mark, who is identifiable by his symbol,
the strange-looking lion above his head,
from which he appears to be waiting for
inspiration. The scroll held in the beast's
paws may represent the transmission of the
text to the evangelist. The Ottonian
ancestry of the decoration is apparent in
its richness, as for example in the
multicoloured column shafts.

58
THE PRESENTATION IN THE TEMPLE, AND THE BAPTISM OF CHRIST

before 1065, wood
panel approximately 18 × 30 in (45·5 × 76 cm)
St Maria im Kapitol, Cologne

The doors originally belonged to the entrance into the north transept of the church dedicated in 1065. The panel illustrated is one of thirteen, all set in borders of interlace. The two scenes show Christ as an infant being presented to Simeon in the Temple, and as a full-grown man at the start of his earthly ministry. The iconography of the Baptism is odd in that the river Jordan is symbolised by a sea monster from Greek mythology, which may be doing double duty as a symbol of evil crushed by the Saviour.

59
CRUCIFIX

c. 1100–30
copper and silver plated with niello
4.6 in (11·7 cm)
Minden Cathedral

The Christ of this fine Romanesque crucifix has all the characteristics of the type known as Christ in Triumph, in which the Saviour is shown as having defeated death on the cross. There is no suggestion that he is suspended from the nails through his palms. Instead he stands on the footrest, seeming to hold his arms out in some form of gesture. There is, however, a sense of pathos, expressed in the set of the shoulders and neck and the cast of the eyes and mouth.

60
THE RELIQUARY SHRINE OF ST HERIBERT

c. 1150–70
copper and gilt, enamel and gems
whole reliquary 27 × 16·5 × 60 in
(68 × 42 × 153 cm)
Heribert Church, Cologne-Deutz

The shrine is a container for the wooden box in which are kept the relics of St Heribert. Heribert, who was Archbishop of Cologne from 999 to 1021, was a friend of the emperor Otto III, who consequently bestowed his patronage on Cologne. The saint's relics were transferred in 1147, but for stylistic reasons it is unlikely that their sumptuous container was made immediately.

61 *far right*
THE FALL

c. 1225
paint on wood
St Michael, Hildesheim

This representation of the Fall of Man forms one of the panels of the celebrated Hildesheim painted ceiling, which is in a perfect state of preservation. The picture is bisected by the Tree of Knowledge, while the pervading influence of the Tree is neatly expressed by the repetition of the apple as a form of pattern over the large circle which encloses the protagonists.

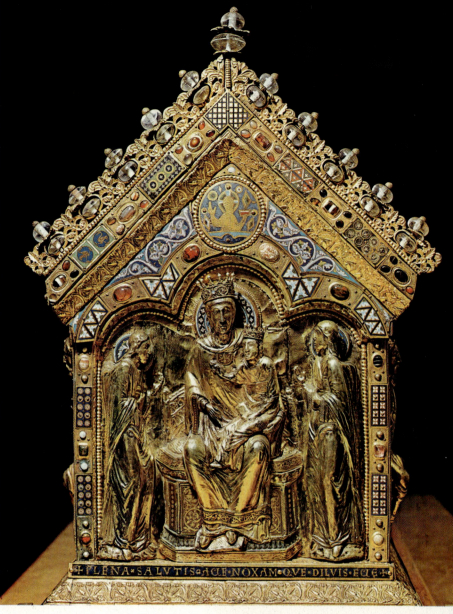

62
DOMED RELIQUARY

c. 1175
gilded copper and walrus ivory
h. 16·4 in (41 cm)
Kunstgewerbemuseum, West Berlin

This reliquary for the head of a saint forms part of the magnificent Guelph treasure, which consists of north German goldwork of the 12th–15th centuries. The treasure was for a long time, until the early 1930s, in the possession of the grand dukes of Brunswick-Lüneburg. The reliquary is constructed in the form of a Byzantine cross church with a dome in the centre. It is decorated with scenes from the Life of Christ and figures of prophets, saints and apostles.

63

**HENRY THE LION
AND HIS WIFE MATHILDA**

c. 1227
stone
Brunswick Cathedral

Henry the Lion had wished to be buried in
the cathedral which he had built at
Brunswick. Unfortunately, however,
this was burned down, and its
replacement was not dedicated until 1227,
over thirty years after Henry's death in
1195. The style of these tomb effigies is
that of the second quarter of the 13th
century. Henry, who is represented as a
man of about thirty although he was
sixty-five when he died, is holding a model
of his cathedral.

48

THE VIRGIN OF THE VISITATION

c. 1230–40
Bamberg Cathedral

The figure of Mary is one of a pair which were probably originally portal sculptures, but which are now inside the church, arranged at right angles to one another and on different levels. It is necessary to imagine the original relationship of the figure of the Virgin with that of the older and more forbidding Elizabeth, in order to make sense of the extraordinarily mannered style of the former, with her dimpled cheek and swaying hip.

64 *left*

CATHEDRAL OF ST GEORGE

completed 1235
Limburg an der Lahn

The Cathedral of St George at Limburg an der Lahn, the building of which was initiated by Henry, Count of Limburg, early in the 13th century, is representative of the transition in architecture from the Romanesque to the Gothic. This view of the interior is taken from the gallery above the ambulatory which runs round the apse. In the foreground lies the sanctuary with the altar.

above

The complex silhouette of Limburg Cathedral, together with its fine setting, give the building a certain romantic appeal. The great number and variety of the towers make it difficult to believe that the church is not a centralised building. It is, in fact, a longitudinal nave with a cross or transept arm. The main tower and spire mark the crossing, while the next largest pair of towers is placed at the west end.

During the early medieval period in Germany cultural life had been dominated by the aristocracy, both secular and ecclesiastical, and imperial patronage had been of particular importance. Significant political and social changes, which were eventually to have their effect on the artistic scene, followed the death of Frederick II, the last great Hohenstaufen emperor, in 1250. From that year until 1273 the Holy Roman Empire suffered the so-called interregnum, or *kaiserlose Zeit* (time without an emperor), which all but plunged the whole of Germany into civil war.

The extinction of the Hohenstaufen dynasty put an end to all chances of a unified Germany under strong centralised government. Power lay in the hands of the seven electors, while the emperors whom they elected, thwarted of real authority, sought to increase the wealth and possessions of their own families and by so doing laid the foundations for the future greatness of dynasties such as the houses of Habsburg, Wittelsbach and Luxemburg. Patronage of the arts thus continued to be an activity of the great noble families as part of their efforts towards self-glorification.

At the same time a new social force – young, vital and dynamically expanding – was emerging in the shape of the bourgeoisie, in whose hands lay the economic growth of Germany. They turned the larger towns into 'free imperial cities' owing allegiance direct to the emperor, and grouped themselves together for mutual protection and to further international trade, forming such leagues as the Hanseatic League. The rising middle classes and the increasing prosperity of the towns were undermining the authority of the nobility, but nearly a hundred years were to elapse after the death of Frederick II before the bourgeoisie was able to make any real impact on German art as a whole.

Continuation of aristocratic patronage

The first half of the 13th century, when the German Romanesque reached its peak and blended happily with the new Gothic style introduced from France, was one of the greatest in the history of German art. The impact of such works as the Bamberg Rider and the Naumburg donor figures was felt in many parts of Germany, but already a new spirit was perceptible which was transforming these classically conceived figures into more individualised, more complex but less noble, less heroic beings. The sculpture of Meissen Cathedral dating from around 1270, which derives directly from Naumburg, exemplifies this. The builder of Naumburg was Bishop Dietrich of Wettin and the series of donor figures mentioned above, typical of the heroic phase of aristocratic feudalism, represent a glorification of the house of Wettin.

The period from the mid-13th to the mid-14th century in Germany, sometimes described as the *ritterliche Spätzeit* (late chivalric age), was heavily dependent on France. The small landowners and petty princes were too impoverished and too preoccupied with their own struggle for survival to sponsor any great artistic projects. They clung to old-fashioned ideas and preferred their art to be reminiscent of past greatness. Superficial charm, generally rather coarser than that of French models, often concealed an underlying emptiness and artificiality.

Nevertheless, under the patronage of the rich nobles and bishops and with the vast resources of the church and of the powerful elector states, aristocratic art was still worthily sponsored, and the period was by no means lacking in works of outstanding quality. New cathedrals and churches were built freely in all parts of the country, now in the fully developed Gothic style. Through the organisation of the building yards, to whom teams of sculptors were attached, the main centres had widespread influence over those parts of the country in which they lay. Cer-

1, 54

67

The Great Age of Religious Art

c. 1250 – 1450

66

INTERIOR OF COLOGNE CATHEDRAL

choir built 1248 – 1322

The model for the new choir of Cologne Cathedral, begun after a fire in 1248, was that of the cathedral at Amiens in France. Cologne Cathedral had originally been founded in the 4th century and was rebuilt on its present site by Archbishop Hildebold around 800 AD. The gift of relics of the Three Wise Men, given to Archbishop Reinald von Dassel in 1164 by Frederick Barbarossa, established the cathedral as one of the great pilgrimage centres of Europe.

67

EMPEROR OTTO I *detail*

c. 1270
Meissen Cathedral

The donor figures of Otto I and the empress Adelheid were originally intended as decoration for the west front of Meissen Cathedral. Though lacking the heroic grandeur of their prototypes at Naumburg, they are nevertheless works of high sculptural quality. They are among the earliest art-works representative of the 'late age of chivalry', and show the typical German characteristics of broad rather fleshy faces and heavy solid bodies. Yet they are already individualised with personal expressions and a superb vitality.

68

COLOGNE CATHEDRAL
external detail

choir built 1248—1322

The rebuilding of Cologne Cathedral after the fire of 1248 was begun at the east end, the choir being completed by 1322. The rest of the building proceeded more slowly. The transept and nave were unfinished when plans for the towers at the west end were made; these, too, were left uncompleted. It was not until the 19th century, after the discovery of the original plans, that the cathedral was finally fully completed (**199**).

tain types of architecture became associated with particular areas; this was the case with the hall church (in which all the aisles are of the same height and share a single roof) in Westphalia and brick buildings in the north.

Early Gothic in Cologne

In Cologne, the new cathedral begun in 1248 adheres rigidly to the formal and technical principles of Gothic architecture. The town itself was eminently suited to be a leading centre for the new age. As well as being the seat of one of the most important archbishoprics, covering an area stretching westwards from Westphalia far into French-speaking territory, it was one of the richest towns, a centre of international trade, with contacts in England, France and the Netherlands. It was thus international in character and wide open to influences on all sides. Here, too, were concentrated the many conflicting spiritual and intellectual features that were so characteristic of the whole period and gave it its varied picture. It was an intellectual centre of the highest order. The great British philosopher Duns Scotus spent some time teaching there, as did Albertus Magnus, one-time professor in Paris. Among his pupils was St Thomas Aquinas, who represents the culmination of medieval scholasticism. In addition, it was also a centre of the new mysticism which swept Germany in the troubled times of the interregnum, offering to the poor and the distressed a personal religion far removed from the traditional feudal conception of the authority of the church. The mystics Master Eckehart and his pupils Heinrich Seuse and Johannes Tauler all lived in the city and were soon exerting their own pressure on the cultural life around them. Finally, the middle classes enjoyed exceptional prosperity and the town is one of the early centres to show the beginning of a bourgeois culture which was to gather more and more momentum as the 14th century advanced.

The almost grotesque contrasts resulting from the juxtaposition of such widely diverse interests in Cologne can be appreciated if we compare the so-called *Gabelcrucifix* (fork crucifix) of 1304 in the Church of St Maria im Kapitol with the only slightly later sculpture in the choir of the cathedral, notably the pillar figures of the Apostles or the *Mailänder Madonna*.

The crucifix is a work of almost shocking horror, with the dead Christ nailed to the forked trunk of a dead tree. A work of this kind, the direct expression of deeply emotional mystic conceptions, reveals a spiritual anguish which is almost unbearable to contemplate. It was by no means an isolated example of its kind. Small figures or figure groups which survive in other parts of the country as well as the Rhineland include a number of Pietàs showing a sorrowing Virgin holding the emaciated body of her son.

The Cologne Cathedral sculpture contains elements of the style sometimes referred to in Germany as the *neue süsse Stil* (new sweet style). This style, which represents a general European trend towards lyrical sweetness of expression, is found in cathedral sculpture throughout Germany, but is particularly centred on Cologne. The *Mailänder Madonna*, which has lost all traces of classicism in form, is a typical example of the use of the Gothic S-curve and of deeply undercut flowing drapery folds evidently inspired by similar cathedral sculpture in France, such as the *Vierge Dorée* of Amiens or the Madonna in the north transept of Notre Dame in Paris. There is, however, a new feature perceptible in the Cologne work. A certain bourgeois attitude can be felt in the whole conception of the figure and especially in the features of the Madonna herself who regards her son with a touch of very down-to-earth smugness. Works such as this, which are very characteristic of the period, remind us of the exceptionally favoured position of the wealthy bourgeoisie in Cologne at this time. They probably contributed a large part of the money for the decoration of their

66, 68

95

69, 7

70

73

cathedral and it is not surprising to find their more sober, less spiritual outlook reflected in the art.

The statue of Otto II

In Magdeburg the cathedral sculpture was still heavily dependent on that of Bamberg. Outside the church in the market square, however, a unique monument was erected before the middle of the 13th century which represents the first free-standing non-religious monument in Germany: 93 this was an equestrian figure of the emperor Otto II. The emperor, who is shown in the costume of the mid-13th century wearing a belted gown and 51 cloak exactly in the manner of the Bamberg Rider, which was obviously the general model for the group, had granted rights of township to Magdeburg and it was the citizens of Magdeburg who were responsible for the monument. Though stylistically it belongs to the 'late chivalric age', the monument is nevertheless representative–even at that early time–of the growing importance of the towns and their citizens.

Devotional and funerary sculpture

Most characteristic of the 'new sweet style' are the small-scale devotional sculptures, visionary and mystic in content, which seem altogether to have been a speciality of German art and are hard to parallel in other parts of Europe at this time. They are individual works made to satisfy individual piety and are by no means all tragic in content. The unrest of the times led many German women of the aristocracy to seek refuge in a religious life, and much of this small-scale sculpture was made for such aristocratic nuns. Very popular, especially in southern Swabia, were the 89 two-figure groups representing Christ and St John the Evangelist, conceived as abbreviated versions of the Last Supper. The youthful St John is seated next to a slightly larger figure of Christ. St John's head rests against Christ's shoulder and he appears sunk in a deep visionary sleep. Christ's arm is placed in a warm protective gesture round his shoulder and contact is further established by the joining of their two hands. A yearning spirituality pervades such groups which are executed with the utmost delicacy and refinement.

Apart from the small devotional figures and groups already mentioned as a characteristic expression of mysticism, sculpture at this time was largely architectural, being used especially to adorn portals, niches and pillars. There was, however, one other category that was very much in evidence during the whole period, namely funerary sculpture. High-ranking members of the church and of the aristocracy in general were anxious to be buried in suitable surroundings and wanted their tombs to be decorated with figural sculpture in which their own effigies were of primary importance. Among the earliest of such works, which are to be found in churches in all parts of the country, is the tombstone of arch-76 bishop Siegfried von Eppstein in Mainz Cathedral, dating from around the middle of the 13th century. It still shows archaic features, such as the over-lifesize figure of the deceased between the much smaller figures of two kings, and is stylistically close to the sculpture of Magdeburg. The full, rather fleshy faces and heavy figures show the slightly coarser style of German as opposed to French art of the period. More than fifty years later, still fully in the spirit of the 'late chivalric age', came the tomb of 71 Landgraf Heinrich I of Hesse, who died in 1308, in the church of St Elisabeth, Marburg. The influence of the mystics is also evident in tomb 90 sculpture, as exemplified in the bronze figure of Bishop Wolfhart von Roth, who died in 1302, in the Cathedral of Augsburg. The emaciated, angular features of the dead bishop have their closest parallel in the small Pietà groups or the crucifixes.

69

APOSTLE FIGURE

c. 1310, stone, Cologne Cathedral

In the figures of the twelve Apostles, each standing against a pillar in the choir of Cologne Cathedral, their role as supporters of the church is expressed both symbolically and physically. The group culminates in the figures of the Virgin and Christ and is crowned by music-making angels.

70

THE RÖTTGEN PIETA

c. 1370, Rheinisches Landesmuseum, Bonn

The grief-stricken figure of the Virgin holding the emaciated tortured body of her dead son is one of the most tragic works of the period–an artistic response to the mysticism that was sweeping Germany. The harsh, distorted features of Christ and his withered form seem reflected in the ugly head and shrunken body of his mother. Together they suggest a mystic unity of physical and spiritual anguish.

Influence of the religious orders

Four of the newer religious orders – the Cistercians, the Teutonic Knights and the mendicant Dominicans and Franciscans – were responsible for much building in the 13th and 14th centuries.

The Cistercians, the powerful order founded in France in 1098 with the aim of putting the rules of St Benedict into strict practice, made a valuable contribution to the development of Gothic style in Germany during the latter part of the 13th century. The emphasis placed by the order on agricultural production, and its strict observance of the rules of poverty (at any rate to begin with) were well expressed in the architecture. On the one hand, the choice of sites away from the towns and preferably in fertile valleys or near good fishing waters provided such picturesque settings as at Chorin in East Germany. On the other hand, a strict limitation of sculptural and painted decoration both inside and outside the buildings, with the resultant emphasis on austerity, led to a special interest in the architecture as such and a preference for high-quality building materials. In the north-eastern sections of Germany, where the Cistercian order enjoyed great popularity, Cistercian Gothic was characterised by a widescale adoption of brick, the material most favoured in that area.

Although at first the greatest patrons of the Cistercians were the territorial princes, who often chose Cistercian abbeys in which to be buried, by the middle of the 13th century the towns were beginning to rival the nobles in active patronage of the order. The prosperity of the towns reached a peak in the 14th and 15th centuries, and the influence of the bourgeoisie soon brought considerable modifications to the style of architecture. Glazed and unglazed tiles gave colour and pattern to the churches, and the Westphalian hall church became popular. Externally, the façades with the low towers approximated more and more to the shape of urban middle-class houses. The Cistercians, with their practical genius for organising agricultural production, were readily welcomed by the townsmen, but the same was not the case with another great religious order, that of the Teutonic Knights, who came to be centralised in Prussia and the Balkan lands which they helped to conquer and colonise. The order, founded in 1198 by German knights in Jerusalem, was exclusively aristocratic in its membership, and was to become extremely powerful and wealthy in Germany. One of the first buildings sponsored by the Teutonic Knights was the church of St Elisabeth in Marburg an der Lahn. Begun as early as 1235, this church, built by masons who were probably trained in France, can lay claim to be one of the first Gothic structures in Germany. Although Rheims, Soissons and Noyon all contributed something to the plan, native Westphalian features such as the hall church form and the broad proportions of the nave, as well as the trefoil choir so popular in the Rhineland, were also incorporated in this magnificent building. St Elisabeth, the young and beautiful princess who had renounced all worldly goods to help the poor, was revered in Germany as a counterpart to St Francis of Assisi. It was not surprising that the order of Teutonic Knights, steeped in the ideals of chivalry, should feel particularly drawn to this aristocratic saint. The splendid and luxuriously equipped building would in fact have been quite contrary to the wishes of St Elisabeth herself, who would have considered the money so lavishly spent on her church better employed to help the poor. The Teutonic Knights remained true to the 'late chivalric age', and their buildings show no trace of bourgeois influence. The order was responsible for many fortified castle sites which included a hospital, chapel and residences within their walls.

71

EFFIGY OF LANDGRAVE HENRY I *detail*

c. 1308
Church of St Elisabeth, Marburg

The dead landgrave lies on the sarcophagus lid, his hands folded in prayer and his head resting on a pillow. His rather broad face looks serene and smiling. An unusual motif is that of the two small angels kneeling on either side of the dead man's head to receive his soul as it escapes from the body through the right ear. French influence is strong in the whole conception of the effigy.

72

THE WEST FAÇADE OF THE CISTERCIAN CHURCH

church begun 1273
Chorin

The church at Chorin, built by the Cistercians in the late 13th century, is an important example of north German brick building in the Gothic period. The façade, despite its simplicity and purity of architectural form, is richly articulated. The lack of flanking towers allows the compact cubic quality of the structure to emerge with full effect. The monastery to which the church belongs was much used by the rulers of this part of Brandenburg.

73
THE MAILÄNDER MADONNA

c. 1320–30
wood
Cologne Cathedral

The *Mailänder Madonna* is attributed to the artist who was also responsible for the apostle figures in the choir of Cologne Cathedral (**69**). Even richer than these and more rhythmic in the drapery-flow, this beautiful group of the Virgin and Child represents the climax of the artist's achievement. The Madonna is also less remote and more human in expression than the apostles as she gazes, with a hint of a smile, at her child.

74
A CHOIR STALL

c. 1315
wood
Cologne Cathedral

The celebrated choir stalls of Cologne Cathedral occupy three bays on each side of the choir and contain 104 seats. The decoration, carried out by various artists, is very elaborate, and in the drolleries of the scrollwork which crowns the seats the influence of English illuminated manuscripts can be seen. Technically these choir stalls are outstanding in the clear precision of the details.

TOMB OF ARCHBISHOP SIEGFRIED VON EPPSTEIN

c. 1249
stone
Mainz Cathedral

This tomb is a fine example of the style of the 'late age of chivalry'. The large, rather fleshy-faced figure of the archbishop in the centre – he died in 1249 – dominates the two small flanking figures, who represent the two kings crowned by him. Other surviving sculpture from the same Mainz workshop testifies to the high quality of its products, which show links with the contemporary sculpture at Bamberg and Magdeburg.

RELIQUARY SHRINE FOR THE ARM OF ST SIMEON

c. 1340
silver-gilt
Cathedral Treasury, Aachen

The precious relic for which this shrine was made is a bone from the arm of St Simeon, embedded in the silver table. At either end stand the silver-wrought figures of the Madonna and St Simeon with outstretched arms. The latter has just received the Christ-child from Mary, who holds a pair of doves in her extended hands. In the centre of the table stands an antique porphyry vase. The charm and sweetness of the figures is typical of Rhenish art of the period.

THE ADORATION OF THE KINGS

1379
Master Bertram d. 1415
Kunsthalle, Hamburg

This is a panel from the Grabow altarpiece, painted for the Church of St Peter in Hamburg. The Madonna, seated on a low throne, holds with both hands the tiny Christ-child as he stands precariously balanced on her knee. The bareheaded kneeling king grips the baby's arm. Despite the attempted recession of the floor the gold background limits the feeling of three-dimensional space. The mood is naive and charming with a tender poetic quality, and already shows something of the preciousness of International Gothic.

78 *right*

THE ANNUNCIATION

c. 1310—40
oak panel
Cologne Master
16·5 × 13·6 in (42 × 34·5 cm)
Wallraf-Richartz Museum, Cologne

The panel probably formed part of an altar-piece, perhaps the left
wing of a triptych. A second panel in the same museum, identical
in size and style and representing the Presentation in the Temple,
may have been the right wing. *The Annunciation* is set against a
gold background, which enhances the spaceless and timeless
nature of the scene. The smooth drapery flow and decorative
linear design, together with the gentle rather dreamy mood, are
typical of the Cologne school of the period.

79 *above*

THE NATIVITY

1424, Master Francke, c. 1405–after 1424
oak panel, 39 × 35 in (99 × 88·8 cm), Kunsthalle, Hamburg

The panel formed part of the St Thomas à Beckett Altar which
was commissioned from Master Francke by the *Englandfahrer-*
gesellschaft (society of travellers to England) in Hamburg for the
church of St John. On the scroll band to Mary's right, are the
words *Dominus meus – Deus meus*. The idyllic scene, set against
a gold-starred red ground, is typical of the German 'soft style',
and the Annunciation to the Shepherds is charmingly depicted.

80 *right*

ULM MINSTER

begun 1377

The minster in Ulm was the pride of the citizens of the town, who
spared no expense on its construction and decoration. The choir
was built by members of the Parler family, while the west spire
was begun by Ulrich von Ensingen. Ensingen, who completed
the porch and lower sections of the spire, planned to mould it
organically to the body of the building. Technical difficulties,
however, caused considerable modification in Ensingen's plans,
and the 530-foot spire was not completed until the 19th century.

81
INTERIOR OF
THE DOMINICAN CHURCH

1245–75
Regensburg

The simplicity of the architecture favoured
by the mendicant orders is well
illustrated in the Dominican church at
Regensburg. The upper walls are bare,
articulated only by the slender pilaster
strips rising from the octagonal pillars and
consoles. Most of the capitals are
undecorated. On the other hand, a certain
painterly quality is introduced by the play
of light and shade on the deeply-moulded
pointed arches of the arcades.

Very different in purpose and spirit were the churches and monasteries
built by the two great mendicant orders, the Dominicans and the Franciscans, both of which embraced the ideal of poverty. As early as the
middle of the 13th century the Dominicans built churches at Esslingen and
Freisach and these were characterised by strict adherence to the rules of
austerity, retaining a basilican form without transepts. Soon, however, the
bourgeoisie came to exert more and more influence on the buildings of
both orders, as lay commissions were formed in the towns to supervise the
planning of their churches. The close association of the Dominicans and
Franciscans with the citizens of the towns rested on their need, as teachers,
to attract ordinary people in large numbers. Because of this need they
usually chose easily accessible sites on the outskirts of the towns on which
to establish themselves. These were often close to the city walls and sometimes even incorporated part of the fortifications. In times of war they
had to abandon such parts of their monasteries to the defenders of the
city, and if the situation was critical the citizens would seek refuge
within the complex. Although the citizens acquired influence over the
architectural style of the two orders, the basic idea of simplicity and
economy of decoration remained, and it is interesting to compare the
churches of the mendicant orders with the more elaborate cathedral
buildings of the same period. At Regensburg, for example, the cathedral,
begun in 1275, is in striking contrast to the Dominican church. The for- **81**
mer, with its elaborate sculptural decoration, was an important centre, the
influence of which radiated to many parts of south-eastern Germany.
Here we find the work of an important sculptor whose style is personal
enough for specific works in other churches to be attributed to his workshop. Known as the 'Erminold Master' after his most important work, the
tomb figure of St Erminold in Prüfening, near Regensburg, he was responsible for some of the finest of the sculpture in Regensburg Cathedral,
including the two pillar figures of the Annunciation.

Late Gothic art

By the middle of the 14th century German Gothic art was developing into
its late phase which was to continue until well into the 16th century.
Characteristic of this late Gothic style is the elaboration of the vaulting
system; the vaults become decorative and non-structural and evolve increasingly complex forms which spin net-like across the surface. The hall
church now spread from its area of origin in Westphalia to many other
parts of Germany, especially in the south and eastwards to Bohemia and
Austria. Parallel to the French flamboyant style of decoration, the German
artist developed an elaborate form of tracery work in which the motif
known as the *Fischblase* (fish bladder) was very popular, while the emphasis on horizontal elements, a feature also developed in England,
meant that the soaring height of the earlier period was no longer the ideal.

This German so-called *Sondergotik* (special Gothic) is partly due to the
emergence of individual artistic personalities whose names are known and
whose work can be traced in various parts of the country. The first and
one of the greatest families of builders was the Parler family. Heinrich
Parler, the founder of the dynasty, came from Cologne and became free
master in Schwäbisch-Gmünd where he built the church of Heiligkreuz,
the choir of which was begun in 1351. Members of the Parler family were
also concerned in the building of one of the first examples of a fully
bourgeois church, the minster in Ulm, where they worked on the choir. **80**
Ulm Minster was built by the townsmen to commemorate their victory
over the counts of Württemberg in 1377. Following this success the small
town expanded rapidly to become one of the leading centres in Swabia, a

free imperial city owing allegiance direct to the emperor and independent of aristocratic domination. The sphere of influence of the Parler family shifted to the east after the emperor Charles IV had called its greatest member, Peter Parler, to Prague to take over work on the cathedral there.

Meanwhile the citizens of Ulm, who took great pride in their cathedral, after 1392 employed Ulrich von Ensingen, another mason from a second important dynasty of builders. He redesigned the nave and produced a monumental plan for a mighty western tower, though this was not finally completed until more than a hundred years after his death, and then with considerable alterations. A third individual artist, the painter and mason Hans von Burghausen (probably identical with Hans Stetthaimer) contributed to a progressive form of late Gothic in Bavaria. The church of St Martin at Landshut, begun in 1392, is one of the most important buildings for which he was responsible. His style was continued in Bavaria by Jörg Ganghofer in the Frauenkirche in Munich, not completed until 1488.

Another town to emerge as a leading bourgeois centre, a position it was to retain until the 16th century, was Nuremberg in Franconia where, as early as the mid-14th century, there was an unparalleled development of bourgeois lay architecture. The public buildings include the hospital (the Heilig-Geist Spital) and its church, founded 1331–41 and considerably enlarged in the late 15th and early 16th centuries. In addition, splendid houses for the wealthy bourgeoisie were erected and the town can also claim some of the finest and earliest fountains to be erected in the market 82 places and main squares of German towns. If the Schöne Brunnen, built under the supervision of the building lodge of the Parlers, is, with its heroic figures, still very much an architectural monument, the small 83 decorative fountain figure of the so-called Brunnen Hänsel, which dates from c. 1380, represents the first example in Nuremberg of the small decorative fountain. Such figures as the little bronze 'Hänsel' of this fountain were frequently set up in small fountains adorning the courtyards of the larger houses and already foreshadow the great age of the bourgeoisie.

Painting and the minor arts

The predominance of surviving works of architecture and sculpture over monumental painting during the late 13th and 14th centuries is not entirely due to the more durable nature of the materials used in the former arts. The Gothic style was in general unsympathetic to mural painting, since the increase in size of the windows limited the space available for painting, and the ever growing demand for stained glass on the one hand and the restriction of decoration prescribed by the mendicant orders on the other combined almost to eliminate mural painting, at any rate in ecclesiastical architecture. However, a new form of painting began to make its appearance around the middle of the 13th century in Germany, namely panel painting either for altar frontals (as at Soest) or for altarpieces. The altarpiece had in fact a great future for the painter, although until the end of the 15th century it was sculpture rather than painting which was most in demand for the decoration of large altarpieces.

Side by side with the new panel painting, manuscript illumination remained the leading branch of painting, and indeed illuminated manuscripts continued to furnish the models for embroidery, stained glass windows and even for the painted panels. Enamel, metal work and jewellery were still in demand, but their previous importance as major branches of art began to decline as they followed, rather than led, the new trends; however, they retained popularity as objets d'art, especially with the wealthier aristocrats. Fewer reliquary shrines were made than formerly, though many processional crosses and church vessels of the

THE SCHÖNE BRUNNEN *detail*

c. 1390
Nuremberg

The Schöne Brunnen in Nuremberg is one of the earliest fountains in Germany. The sculpture was probably executed in the workshop of the Parler family, and the rich figural sculpture, representing the seven electors and seven heroes, is in the International Gothic style. The idealised figures standing beneath Gothic canopies blend with the architectural setting.

83

BRUNNEN HÄNSEL

c. 1380
bronze
h. 44·5 in (113 cm)
Germanisches Nationalmuseum, Nuremberg

This delightful little boy musician once crowned the top of a small fountain in the courtyard of the Heilig-Geist Spital in Nuremberg. Such decorative figural fountains were soon to become popular for the small courtyards of patrician and middle-class houses; Brunnen Hänsel is the earliest known example. The elegant little figure, modishly attired in a tightly buttoned jacket and wearing long pointed shoes, is blowing lustily into a musical instrument.

period are still to be found in ecclesiastical treasuries and museums. Generally speaking, painting and the minor arts followed the trend of sculpture during the 'late chivalric age'.

Ideals of chivalry are well expressed in some charming illuminated manuscripts dating from around 1300, and now divided between the libraries of Heidelberg and Weingarten. These are collections of *Minnelieder* (love songs) by courtly poets, who are portrayed in full-page illustrations at the beginning of their works, as courtly knights engaged in hunting, wooing or jousting. The same linear rhythms and sweetness of expression are also to be found in the religious painting of the period.

The rising influence of the middle classes on painting can be seen in the increasing appearance, during the 14th century, of everyday objects in the religious scenes. In such works as the painted panel of the Erfurt Master of *c.* 1350 made for the Augustinian church and now in the museum at Erfurt, an increased sense of realism is given by the partial abandonment of gold background and the greater interest in three-dimensional space.

Charles IV and the introduction of International Gothic

During the last three decades of the 14th century Germany, like most other European countries, was caught up in the style known as the International Gothic. In the case of Germany the adoption of this style was considerably accelerated by the cultural relationship with Prague, since 1347 the seat of the emperor Charles IV, and a great historical and cultural centre in which art took on a truly international character. Charles IV, a member of the house of Luxemburg, had been educated in France, and in addition to French culture had also acquired Italian interests. He was in contact with Petrarch and called many Italians to his court at Burg Karlstein near Prague. In the many surviving International Gothic works in Germany, which include illuminated manuscripts, panel paintings, wood engravings, textiles, jewellery, metalwork and sculptures, the debt to the Bohemian school is very much in evidence.

In Germany the International Gothic, which is known there as the *weiche Stil* (soft style), lasted for a considerable time (in some of the more remote centres until the middle of the 15th century). Owing to her geographical position, Germany was able to absorb influences from east and west – from the Prague court, from French art, especially Parisian illuminated manuscripts and, around 1400, from the increasingly important Franco-Burgundian school. Moreover Germany, like so many other European centres, was also influenced by Italian, more especially Sienese art.

The development of panel painting

The first great artistic personality to emerge in Germany at this period was Master Bertram, an artist from Minden in Westphalia who, from 1367, is documented in Hamburg. One of his earliest major works, the Grabow altarpiece, dating from around 1380, was originally made for the church of St Peter in Hamburg. The large work consists of a sculptured shrine (probably also the work of Master Bertram who was a sculptor as well as a painter) and double folding wings containing twenty-four scenes from the Creation and the Childhood of Christ painted in two registers. In its naïve charm and smooth soft drapery flow, as well as in the gay colouring, lavish use of gold and decorative elements, it is fully in the spirit of International Gothic, but the squat rather broad-faced figures and the emphasis on naturalistic details show both a knowledge of Franco-Burgundian manuscripts and also Bohemian influence. Conrad of Soest, who was active in Westphalia from the 1390s to the 1420s and whose two major works are in Dortmund and Soest, also represents the International Gothic style with strong western influences. A third representative artist is Master

75

Francke, who is documented in Hamburg from 1407–14 and who is one of the most charming artists of the 'soft style'.

The large number of surviving panels from the late 14th and early 15th centuries testify to the rapid rise of this branch of painting which was patronised by members of the bourgeoisie as well as by the church. The famous Imhof altarpiece by a Nuremberg artist (now in the Germanisches Nationalmuseum in Nuremberg) was commissioned for the church of St Lorenz by Konrad Imhof, a citizen of the town, between 1418 and 1422. It is an excellent example of the style of painting in this free and independent middle-class town. As could be expected the great international city of Cologne, which played such a leading part in the development of architecture and sculpture, was of considerable importance in the field of painting. The altar panels of the early 14th century, with their abstract linear rhythms and the other-worldly charm of their madonnas, saints and angels, merge almost imperceptibly and under strong western influence into the International Gothic style of the 1400s. The Rhineland, with its strong western connections, was a natural centre of the style, and there are a number of delightful works from this region. The idea of the Madonna seated in front of a rose hedge or in a walled garden, in which a wealth of individualised flowers appear in full bloom, was extremely popular. One of the most poetic examples is the little painting known as the *Garden of Paradise*. Even in more orthodox biblical scenes such as the Passion of Christ the same lyrical spirit prevails. A sweet melancholy sadness pervades the figures of the Virgin and St John flanking the Crucifixion in the Pähl altar panel, now in Munich, by a Bavarian artist *c.* 1400.

Perhaps the last great master of the 'soft style' in Cologne was Stephan Lochner who, though not a native of the city, nevertheless spent most of his working life there (his presence is documented from *c.* 1430 until his death in 1451). Lochner, who came originally from Meersburg, was an artist of great lyrical charm, as can be seen in his *Madonna in the Rosegarden* in Cologne. The artist's main work, the *Altarpiece of the Magi* in Cologne Cathedral, already shows a new understanding of three-dimensional space.

Sculpture of the late Gothic

Of the many works of sculpture in the 'soft style' that are to be found in churches and museums all over the country, not all were by German masters. The popular type of *schöne Madonnen* (beautiful madonnas) were generally produced by Bohemian and Austrian sculptors, often in small monasteries in those countries.

Some very expressive sculpture was produced in Swabia, such as the group of mourning women (now in Berlin) which is ascribed to a master from Middle Bibrach. The intensity of expression and the contrast between the swooning figure of the Virgin Mary and the passionate grief of the women supporting her is made all the more effective by the restraint of the formal rhythm of the group. The same restraint, though poetic rather than emotional, can be seen in the many Pietà groups of the International Gothic style. In mood they differ profoundly from the harshly expressive interpretations of the similar groups produced nearly a hundred years earlier. International Gothic is already giving way to a new, more realistic style in one of the last works of the period, the Tiefenbronn Altarpiece, dated 1431, by Lucas Moser of Weilderstadt. This work, a curious mixture of medieval other-worldliness and a new visual conception of reality, represents the first German work that shows some awareness of the problems with which the contemporary Flemish school had already come to grips.

Marguerite Kay

84 *facing page*

THE MAGDALEN ALTARPIECE

1431
Lucas Moser, first half of 15th century
wood panel
left-hand panel 58·7 × 25·25 in (149 × 59 cm)
Tiefenbronn Church, near Pforzheim

The altarpiece of Mary Magdalen is still in the church for which it was painted. The artist is in many ways an innovator, showing a new sense of space and realism in the sea- and landscape setting, but he retains the overall linear patterning of the 'soft style'.

85

THE PÄHL ALTARPIECE

c. 1400–10
canvas mounted on wood
centre panel 48·5 × 34·5 in
(123 × 87·5 cm)
Bayerisches Nationalmuseum, Munich

The triptych of which this is the centre panel was purchased in 1857 from Pähl on the Ammersee near Augsburg, and allegedly came fron the Palace Chapel there. A major work of the south German International Gothic style, it is one of the earliest surviving altarpieces with wings. On the front, the wings show St John the Baptist and St Barbara, and on the back, Christ as Man of Sorrows and the Madonna and Child. The artist was strongly influenced by the Bohemian School.

87
MADONNA
WITH THE VETCH PLANT

c. 1420, oak panel
20·9 × 13·4 in (53 × 34 cm)
Wallraf-Richartz Museum, Cologne

This is the centre panel of a triptych, the wings of which show St Barbara and St Catharine. The anonymous artist is known to have worked in Cologne, Westphalia and Lower Saxony. The Madonna and Child as depicted here are a painted version of the carved 'beautiful madonnas' which are so characteristic of the International Gothic in Bohemia and Austria (**96**).

88 *centre*
EPITAPH OF BISHOP FRIEDRICH
OF HOHENLOHE

c. 1351
stone, Bamberg Cathedral

This tombstone is one of the finest works of mid-14th-century German Gothic. The haggard, aristocratic and deeply intellectual face of the bishop is impersonal and remote, despite a certain individualis-ation of expression. The drapery, deeply hollowed out and falling in long unbroken folds, is beautifully executed, and enhances the spiritualised aspect of the dead bishop.

86 *below*
THE MADONNA
IN THE GARDEN OF PARADISE

c. 1410/20
Master of the Garden of Paradise
oil on panel
9·5 × 12·25 in (24 × 31 cm)
Städelsches Institut, Frankfurt am Main

This exquisite miniature-like painting is one of the masterpieces of the International Gothic style in Germany. The Madonna is seated in a walled garden reading her bible, while the Christ-child, attended by a female saint, plays with a musical instrument. Other saints represented are St Dorothy (plucking fruit), St George and St Michael. The idyllic mood is enhanced by the luxurious detail of foliage and flowers.

89

CHRIST AND ST JOHN

c. 1320
polychrome wood
h. 35 in (58·5 cm)
Deutsches Museum, West Berlin

The beautiful group is an example of a
devotional type of work much favoured in
the early 14th century, especially in
Swabia. It shows the sleeping St John with
his head resting on Christ's shoulder. The
lyrical other-worldly expression and
extreme spirituality of the relationship
between the two figures makes it a work
pre-eminently suitable for mystic
contemplation.

90 *below*

TOMB OF BISHOP WOLFHART VON ROTH

c. 1302
Master Otto and Master Konrad
bronze
Augsburg Cathedral

According to the inscription, Master
Otto made the wax model for this effigy
while Master Konrad cast it in bronze. The
bishop, a strikingly realistic figure, seems
tense even in death. His ascetic, haggard
face with the sharp, angular features and
hollowed cheeks has deeply-etched lines,
which enhance the morose and withdrawn
expression. The whole figure seems
consumed by an inner fire, a spirituality
that has outlasted the physical world.

91

THE CHURCH OF
ST ELISABETH

begun 1235
Marburg

This church, one of the earliest Gothic
churches in Germany, was built by the
Knights of the Teutonic Order, as a
memorial to St Elisabeth, on the site of
the hospital and modest little church she
herself had founded. Although it is
modelled on French Gothic cathedrals
such as Soissons and Noyon, it shows
native characteristics, for instance in the
use of the Swabian hall-church structure.

92 *right*

THE WEST FRONT
OF MINDEN CATHEDRAL

c. 1060–1270

The massive compact aspect of the
cathedral is determined by the
Romanesque form of the porch and the
lower sections of the front. The upper part,
with its steep saddle roofs, and the slender
pointed spire are later alterations, but only
the well-proportioned hall-type nave, its
large windows furnished with rich Gothic
tracery, is in the true Gothic style and
dates from around 1270.

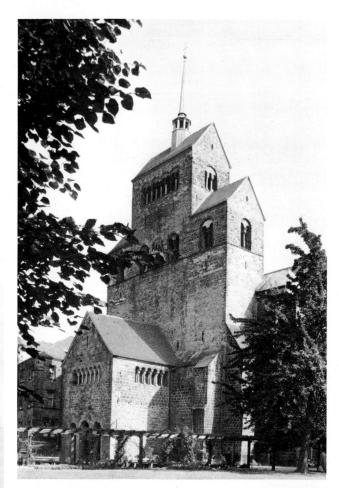

93

EQUESTRIAN STATUE OF OTTO THE GREAT

c. 1245
The market square, Magdeburg

The magnificent group showing Otto the Great on horseback and two accompanying maidens with shields is the earliest large-scale freestanding secular monument in Germany. Originally it stood under a Gothic covering. It was erected by the citizens of Magdeburg to commemorate the city charter conferred by Otto II. Though it owes much to the famous Bamberg Rider (**51**) this equestrian figure is rather simpler and heavier than the earlier group. It is a fine example of the art of the 'late chivalric age'.

94 *left*

THE CHOIR OF FREIBURG MINSTER

begun mid-14th century

The choir of Freiburg Minster carries on the tradition of the Parler school. The ambulatory and radiating chapels give the required depth to the east end, which forms, on the outside, a magnificent counterpart to the splendid single tower rising at the west end. The elaborate vaulting of the nave shows the late Gothic tendency to arrange the ribs in a net-like pattern across the surface.

95 *facing page*

THE GABELKRUZIFIX

c. 1304, carved wood
St Maria im Kapitol, Cologne

This highly expressionistic work, which
reflects the mysticism centred in Cologne,
made a profound impact on other parts of
Germany. Replicas survive in Rhenish and
Westphalian churches. However, when in
1306 an English priest purchased one of
these, the bishop of London ordered that
it should be returned. Though the carving
of the head, hair and loin cloth are
stylistically related to the sculpture on the
west front of Strasbourg Minster, the
realism of the skeleton-like corpse is the
result of the artist's personal vision.

96

MADONNA AND CHILD

c. 1430, painted and gilded wood
h. 42·5 in (108 cm)
Bayerisches Nationalmuseum, Munich

This late example of the 'beautiful
madonna' type of the International Gothic
style was originally in the monastery at
Seeon, Upper Bavaria, and is one of a
group of works influenced by the Salzburg
School. The drapery still flows
rhythmically and cascades richly on
either side, but the folds between the legs
of the Madonna show a tendency towards
the angularity that characterises drapery in
the following decades.

97

ST GEORGE AND THE DRAGON

c. 1390, limewood
h. 4 ft 4 in (132 cm)
Bayeriches Nationalmuseum, Munich

Because of the similarity in style to
contemporary Bavarian funerary
sculpture, this piece is generally
attributed to an anonymous Bavarian
artist. The aristocratic aloofness and slender
elegence of the figure are typical of the
International Gothic. St George seems
more spiritually than physically involved
in the situation, and the toy-like dragon is
more of a symbol than an actual vicious
beast. The group, with its mannered
Gothic S-curves, lacks stability, but
balance is established by skilful
composition.

98

GROUP OF
MOURNING WOMEN

c. 1420
Master of Biberach
wood
h. 45·75 in (116 cm)
Staatliche Museen, West Berlin

This highly expressive group of mourning
women, probably a fragment from a
Crucifixion, shows the very personal style
of an anonymous Upper Swabian master.
The central figure, supported by the two
standing women, probably represents the
Virgin Mary. Though the elegant, richly
carved drapery flow is in keeping with the
International Gothic style, the emotional
intensity of the women is unusual at this
early date and seems to foreshadow the
art of Matthias Grünewald.

99

THE ADORATION OF THE KINGS

1430s
Stephen Lochner, after 1410/15 – 1451/52
panel
98·8 × 111 in (251 × 282 cm)
Cologne Cathedral

This is the centre panel of the altarpiece, painted by Lochner for
the Ratskapelle in Cologne Cathedral. The altarpiece is not only
the chief work of Lochner, but also of the Cologne school of the
period. The sweet lyrical expression and rhythmic linear
design of the painting link it with the International Gothic style,
but the composition and spatial arrangement of the figure-groups
show a new sense of realism.

100

RELIQUARY BUST OF CHARLEMAGNE

c. 1349
silver, chased and jewelled
Cathedral Treasury, Aachen

This bust was made to hold the brain-case of Charlemagne, which
had been taken from the 13th-century Charlemagne shrine, also
in the Aachen treasury (**44**). The finely-modelled head is one of
the major works of the Aachen goldsmith's art, which reached a
peak in the mid-14th century. The French interest in
Charlemagne, which was more intense than that of the Germans
(who preferred Frederick Barbarossa as their national hero) led
to the later addition of the fleurs-de-lis decoration on the bust.

1500
AD

Albertus Durerus Noricus
ipsum me proprijs sic effin
gebam coloribus ætatis
anno XXVIII

During the 15th and early 16th centuries the German bourgeoisie was at its height and the towns were the chief centres of cultural and artistic development. New technical inventions, first and foremost that of printing, helped to lay the foundations for a wider education among the people, while trade, with its international contacts, strengthened the links of the merchant class with other countries. Geographical exploration, culminating in the discovery of America by Christopher Columbus, opened exciting new horizons to the limited outlook of middle-class life and sharpened cultural appetites. Man became conscious of his own powers, and a new sense of individuality emerged. But these possibilties were clouded by the deterioration of social conditions and the appalling poverty of the lower classes, and everywhere tormenting religious doubts appeared. The Church, whose authority had been absolute, was now seriously questioned as many of its abuses were exposed. The seeds of doubt sown by the earlier mystics finally erupted when, in 1517, Martin Luther nailed his theses to the door of the Wittenberg Castle Church. The subsequent outbreak and harsh suppression of the peasant revolt of 1525 threw the whole country into a turmoil. Throughout the 16th century religious and political conflicts sharpened and finally, in 1618, exploded into the Thirty Years War, which virtually ended cultural progress.

The late Gothic artist

For most of the 15th century German artists continued to look to the west, especially to France and the southern Netherlands, and it was not until the end of the century, when there was an unparalleled concentration of artistic talent, that a real awareness of Italian Renaissance art began to make itself felt, in painting and sculpture more than in architecture.

At first artistic initiative was predominantly in the hands of the sculptors. Since few important new churches were being built, the sculptors, deprived of their former main task of decorating religious buildings, turned to the carving of large altarpieces, which were now more and more in demand in Germany. In fact, these monumental works still remained, in a sense, linked to architecture, for the often highly elaborate superstructures conformed to the late Gothic style of the churches in which they stood. The invariable custom of gilding and painting the structures and the carved shrines gave painters too a share in the work; indeed the panels of the folding wings were often painted with religious scenes. The completed work thus showed a combination of all three arts, and was usually the product of one workshop.

Such workshops were now organised into guilds, and in most of the towns the guild system was strictly enforced, a practice which considerably limited the freedom of the artists. Training followed a rigid pattern of apprenticeship at a very early age, followed by a period of travel and, finally, acceptance into the appropriate guild with the obligation of taking on pupils to train. The head of the workshop was officially responsible for the education and schooling of his young apprentices, but in practice this frequently amounted to mere instruction in reading and writing with little emphasis on a wider education. This was probably one of the reasons why the advanced forms of learning eagerly sought in Italy were so slow in reaching the many talented artists working in Germany.

During the first half of the 15th century the idealism of the *weiche Stil* (soft style) began to give way to a new, more down-to-earth form of art, with increasing emphasis on everyday life. The sweeping linear rhythms of the drapery were replaced by angular, broken folds, often extremely elaborate. This can first be seen in the work of two important artists, both of Swabian origin, Hans Multscher and Konrad Witz. In 1427 Multscher,

The Middle Classes and the German Renaissance

c. 1450 – 1618

101

SELF-PORTRAIT

1500
Albrecht Dürer 1471 – 1528
limewood
26·4 × 19·3 in (67 × 49 cm)
Alte Pinakothek, Munich

This is probably the best known of all Dürer's self-portraits. The artist has chosen to portray himself in a solemn, somewhat hieratic manner, which earned the picture the title of *Christusbild* (picture of Christ). The completely symmetrical and frontal attitude of the sitter makes this a most unusual self-portrait, and the picture shows something of the polish and humanism that Dürer had learned in Italy.

102, 136
a sculptor-painter, settled in Ulm, one of the strongholds of the German bourgeoisie, where he worked on the town hall and subsequently on the minster. He soon became head of a large workshop which supplied altar-pieces, with the now fashionable arrangement of carved shrine and painted wings, to many parts of Germany. As can be seen from the sur-

103
viving painted panels of the Wurzach altarpiece (now in the Dahlem Museum, Berlin), which the artist signed and dated 1437, the paintings also showed the new feeling for material weight and physical reality.

If Multscher was the first outstanding sculptor of the new age, Konrad
110
Witz, who was born at Rottweil around 1400, was certainly the greatest painter. In his comparatively short life (he died before 1446) he intro-duced into painting the new realistic style that was already in full swing in the Netherlands.

Neither Multscher nor Witz had any real successors among German artists working around the middle of the 15th century, though there were sufficient competent artists to satisfy the continuously increasing demands for large altarpieces, tombs and decorative work for churches and cathe-drals, especially in the larger towns. The main focus of interest during the second half of the century remained the Netherlands. Works by
106
Rogier van der Weyden and Thiery Bouts made their way early into Ger-many and are still to be seen in many museums and galleries there. Some Netherlandish artists actually came to work in Germany, the outstanding example being the sculptor Nicolaus Gerhaert of Leyden. His earliest dated work, done at Trier for Archbishop Jacob von Sierck, was the archbishop's tomb, of which only the carved lid (now in the Episcopal Museum in Trier) survives. The highly personal, almost introvert, expres-sion of Gerhaert's Crucifix (dating from 1467) in the old cemetery at Baden Baden, gives some idea of the quality of his art, in which the older, idealistic style seems to have merged into a new and monumental, almost classic aloofness. His art was to have wide repercussions in Germany.

The beginnings of the German Renaissance

The years after 1470 witness a great change in the development of German art. If previously there were relatively few artists whose work can claim international status, the last decades of the 15th century and the first three decades of the 16th can be regarded as one of the greatest periods in the whole history of German culture. The earlier years of the 15th century appear in the nature of a preparation for the coming efflorescence, a period of ferment when new ideas were being assimilated and slowly blended with native feeling. A harsh, sometimes brutal realism, an awareness of space and of physical reality and a sensitive response to the beauties of nature were combined with strong emotionalism and a searching moral introspection to evolve a new formal expression in late Gothic sculpture and painting. These developments were mainly concentrated in southern Germany, and even here the many individual centres reflected a variety of responses. Whereas artists of Cologne and the Rhineland emphasised tenderness and retained a certain refinement (the painter and engraver
107
Martin Schongauer is the outstanding example), artists in Swabia, especially Ulm and Augsburg, concentrated on intensified expression, and showed a strong talent for portraiture. The choir stalls of Ulm Min-
104
ster by Jörg Syrlin the Elder or the silver-point portrait drawings of Hans Holbein the Elder are good examples. By the beginning of the 16th century painters and graphic artists rather than sculptors occupy pride of place in German art, and it is in their hands that the northern Renaissance finds its most brilliant expression. The three greatest German artists of the earlier 16th century, Albrecht Dürer, Matthias Grünewald and Hans

102

CHARLES THE GREAT AND TWO SHIELD-BEARING PAGES

c. 1427
Hans Multscher c. 1400–67
Ulm Museum

The group was commissioned from Multscher by the Ulm civic authorities to decorate the town hall, sculpture for which had already been completed by earlier masters. Multscher's group is by far the finest and most progressive of the series, showing his knowledge and interest in the realistic art of Claus Sluter and the Franco-Burgundian and Netherlandish schools in general.

103
THE RESURRECTION

1437
Hans Multscher c. 1400–67
pinewood panel
panel 58·25 × 55·1 in (148 × 140 cm)
Gemäldegalerie, West Berlin

The Resurrection forms one of four panels of an altarpiece painted on both sides, commissioned from Multscher for the church at Wurzach in Allgäu. Although Hans Multscher, who was head of a large workshop at Ulm, signed the work, he probably did little of the actual painting and only supervised the work. It is, however, something of a landmark in the development of the Swabian school, because of the impressive sculpturesque figure of Christ seated on the sarcophagus, and the spacious setting, which shows a new sense of realism.

104
SENECA

1468/69–1474
Jörg Syrlin the Elder d. 1491
oakwood
Ulm Minster

The Ulm choir stalls, of which this bust is a detail, are a landmark in 15th-century Swabian art. The humanistic programme of the artist determined the arrangement of the decoration and relief panels on the backs of the seats, and the series of ninety-nine busts in front. These busts represent the sibyls prophesying the coming of Christ, and the philosophers, poets and scholars of antiquity, all linked to the Christian idea of salvation.

Holbein the Younger, were all painters and graphic artists, and they were surrounded and followed by a great number of painters of hardly lesser talent.

When late Gothic art was at its height a new and enriching influence, that of the Italian Renaissance, was superimposed from without. By the close of the 15th century the import of Italian engravings of works by the great masters began to make a real impression on German artists, but even more significant for the introduction of Renaissance art was the increasing activity of bourgeois patrons. Humanistic culture was at first exclusively confined to the wealthy bourgeoisie, whose trading links with Italy brought it early into contact with the new Renaissance ideas prevailing there. Prosperous and by now with a well-established sense of security, the middle classes turned increasingly to cultural pursuits. Study at the universities brought them into contact with humanistic thought and enabled them to appreciate Italian art, which they saw during their business trips to Italy. They also established contact with leading scholars outside Italy, for example Erasmus of Rotterdam, who was friendly with many personalities, such as Martin Luther and Willibald Pirckheimer, one of the foremost humanists in Germany and a friend of Dürer.

Augsburg and Nuremberg, both of which were flourishing bourgeois strongholds, became the most prominent centres for the development and expansion of the graphic arts, which were to some extent pioneered in Germany. Even before the invention of printing, a simple form of wood engraving known as *Einblattholzschnitt* had been developed and was widely used to illustrate manuscripts. In the second half of the century, after the invention of printing, woodcuts became the most popular form of graphic illustration, and copper-plate engraving was also widely used. Since a large number of sheets could be produced from one block or plate and were easily transported, woodcuts and engravings were instrumental in spreading knowledge of artistic style, not only from one workshop or town to another but also from one country to another. Although Albrecht Dürer stands supreme as the greatest graphic artist in Germany, **134** the second half of the 15th century was not lacking in gifted engravers.

Of Dürer's immediate predecessors the most influential and talented was Martin Schongauer, a native of Augsburg who spent most of his life in Colmar (now in France). He was extraordinarily sensitive to the possibilities of expression through a rich and varied use of line, which he handled with the utmost sensitivity. Though he was well known as a painter, few of his works in this field have come down to us, but as an engraver he was extraordinarily prolific and was perhaps the first German artist to acquire international fame. Small wonder that Dürer was anxious to meet Schongauer for there was nothing in Nuremberg at that time that could in any way compare with his work. In fact, as soon as he had finished his apprenticeship, Dürer went to Colmar with the express intention of meeting the artist, but he arrived too late, for Schongauer had died some months previously.

The flowering of sculpture

The great period of German sculpture came a little earlier than that of painting. Moreover, sculptors clung much more tenaciously to late Gothic tradition than did painters. This characteristic is well illustrated in the work of Michael Pacher, who, though a native of Austria and established since 1461 in Bruneck in the Tyrol, was also a source of inspiration in southern Germany. His workshop produced numerous large altarpieces which were exported to many centres. He is the classic example of the sculptor-painter, and in the magnificent architectural detail of his altar superstructures he achieved a new and splendid harmony between the three arts of architecture, sculpture and painting. Late Gothic tradition is preserved in his sculpture whereas his paintings show a well-assimilated knowledge of north Italian art, the main source of which must have been the art of Mantegna in Padua. This Italian element is also very apparent in the painted wings of the Church Fathers' altarpiece from Neustift in the Tyrol, now in Munich.

The influence of Nicolaus Gerhaert is discernible in the major works executed by a number of talented sculptors in Swabia, especially in Ulm Minster. Here the choir stalls executed between 1469 and 1474 under the direction of Jörg Syrlin the Elder constitute the most magnificent achievement. One of the artists employed on this work may have been Michael Erhart, whose work includes the beautiful *Virgin of the Misericord* originally done for Ravensburg and now in Berlin. Michael Erhart's son Gregor carried on his father's manner, especially in the carving of individual and highly realistic figures.

In 1494 Gregor Erhart moved to Augsburg, the home of the famous Fugger family of businessmen (later bankers) and the favoured town of the emperor Maximilian I. Augsburg was shortly to become one of the leading centres of German Renaissance. The development in Bavaria was less spectacular, for here enlightened middle-class patronage was lacking, but there was a certain amount of late Gothic sculpture of an original kind. Erasmus Grasser, who worked in the 1480s and 1490s, is one of the best-known Bavarian artists of the time. In addition to many religious works, including the beautiful figures from a Crucifixion for the high altar at Piping, now in Munich, there was a more popular side to his art, well represented by a curious series of sculpted wood Morris Dancers, which combine the lusty zestful vigour and rather coarse humour of Bavarian peasant art with a superb sense of dynamic rhythm and a strong ornamental quality. They were commissioned in 1428 for the town hall in Munich and are still to be seen there.

In northern Germany Lübeck was the chief centre for an artistic development, which culminated in the late Gothic art of Bernt Notke, a native of Lassan in Pomerania and evidently a member of a patrician Hanseatic family. This status, unusual for a German late Gothic artist, secured him a favoured position in Lübeck, where he was patronised by the mayor and by high ecclesiastics. He was not compelled to join the Lübeck guild of artists, but worked independently. For Lübeck he carved the Triumphal Cross now in the St Annen Museum, a work of great expressive quality. Notke's most outstanding work as a painter is the altar panel of the Mass of St Gregory done for the Church of St Mary in Lübeck, where it remains.

The great sculptors of Nuremberg

The progressive centres for sculpture and painting were not, however, in northern Germany. Both in the culmination of a brilliant late Gothic style and in the beginnings of a new humanism, the south became the main focus, and the importance of Nuremberg can hardly be overestimated. There, the cultured and wealthy middle-class families, who considered themselves far superior to the ordinary citizens, formed a kind of aristocracy. Not only did they commission splendid funerary monuments for themselves and their families, but they also paid for artistic works to decorate the town and the churches. Moreover, they sought to increase their own standards of living and required better constructed houses with roomier living accommodation. This led to a big increase in domestic architecture, but until well into the 16th century the general style re-

105
ROTHENBURG TOWN HALL
c. 1570

In the 16th-century town hall of Rothenburg ob der Tauber, the blending of the late Gothic and Renaissance elements has not yet been successfully achieved. The curving lines of the gable are almost Baroque in their dynamic movement. The town hall is nevertheless impressive in its combination of architectural forms, and it is regarded as one of the best buildings of its day in Franconia.

106

ADORATION OF THE KINGS

c. 1450
Rogier van der Weyden 1399/1400 – 1464
oak panel
54·4 × 60 in (138 × 153 cm)
Alte Pinakothek, Munich

This is the central panel of the St Columba altarpiece, commissioned by Goddert Wasseras for his chapel in the church of St Columba, Cologne. The work, with its rich colouring, the details of the costly brocades and the exquisite town- and landscape in the background, is generally dated after the artist's visit to Italy. The tenderness expressed in the group with the kneeling king is particularly suggestive of Italian influence.

107

THE NATIVITY

attributed to Martin Schongauer
c. 1430/35 – 1491
limewood panel
10·25 × 6·7 in (26 × 17 cm)
Alte Pinakothek, Munich

The panel, which is unsigned, is attributed to Schongauer on stylistic grounds. Of the small number of paintings which have been attributed to this artist (he is now mainly known for his engravings), the *Madonna of the Rose Hedge*, in Colmar Museum, is the one most generally accepted as his. *The Nativity* would appear to be earlier than this work, less sophisticated and with some awkwardness in the proportions. The figures and details, however, are charmingly depicted.

108

THE ANNUNCIATION

c. 1440 – 45
Konrad Witz 1400/10 – 1445/46
Germanisches Nationalmuseum, Nuremberg

The Annunciation probably formed part of an altarpiece, now dismantled, of which three other panels have been identified. In this late work Witz has succeeded, by the simplest of means, in suggesting the momentous nature of the scene. The sensitive observation of light and the feeling for space make this realistic depiction of an interior something of a landmark in German art.

109

FAÇADE OF
A MIDDLE-CLASS HOUSE

early 16th century
The market-place, Greifswald

This is a very fine example of a bourgeois brick house from north-east Germany. The slender proportions and pointed arches of the window arcades are Gothic elements. The vertical and horizontal axes are both equally emphasised and the rich decorative upper part of the façade rises lightly from the sober brick pedestal-like ground floor. This type of middle-class building had great influence on the façades of Cistercian brick churches in the area.

110 *far right*
SALVE REGINA

1517 – 18
Veit Stoss 1438/47 – 1533
polychrome stone
Church of St Lorenz, Nuremberg

This very popular work was executed by Veit Stoss in his old age. It is an Annunciation scene, showing the Angel and the Virgin Mary within a large rosette circle surmounted by a representation of God the Father in glory. Medallions with biblical scenes and a framing rosary enliven the frame, and dynamic little angels lend a festive note to the original and highly personal conception.

mained late Gothic, as the Renaissance style roused no particular interest either in the patrons or in the artists themselves. At the most, decorative elements with Renaissance ornament were used on the outside of the buildings, bay-window surrounds or portal ornaments often being plastered on to late Gothic fronts. Stone, too, began to replace wood as a building material, but in general the towns remained conservative in appearance. Nuremberg, once a magnificent example of a late 15th-century south German town, was unfortunately so severely damaged in the Second World War that, in spite of an intensive rebuilding programme, it is now impossible to form any real idea of what the town once looked like. Fortunately, the monuments in the churches and the public squares were well protected and many of them have been restored to their original sites. This applies to the major works of Veit Stoss, Adam Krafft and Peter Vischer, all of whom were working in Nuremberg at the end of the 15th century, and contributed to the decoration of the churches and of the town as a whole.

Veit Stoss, perhaps the greatest and most imaginative of all German sculptors, never went beyond a personal and highly dynamic form of late Gothic and, though he influenced a large number of lesser artists, had no real successors. A native of Horb in Swabia, he acquired Nuremberg citizenship in 1477, but then spent almost twenty years in Cracow. He returned to Germany and resumed his Nuremberg citizenship in 1496, his first commission after this being for three reliefs of the Passion for the Church of St Sebaldus. These works, commissioned by Paul Volckamer, were part of an intensive programme undertaken by the patrician families of Nuremberg to beautify the church. Shortly afterwards Stoss came into legal conflict with the Nuremberg authorities, and the bitterness with which the matter was pursued by both sides clouded the rest of his life. He suffered the harsh penalty of branding on both cheeks and also a term of imprisonment. During this conflict Stoss appealed direct to the emperor Maximilian I, who granted him a free pardon and also commissioned work from him. It says much for the independence of the citizens that they never really accepted the emperor's decree. It is also symptomatic of the growing interest in the fine arts that, in spite of the dishonour attached to his name, Stoss was consistently employed by the leading families. Something of the visionary grandeur of his art can be seen in his famous *Salve Regina* in the choir of St Lorenz, a late work executed between 1517–19. This work is enhanced by gilding and painting, but in fact the universal practice of colouring sculpture was at last beginning to die out. For the impact of Renaissance ideas was creating a feeling for the effectiveness of the materials themselves, as well as a new awareness of the autonomy of sculpture. In one of Veit Stoss's latest works, the high altar commissioned by the prior Andreas Stoss (the son of the artist by his first marriage) for the Carmelite monastery in Nuremberg, he expressly stated that 'it was never to be thoughtlessly coloured'.

The two great contemporaries of Veit Stoss, Adam Krafft and Peter Vischer, close friends throughout their lives, were highly divergent in their art and in the aims they pursued, though both developed away from late Gothic style and opened the way for the triumph of the Renaissance. The best-known works of Adam Krafft are the Sacrament Tabernacle for St Lorenz's, with its famous self-portrait of the artist shown with two assistants kneeling as supporting figures for the structure, and the reliefs of the Stations of the Cross for St Peter's in Nuremberg. They show a new interest in human types in strongly realistic attitudes. Adam Krafft's first known work was the result of an unusual commission given by two lead-

III

EVE *detail*

1491–93
Tilman Riemenschneider c. 1460–1531
grey-green sandstone
Mainfränkisches Museum, Würzburg

This figure of Eve is part of the group of Adam and Eve formerly in the south porch of the Chapel of the Virgin in Würzburg. An early work, the group was the first important commission given to the artist by the civic authorities. The two figures are in striking contrast. Eve is self-assured and aware of her powers, whilst Adam's expression is thoughful and strained, almost as if he is guiltily aware of the consequences of their action.

112

SHRINE OF ST SEBALDUS

1508–19
Peter Vischer the Elder c. 1455–1529
bronze
Church of St Sebaldus, Nuremberg

The elaborate shrine, with its wealth of small figural decorations, is a tall canopied structure of late Gothic form. The details, however, already show the influence of the Italian Renaissance, which had been absorbed by two of Vischer's sons, Peter the Younger and Hermann, both of whom had visited Italy and who assisted their father in the work. The Renaissance style was, in fact, very slow in spreading throughout Germany, possibly because its classical ideals were uncongenial to the German temperament.

ing Nuremberg families, the Schreyers and the Landauers, namely to carve in stone relief, outside the choir of St Sebaldus, copies of the paint- **138** ings which hung above the burial place of the two families inside.

Peter Vischer the Elder was the son of the bronze founder Hermann Vischer, who had settled in Nuremberg in 1453. Peter himself became a specialist in bronze sculpture and gave a new importance to a material that had been somewhat neglected in previous late Gothic sculpture. His two sons, Hermann and Peter, who both predeceased their father, were among the first German sculptors to introduce Italian Renaissance art to Germany, mainly through small-scale bronze figures of mythological or biblical content. Both sons visited Italy, Hermann even being recorded as having travelled to Rome at his own expense for the sake of his art. The major monumental work associated with the Vischer workshop, in its present form the result of a collaboration between father and sons, is the tomb of St Sebaldus in the church of that name. It is a vast undertaking, and its **112** many parts show late Gothic and Renaissance forms in the figures, although the overall style of the shrine itself is late Gothic. First commissioned from the elder Vischer in 1488, it was then conceived in purely late Gothic terms. However, this plan was never carried out and a second commission was given in 1508. This was then completed, with interruptions, by 1519.

Conrad Meit and Tilman Riemenschneider

Although patronage by the wealthy bourgeoisie in the free imperial cities played the most important part in the progressive development of German sculpture, this does not mean that there was stagnation in other parts. Conrad Meit of Worms, one of the oldest artistic centres in Germany, also took a decisive step in introducing Renaissance art. He worked first in Wittenberg and then, from 1512, in the Netherlands for archduchess Margaret of Austria, daughter of Emperor Maximilian I. Meit's works include a number of small-scale bronze figures.

Würzburg, one of the three important bishoprics in Franconia, was the town chosen by Tilman Riemenschneider in which to establish himself. He was a native of Osterode in the Harz mountains, but from 1478–79 he is documented in Würzburg. His patrons included the bishop himself, and members of the Franconian nobility and of the town council. For all his personal originality, Riemenschneider remained fundamentally a late Gothic artist. His work shows a tender lyrical expressiveness and a superb sense of craftsmanship; he took great care in his choice of materials, whether wood, stone or alabaster, which he worked with equal skill, and he knew how to exploit effects of light and shade. He was also one of the first German sculptors to break consistently with the tradition of gilding and painting his work. His earlier work, such as the beautiful figures of
III Adam and Eve, made originally for the Chapel of the Virgin in Würzburg,
113 or the sandstone figure of the Virgin, suggests some familiarity with Swabian and Netherlandish art. Of Riemenschneider's later works, the Altar of the Virgin in the little church of Creglingen in Bavaria is one of the most impressive.

Albrecht Dürer and Matthias Grünewald

The rich array of talent concentrated in Nuremberg at the end of the 15th century was certainly impressive. Moreover, it was the birthplace
91, 134, and main centre of activity of Albrecht Dürer, the dominant master of
146 the northern Renaissance. Born in 1471 the son of a goldsmith who had emigrated from Hungary, his first training was in his father's workshop. At fifteen, however, he was apprenticed to the leading Nuremberg painter of the day, Michael Wolgemut. Wolgemut was in contact with the most important publishers of the day, and he supplied them with designs for woodcuts and engravings. Dürer, with his superb skill as a draughtsman and his knowledge of the exacting goldsmith's technique, must have been invaluable to him.

The tremendous revelation of Italian art was a major factor in the formation of Dürer's personal style. He knew the work of the great artists of the High Renaissance and was in correspondence with Raphael, with whom he exchanged drawings. He was able to appreciate the significance
146 of Italian humanism and was the first to apply this understanding to his art. His intellectual qualities raised him far above his contemporaries, and he enjoyed the friendship of enlightened scholars outside his own social milieu at a time when artists in Germany were still regarded as mere artisans. From Italy, where Dürer was very conscious of the different cultural atmosphere, the artist wrote to the humanist Willibald Pirckheimer: 'Here I am a gentleman, at home a nobody'.

Dürer enjoyed the patronage of both the aristocracy and the bourgeoisie. The elector Frederick the Wise of Saxony was a great admirer of the artist, and Dürer's first commissions for paintings came from him.

113
ALTAR OF THE VIRGIN
detail
c. 1505–10
Tilman Riemenschneider c. 1460–1531
wood
Herrgottskirche, Creglingen

The heads of Apostles illustrated here are part of the carved decoration on the shrine of an altarpiece showing the Ascension of the Virgin. The twelve Apostles kneel praying on either side of the figure of the Virgin. The dominant mood is one of sadness and contemplation. The refinement and personal mannerism of the artist are well reflected in the faces and in the general treatment of the decoration.

Dürer was also court painter to the emperors Maximilian I and Charles V, but his work for them was mainly graphic. It includes the well-known prayer-book of Maximilian. Among work carried out for wealthy bourgeois families was the Heller altarpiece for the Dominican church at Frankfurt am Main (now existing only in copies), commissioned by Jakob Heller. The Paumgärtner altarpiece, probably commissioned by the Paumgärtner family, traditionally contains portraits of Georg and Lucas Paumgärtner in the figures of St George and St Erasmus.

An exact contemporary who represents, as it were, the opposite pole of German art to Dürer was Matthias Grünewald, a mystic who was anti-classical and essentially in tune with medieval ideals. The artist who is regarded today as perhaps the greatest German painter remains almost intangible as a person. Whereas Dürer was interested in the human aspects of religion as it affected man on earth, Grünewald–and in this he appears rooted in medieval spirituality–was transcendental and absorbed in the divine, which he experienced with all the passionate intensity of the mystic. A source of inspiration for his art can be found in the writings of St Brigid of Sweden whose *Revelations* had been published with woodcut illustrations in Nuremberg in 1502. Its sombre mood and threats of perdition were in tune with the popular mood of the day, and, indeed, inspired other artists, such as Lucas Cranach in his early work. Only Grünewald, however, was able to translate into pictorial terms the immediacy and burning sincerity of the work.

Seligenstadt, where Grünewald established himself in 1500, was ruled by the archbishop of Mainz, and the artist became court painter to two archbishops, Uriel Gemmingen and Cardinal Albrecht of Hohenzollern. The work for which Grünewald is most famous, the magnificent high altarpiece for the church in Isenheim, Alsace, now forms part of the art heritage of France, but other fine works by the artist are to be seen in Germany. His earliest known work is *The Mocking of Christ*, painted for the Collegiate Church of Aschaffenburg. As far as we know Grünewald painted only religious subjects. His nearest approach to portraiture is the panel showing the meeting of St Erasmus and St Maurice in which the figure of Erasmus bears the features of Albrecht of Brandenburg, Cardinal Archbishop of Mainz, by whom the work was commissioned for the Collegiate Church of St Maurice and Mary Magdalen at Halle. Grünewald, like so many other artists, seems to have had Lutheran sympathies and, after the suppression of the peasant revolt, to have been dismissed from the archbishop's service.

The Danube School

It says much for the wealth of talented painters in Germany during the early decades of the 16th century that, despite the overwhelming genius of Dürer and Grünewald, other artists were able to maintain a considerable degree of independence, so that neither of the great painters had successors in the strict sense of the word. It is as if the many independent units into which the country was split politically encouraged the establishment of local artists who were able to pursue their own aims or else adapt them to suit the requirements of their patrons. Something of an exception to this tendency towards local development is the Danube School, which covered a wide area stretching from Regensburg to Switzerland. The general characteristics of this school were a manneristic treatment of the human figure and, above all, a very special form of landscape painting.

The first artist to develop the style was Lucas Cranach the Elder, who was born in 1471 in Kronach in Upper Franconia. Cranach was called as court painter to the elector of Saxony in 1505, and in the Protestant centre

114

PAGE FROM THE PRAYER BOOK OF EMPEROR MAXIMILIAN I

printed 1512–13;
Dürer's marginal designs 1514
Albrecht Dürer 1471–1528
Staatsbibliothek, Munich

The prayer book was one of the pet projects of the emperor, who wrote the text for the Knights of the Order of St George, founded in 1469. The leading court artists were called to decorate the borders. The first was Dürer, who began the marginal decorations, and he was followed by Lucas Cranach, Hans Burgkmair, Hans Baldung Grien, Jörg Breu and Jörg Kölderer. The drawings supplement the text of the book in allegorical form.

115

MORRIS DANCER

1480
Erasmus Grasser c. 1450–1526
wood
Historisches Stadtmuseum, Munich

The Morris dancer is one of ten such figures carved by Erasmus Grasser for the frieze in the long room of the old town hall in Munich. With these figures, Grasser created a new popular type of Bavarian art. The grotesque movement of the long-limbed, squat-bodied dancers has perhaps more decorative than sculptural qualities, but their coarse vitality gives them an irrestible attraction.

116

THE BIRTH OF THE VIRGIN

c. 1460
Master of the Life of the Virgin
active in Cologne 1460–80
oak panel
33·5 × 41·75 in (85 × 106 cm)
Alte Pinakothek, Munich

This is one of six panels, all in Munich, of an altarpiece dedicated to the Life of the Virgin Mary. The anonymous artist, named after the Munich panels, is also known from other surviving works and must have headed an important workshop in Cologne during his lifetime. The work shows strong Netherlandish influence, especially in the detailed execution of the unusually spacious interior, but the slightly mannered gestures, small features and demure expressions of the women show a very personal conception.

117 *below*

THE DEATH OF ST KORBINIAN

1483
Jan Polack d. 1519
pinewood
57·9 × 50·8 in (147 × 129 cm)
Alte Pinakothek, Munich

Jan Polack, as his name suggests, was of
Polish descent. He is documented in
Munich from about 1480 until his death.
This panel from the high altar of the
Church of Weihenstephan shows in the
foreground the elongated figure of St
Korbinian on his death-bed, surrounded by
praying companions. Through the open
arcades at the back is a view of the town
of Freising. The rather harsh austerity of
the work and the restless movement are
typical of Bavarian late Gothic art.

118

VIRGIN OF
THE MISERICORD

1480s
attributed to Michael Erhart
active 1469 – 1518
wood
h. 53·1 in (134 cm)
Staatliche Museen, West Berlin

The narrow figure of the Madonna and the
sharp angular folds of the drapery are
typical of the late Gothic style of the last
decades of the 15th century. Also
characteristic of this period is the concept
of Mary as a feudal protectress, expressed
here by the contrast between her towering
figure and the tiny kneeling people
sheltering inside her cloak. The attempt
to depict individual faces relates the group
to the choir-stalls of Ulm Minster from
the workshop where Michael Erhart was
trained. The group was acquired from
Ravensburg.

119 *left*

THE MADONNA AND CHILD

early 16th century
Veit Stoss 1438/47 – 1533
limewood
Germanisches Nationalmuseum, Nuremberg

This work, which shows the mature style
of the artist, was originally carved for his
own house. The Madonna, who is standing
on a lunar disc, is a noble dignified figure,
solid and firmly modelled. The Christ-
child rests against his mother's right
shoulder, wriggling his legs and playing
with her drapery and an apple. His chubby
face and plump little body are beautifully
modelled to show the soft flesh tones.

120 *below*

THE CHURCH FATHERS'
ALTARPIECE

c. 1483
Michael Pacher c. 1435 – 98
cedarwood panel
central panel 85 × 77 in (215 × 195 cm)
Alte Pinakothek, Munich

This altarpiece, with its representations of
St Jerome, St Augustine, St Gregory and
St Ambrosius, was commissioned from the
artist for the Stiftskirche in Brixen,
probably by the provost Leonhard Pacher.
In contrast to the elaborate late Gothic
detail of the canopies, the figures of the
Church Fathers show Pacher's familiarity
with north Italian painting. But the
psychological interpretation, the
manneristic attitudes and gestures of each
figure and the emotional climate are
Pacher's own.

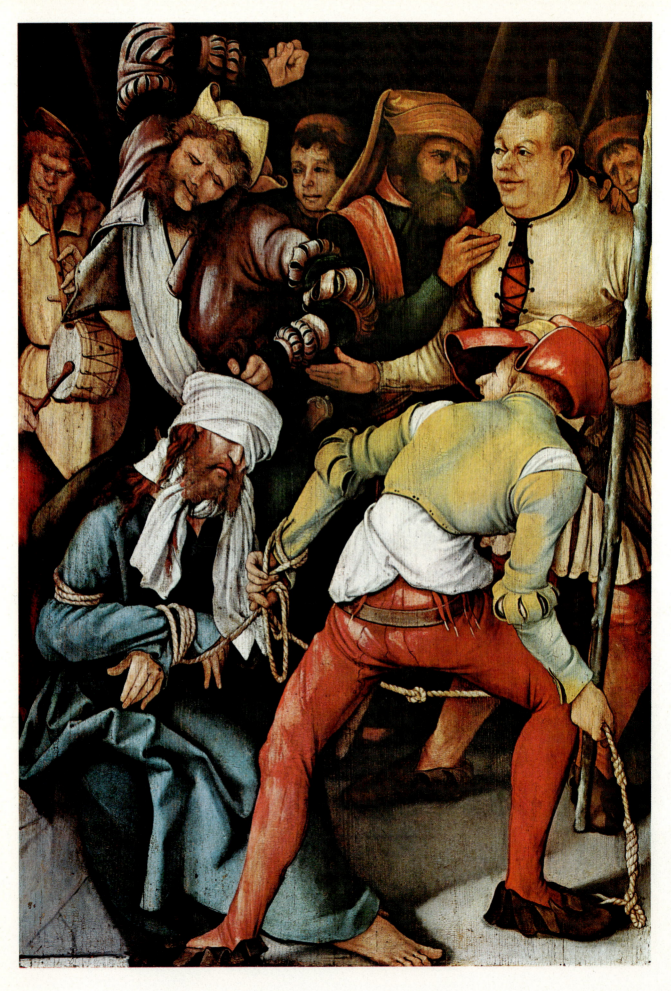

of Wittenberg (where Martin Luther taught as professor at the newly-founded university) he changed his style radically, abandoning the religious scenes and portraits with romantic landscape settings which he had formerly favoured. His new manner consisted of a charming adaptation of Italian mythological themes to a highly individual form of German Mannerism, with particular emphasis on piquant and exquisitely executed nude figures. There was of course little scope in this Protestant stronghold for the development of religious painting, and the bulk of the religious material produced in the Cranach workshop was propaganda for the Lutheran cause. The prestige of the workshop, in which both the artist's sons and many other assistants worked, was far-reaching, especially in Protestant northern Germany where its products were in demand at the courts and among the aristocracy. Lucas Cranach himself was at all times highly esteemed as a portrait painter, and his portraits of Martin Luther, his wife and his parents are historical and artistic documents of great value.

Of the many artists associated with the Danube School, Albrecht Altdorfer of Regensburg was by far the most significant. He was the first German artist, perhaps the first anywhere, to paint independent panels of pure landscape with no figures. Even in his early religious pictures the figures are often so small that they are all but lost in the landscape settings. Altdorfer also specialised in landscape drawings, for which there seems to have been some demand at the time among the aristocracy. Wolf Huber, too, a contemporary of Altdorfer and also a native of Regensburg, supplied many drawings for the same type of clients. Altdorfer's genius, however, soon led to a demand for more orthodox types of paintings by his hand, especially religious altarpieces for churches and monasteries mainly in the Catholic areas.

The 'Little Masters' and Hans Baldung Grien

In addition to landscape and portraiture, classical themes became increasingly popular, especially during the early decades of the 16th century, while the demand for graphic works of all kinds often made these the main field of activity for many of the so-called 'Little Masters', who began to include genre subjects and decorative designs for architectural ornament, jewellery and metalwork in their engraved pattern books and single engravings. Popular figures, such as the Gänsemännchen on the top of a fountain in Nuremberg, appeared everywhere.

Hans Baldung Grien, an artist of Swabian origin and at one time a pupil of Dürer, worked in Strasbourg and Freiburg; his most important altarpiece is still to be seen in the minster of the latter town. Baldung was an original artist who was interested in many branches of art, especially in drawing and engraving. His subject matter included a wide range of nude female figures with both mythological and allegorical significance.

Art and patronage before the Thirty Years War

Augsburg, the home of the Holbein family and the chief centre of activity of the painter Hans Burgkmair the Elder, was also the first town in Germany to introduce a Renaissance building in the true Italian style. This was the chapel built from 1509–18 for the Fugger family in the late Gothic church of St Anne. The leading artists of the day were employed, and it is generally believed that many of the sculptured monuments, though executed by a variety of sculptors, owed much to Dürer. This chapel, though it remained for long an isolated example in Germany, was one of the first works to show a type of patronage in any way comparable to that of the great Italian Renaissance patrons. The Fuggers enjoyed the special protection of the German emperors, for their wealth was a decisive

121
THE MOCKING OF CHRIST

1503
Matthias Grünewald, d. 1528
pinewood
43 × 29 in (109 × 73·5 cm)
Alte Pinakothek, Munich

This, the earliest dated work by Grünewald, was originally painted for the collegiate church of Aschaffenburg. In 1613 it was presented to Duke William V of Bavaria. The passive suffering figure of Christ, the crowding of the figures into a shallow space and the twisted stance of the figure in the left foreground are all late Gothic Mannerist qualities which confirm the picture as an early work. Yet the sophisticated colours and emotional tension are typical of Grünewald.

122
GÄNSEMÄNNCHEN FOUNTAIN

c. 1550
attributed to Pankraz Labenwolf d. 1563
bronze
Nuremberg

The figure of the Gänsemännchen is one of a number of popular folk types used for town monuments, especially fountain heads, in the mid-16th century. The wooden model in the Germanisches Nationalmuseum, Nuremberg, bears the signature of Pankraz Labenwolf. Like so many public works of the kind, however, the fountain may have been the result of collaboration between various artists and their workshops. The immense popularity of the work is probably due rather to the subject matter than to any particular artistic quality in the work.

factor in the political field. Jacob Fugger the Rich had financed three emperors, Maximilian I, Charles V and Ferdinand I, and was probably the most powerful man in Germany. But both he and his immediate successors were restrained in their patronage of the arts, which they did not conceive in the grand manner of their contemporaries in Italy. Nor did the emperor Maximilian I, though he fancied himself as the great patron of art, ever assimilate Italian taste or try to emulate the ambitious projects of the French king, Francis I, who not only succeeded in bringing Leonardo da Vinci to France, but at Fontainebleau was employing leading Italian architects and artists. No immigrant Italians played any decisive role in German art until the second half of the 16th century, when the German aristocracy was once again the main arbiter of taste and the bourgeoisie had lost its dominant position. For the aristocracy were quick to take advantage of the increasing poverty which was the outcome of the peasant revolt and which soon spread from the country to the towns, seriously affecting the ordinary middle-class citizens. In such circumstances only the really wealthy could weather the storm.

The Peace of Augsburg of 1555 brought about an uneasy truce in the religious conflicts, but in the event this proved to be only a lull before the storm of the religious wars in the 17th century. In the latter part of the 16th century the ideals of the Renaissance were adopted everywhere in Germany and the now dominant aristocracy turned increasingly to Italy or the Netherlands to bring architects and sculptors to the country. It seems as if the great creative period in Germany had spent itself and there were no outstanding artists to satisfy the aristocratic patrons. Hans Holbein

142 the Younger, one of the greatest of all portrait painters, left his native Augsburg when he was still in his teens and settled first at Basle and then in England, where he became famous as court painter to Henry VIII. His early death in 1543 and the death of Lucas Cranach in 1551 virtually ended the specifically German aspect of the Renaissance. In Augsburg the Fuggers too called in foreign artists for their projects. The Netherlandish sculptor Hubert Gerhard, who had studied in Florence, worked for the Fuggers in Augsburg around 1581. Later he went to Munich where his major work was the huge figure of St Michael for the façade of the church of the Jesuit college of St Michael.

One of the few native architects at this time was Elias Holl of Augsburg. He had visited Venice and was then able to display a monumental classical

143 style in the new town hall of Augsburg which he built in 1615–20. Ignoring the trend for Mannerism and Baroque noticeable in so many of the new buildings going up at great speed, especially in Franconia, Holl produced a simple geometric structure relying entirely on purity of line and form for decorative effects. However, the most popular of all Renaissance

124 buildings in Germany is the Ottheinrich tract of Heidelberg Castle, built during the reign of the elector Ottheinrich (1556–59). As opposed to Holl's town hall, this building is richly decorated and has a lively and varied façade. The German love of exuberant and rather overloaded ornament is nowhere better expressed than in the wood carvings, mainly by

123 Ebert Wolff the Younger, for the Golden Hall in Schloss Bückeburg.

Thus, before the outbreak of the Thirty Years War the German Renaissance was established in a rich variety of forms ranging from the classical through Mannerism to the beginnings of a dynamic form of early Baroque. These developments were, however, interrupted by the war, during which Germany was the main battleground, with the result that they did not bear fruit until the very end of the 17th century.

Marguerite Kay

123
THE GOLDEN HALL
decorated 1605
Ebert the Younger and Jonas Wolff
Bückeburg Castle, Lower Saxony

The castle was originally built in the 14th century, but was completely restored in 1601–08, at which time the decorations for the famous Golden Room were commissioned by Count Ernst of Schaumburg. The heavy coffered ceiling was fitted with inset oil paintings in the Venetian manner. The greatest wealth of ornament was lavished on the main doorway. Figures of Mars and Venus frame the entrance, and Mercury, supported by satyrs, hovers above the door.

124 *far left*

THE OTTHEINRICHSBAU

1556—59
Heidelberg Castle

The elector Ottheinrich of the Palatinate commissioned this, the most celebrated and popular part of the great complex of Heidelberg Castle. The elector was a man of taste and a keen collector, and he took an active part in designing the work. The whole tract was severely damaged by French troops in 1689 and 1693 and has remained a ruin ever since.

125 *left*

THE ENTRANCE GATE
TO THE MUNICH RESIDENZ

1612—18

The old castle in Munich received its main alterations and enlargements under the elector Maximilian I. His superintendent of work was Hans Krumper, who was responsible for the Perseus fountain in the Grotto Court and for the Patrona Bavariae figure in the central portal niche (**126**). The gateway is very much in the Italian manner, consisting of a two-storeyed regular front with two different orders and a large entrance door flanked by two smaller gates. The whole is rather massive in accordance with Bavarian taste.

126 *left*

PATRONA BAVARIAE

1616
Hans Krumper d. 1632
bronze
over life-size
The Residenz, Munich

This popular figure, one of the landmarks of Munich, was the work of a Netherlandish artist who rose to a leading position at the Munich court, first under Duke William V, who sent him to Italy, and later under the elector Maximilian I of Bavaria. The figure was originally planned on a much smaller scale, but then enlarged to monumental size and set in the heavy red marble niche of the central portal of the Residenz façade.

127

AN ARCADE ARCH *detail*

1595—1612
Lüder von Bentheim
The Town Hall, Bremen

The figures of Love and Justice in the spandrels are balanced by allegorical themes on the relief frieze above. They are typical of the extremely elaborate decoration of the town hall and of the complex themes represented. The entire work seems to have been the result of a collaboration between the architect and the Mayor of Bremen, Hinrich Krefting, who acted as intellectual supervisor. The result is one of the most Italianate compositions to be constructed around an earlier Gothic building.

128

THE HERCULES FOUNTAIN

1596–1602
Adriaen de Vries c. 1546–1626
bronze
Augsburg

This fountain, together with the Mercury
fountain, was commissioned in 1596 by
the city of Augsburg from Adriaen de
Vries, a sculptor born in The Hague and
trained in Italy in the Florentine school of
Giovanni Bologna. He had previously
worked for Emperor Rudolf II in Prague.
The many sculptured figures crowned by
the powerful Hercules at the top are
remarkable for their rich full modelling
and still show the strong influence of
Bologna.

129

A JEWEL CHEST *detail*

c. 1580
designed by Wenzel Jamnitzer 1508–85
mother-of-pearl, gems, pearls,
wood covered with silver, parcel gilt
19·7 × 21·25 × 14·2 in (50 × 54 × 36 cm)
Grünes Gewölbe, Dresden

Jamnitzer's sketch for this remarkable
jewel chest has survived, and is today in
Leningrad. The work itself was executed
by the master goldsmith Nicolaus Schmidt,
who was a master in Nuremberg in 1582.
The three standing figures in the niches
represent Chastity, in the centre, with
Justice and Faith on the left and right
respectively. Between these niches, in
canopy-like structures, are two kings.

130 *centre*

CARDINAL ALBRECHT
VON BRANDENBURG
BEFORE THE CROSS

after 1520
Lucas Cranach the Elder 1472–1553
pinewood panel
62·2 × 44·1 in (158 × 112 cm)
Alte Pinakothek, Munich

Although Cranach was court painter to the
protestant electors of Saxony and lived in
Wittenberg, he also worked for non-
protestant princes. He did a number of
paintings for Cardinal Albrecht, Elector of
Brandenburg, of which this is one of the
finest. The work shows the cardinal
kneeling in a lonely landscape with a heavy
threatening sky above.

132

ADAM AND EVE

c. 1510/12
Lucas Cranach the Elder 1472–1553
limewood
18·5 × 13·8 in (47 × 35 cm)
Alte Pinakothek, Munich

Cranach painted this subject many times
throughout his life. The Munich example
is probably the earliest surviving one and
shows similarities with Dürer's famous
engraving of 1504. It also shows, especially
in the figure of Eve, something of the
artist's Mannerist style, which he
developed after he entered the service of
Frederick the Wise, Elector of Saxony.

131 *right*

THE ST JOHN ALTARPIECE
detail

1518
Hans Burgkmair the Elder 1473–1531/32
pinewood, 60·25 × 48·9 in (153 × 124·7 cm)
Alte Pinakothek, Munich

This altarpiece was recorded as being in
the private gallery of Emperor Maximilian I
before 1627. A mature work, it shows
very clearly the influence of the artist's
studies in Italy – Burgkmair was
instrumental in introducing the
Renaissance style into southern Germany.
He was patronised by Frederick the Wise,
Elector of Saxony, and by the wealthy
Fugger family, and was the favourite
court painter of Maximilian I.

ALEXANDER M. DARIVM VLT: SVPERAT
CAESIS IN ACIE PERSAR: PEDIT. C M. EQVIT
VERO X M. INTERFECTIS. MATRE QVOQVE
CONIVGE LIBERIS DARII REGCVM M. HAVD
AMPLIVS EQVITIB: FVGA DILAPSI CAPTIS.

133
THE BATTLE OF ALEXANDER

1529, Albrecht Altdorfer c. 1480–1538
limewood, 62 × 47 in (158·4 × 120·3 cm)
Bayerisches Nationalmuseum, Munich

The picture, which is signed and dated, was commissioned from
the artist by Duke William IV of Bavaria for his new
Lustschloss. It shows the victory of Alexander over the Persians at
Issus, and the historical events are faithfully depicted in the
myriads of tiny soldiers. In contrast to this, the superbly painted
landscape and sky above have a cosmic quality. The scene is one
of the first examples of a new genre – the history piece.

134
THE KNIGHT, DEATH AND THE DEVIL

1513, Albrecht Dürer 1471–1528, copperplate engraving
9·7 × 7·5 in (24·6 × 19 cm)

This is one of the three so-called master engravings produced by
Dürer in 1513–14, the other two being *St Jerome in his Study* and
Melancolia. In this work Dürer portrays the Christian Knight
riding steadfastly towards his destiny, ignoring the figures of
Death on his right and of the Devil behind him. His magnificent
horse, perhaps modelled on Leonardo's studies for the
equestrian monument to Duke Francesco Sforza, forms a striking
contrast to the tired nag ridden by the melancholy figure of Death.

135 *above*

THE CORONATION
OF THE VIRGIN

*1516, Hans Baldung Grien 1484/85 – 1545
panel, 112·2 × 90·9 in (285 × 231 cm)
Freiburg Minster*

This is the central panel of the high altar
in Freiburg Minster. The painting still
shows the influence of Baldung's earlier
stay in Nuremberg, in Dürer's workshop,
especially in the figure of the Madonna.
But it already shows the artist's very
personal style. The richly-carved original
frame, in which Italian influence seems
to have run riot, and the tiny putti-angels
assisting joyously at the coronation scene,
are typical for this artist.

136 *right*

CHRIST AS MAN OF SORROWS

*c. 1429, Hans Multscher c. 1400 – 67, stone
Ulm Minster*

The figure of Christ, amazingly realistic
for its date, still stands on the site for which
it was made, against the central pillar of the
porch of the great tower of Ulm Minster.
Christ leans slightly forward and points
accusingly with his right hand to the
wound in his side. The drapery is treated
with a new sense of its relationship to the
body, no longer in the linear ornamental
manner of International Gothic.

137 *below*

THE ANNUNCIATION

1502, Hans Holbein the Elder, active 1493–c. 1526
pinewood panel, 55·5 × 33·1 in (141 × 84 cm)
Alte Pinakothek, Munich

The panel, which is signed Hanns Holbon, formed one of the painted wings of an altarpiece, the carved central shrine of which (now lost) was by Gregor Erhart. It was commissioned by Abbot Georg Kastner for the high altar in the church at Kaisheim. The eight panels show scenes from the Passion of Christ on the outside and the Life of the Virgin on the inside.

138 *left*

TOMB OF THE SCHREYER FAMILY *detail*

1492, Adam Krafft c. 1455–1509, stone
Church of St Sebaldus, Nuremberg

This monumental tomb outside the choir of the church of St Sebaldus in Nuremberg was made for one of the leading patrician families. The scenes depicted are the Carrying of the Cross (shown here), the Entombment and the Resurrection. A new sense of realism can be seen in the rather heavy, austere figures with heads which appear to be taken from life. Adam Krafft owed less to Italy than did his friend Peter Vischer, but the work does show a more individualised conception.

139

ST GEORGE AND THE DRAGON

1582
Hans Keller
Grünes Gewölbe, Dresden

St George, on a leaping horse, raises his
sword to slay the dragon which already
has a spear sticking through its throat. In
the saint's left hand is an oval shield with
the monogram FAC and the electoral hat
of Augustus the Strong of Saxony, added
at a later date. The piece was originally
presented to the elector Christian II by his
brother Johann Georg before 1610. The
piece bears the mastermark of Hans Keller,
R. 3142.

140 *top left*

A DECORATIVE VESSEL

c. 1570
Wenzel Jamnitzer 1508–85
gold, enamel, mother-of-pearl and shell
Residenz-Schatzkammer, Munich

The Viennese goldsmith Wenzel Jamnitzer
established a highly successful workshop
in Nuremberg. This middle-class
stronghold was the major centre for the
minor arts in Germany in the later 16th
century. Jamnitzer, however, was also
favoured by four emperors. The vessel
illustrated is one of his best works,
satisfying in both form and structure.

141

THE SCHLÜSSELFELD SHIP

1503, Peter Vischer the Elder
silver, partly gilded
31·25 × 17·2 in (79 × 43·5 cm)
Germanisches Nationalmuseum, Nuremberg

The first known owner of this table-piece
was Wilhelm Schlüsselfeld, who probably
inherited it from his uncle Matthäus
Landauer, for whom it was originally
made. It is thus connected with leading
patrician families in Nuremberg and is an
excellent example of the high-quality
goldwork produced in Nuremberg
during this period.

142
THE HANSEATIC MERCHANT GEORGE GISZE OF DANZIG

Hans Holbein the Younger 1497/98 – 1543
1532, oil and tempera on oak panel
37·6 × 33·75 in (96 × 85·7 cm)
Gemäldegalerie, West Berlin

Before he was appointed official court painter to Henry VIII of England many of Holbein's clients were members of the Hanseatic Merchants in London. Such merchants were representative of the wealthy middle class, whose rise to prominence in the 15th – 16th century had a considerable effect on German art.

143
AUGSBURG TOWN HALL

1615 – 20, Elias Holl 1573 – 1646

The new town hall, commissioned from Elias Holl by the Augsburg municipal authorities, is generally regarded as this architect's most successful achievement. Though partially destroyed in World War II, it has since been restored. The centre of the building, emphasised on the outside by the dominant central tract, was occupied by the three-storey high Golden Hall. The two towers with bulbous domes, added in 1618, complete the heavy cubic symmetry of the building, which is conceived in the manner of Roman Renaissance architecture.

144

STATUETTE OF ST GEORGE

c. 1590, Hans Schleich
gold, enamel, precious stones, pearls
Residenzmuseum, Munich

This exquisite piece of goldwork was commissioned by Duke Wilhelm of Bavaria and has never left Munich. It was executed by the goldsmith Hans Schleich, probably from designs by the Netherlandish artist Jan van Schwanenburg of Utrecht. In detail, the style of the ornament is of the Italian Renaissance, but the rich accumulation of rubies, emeralds and pearls that decorate the pedestal, and the slightly bulging forms of its structure are more Baroque in feeling.

145

SUSANNA BATHING

1526, Albrecht Altdorfer c. 1480 – 1538
limewood
29·5 × 24·2 in (74·8 × 61·2 cm)
Alte Pinakothek, Munich

This picture, which is signed and dated, is a late work by the artist, who has given free reign to his imagination in the interpretation of the story. Susanna is depicted as fully dressed, with only her legs exposed, and being attended by her maidens. The rather romantic landscape setting is in the style of the Danube School.

146 *right*

THE FOUR APOSTLES *detail*

1526, Albrecht Dürer 1471 – 1528
oil on wood, 7 ft × 2 ft 6 in (2·15 × ·76 m)
Alte Pinakothek, Munich

The two panels, perhaps originally planned as wings of a triptych whose central panel was never painted, form Dürer's last major work. They were uncommissioned, being intended as a gift by the artist to his native city of Nuremberg. They sum up in monumental form his final synthesis of Italian and Northern art and represent his personal conception of religious humanism. Represented are St John and St Peter on one panel and St Paul and St Mark on the other.

147

PORTRAIT MEDALLION OF A KNIGHT OF THE GOLDEN FLEECE

c. 1450, gold enamel and chalcedony, diameter 3·5 in (9 cm)
Residenzmuseum, Munich

The identity of the sitter has not been definitely established, but he is probably Duke Philip the Good of Burgundy, who founded the Order of the Golden Fleece in 1430. The work is Burgundian and of very high quality. The realism of the face in the cameo-like medallion is striking, and the artist has made no attempt to soften the features, although the modelling is sensitive and the eye keen and expressive.

148 *below right*

THE DISPUTATION OF ST ERASMUS AND ST MAURICE

1524–25, Matthias Grünewald, d. 1528
pinewood, 89 × 69·25 in (226 × 176 cm)
Alte Pinakothek, Munich

The painting was commissioned by Cardinal Albrecht, elector of Mainz, for his new collegiate church at Halle where it formed part of a vast decorative scheme. The arms of the archbishoprics of Mainz and Magdeburg and of the bishopric of Halberstadt are embroidered in pearls at Erasmus's feet. Erasmus, identified by the windlass and intestines in his right hand (he was supposedly martyred by having his intestines wound out of his body on a windlass) is a portrait of the cardinal.

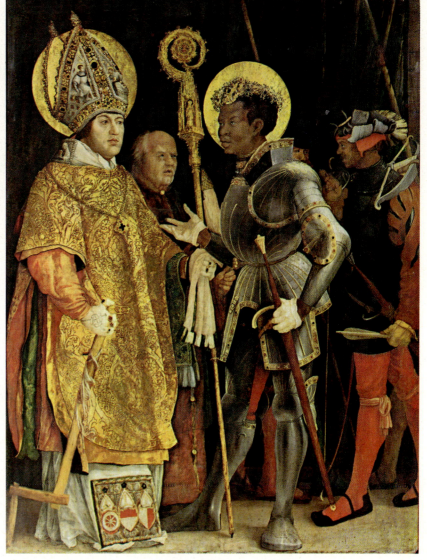

Charles V's great dream of the Holy Roman Empire as a coherent political entity under a single ruler was finally shattered by the Thirty Years War, and the resultant complete political fragmentation of Germany is an important factor in the evolution of art and patronage in the century and a half which preceded the Napoleonic upheavals. No area of Germany escaped entirely the effects of the war, and the works of art created there during the period are, with few exceptions, of limited interest.

The sudden changes of fortune so often characteristic of war are inimical to large-scale patronage of the arts, but such times can nevertheless provide opportunities for collectors which would otherwise be impossible. One collector who took full advantage of the opportunities was Duke Maximilian of Bavaria who, as a powerful member of the Catholic League, was systematic in the additions he made to his Kunstkammer in Munich. He had already in 1617 commissioned four hunting pictures from Rubens to decorate Altschleissheim, his hunting lodge, which formerly stood on the site of Schloss Schleissheim a few miles north of Munich. But above all he had developed a passion for the paintings of Dürer. When the army of the Catholic League turned its attention to the great Protestant city of Nuremberg, Maximilian extracted Dürer's *Apostles* from the city fathers in exchange for leaving the city unmolested. Later, in 1627, he obtained Dürer's *Lamentation* by comparable means from Wittenberg, and his troops received precise instructions as to where paintings he desired were to be found. The intervention of the Protestant Swedish army headed by Gustavus Adolphus temporarily reversed the fortunes of the war, but Maximilian succeeded in hiding most of his collection when Munich was captured by the Swedes.

After the Thirty Years War the real political power rested not with the emperor in distant Vienna but with his electors and those few princes whose domains were sufficiently large and prosperous to survive as viable economic units, while the fifty or so independent imperial cities, such as Hamburg, Nuremberg and Augsburg, became increasingly less important as centres of artistic patronage. When the memories of the war had retreated into the past, the antagonism between the Catholic and Protestant rulers diminished, and in fact several important princes, such as the elector of Saxony, felt able to change their religious allegiances for purely political advantage. The years round 1675 saw a stable, if chaotic, political system flourishing in Germany, and during the last quarter of the 17th century the groundwork was laid for the brilliant flowering of the arts that took place in the 18th century.

By 1675 a pattern had evolved whereby the predominantly Protestant areas of northern Germany tended to look to the Netherlands for inspiration, while the predominantly Catholic areas of southern Germany looked south to Italy. The situation is complicated by the influence of Rubens, and at first it was his northern High Baroque style which was the most powerful force for the introduction of the 'Baroque', as against the merely 'Italianate', into Germany. Matthias Rauchmiller's tomb of Bishop Karl von Metternich of *c.* 1675 in the Liebfrauenkirche at Trier is one of the earliest examples of German sculpture to reveal the impact of the Italian sculptor Gian Lorenzo Bernini, while Italian High Baroque painting took longer to penetrate.

Patronage at the Palatine court

From the 1680s onwards foreign patrons became increasingly important in Italy, and, with the economic revival of Germany, the German rulers were in the forefront of this movement, while the increasing numbers of marriages between the Northern and Italian houses provided an additional

Patrons and Collectors in the Baroque Age

1618 – c. 1800

149

ST GEORGE AND THE DRAGON
1721
Egid Quirin Asam 1692–1750
wood, with silver, gilt and polychrome over life-size
High altar of the Abbey Church, Weltenburg

Abbot Maurus Bächl commissioned the young brothers Cosmas Damian and Egid Quirin Asam to rebuild the abbey church of Weltenburg in 1714, and the high altar was completed in 1721. The Asam brothers were responsible for introducing the powerful Baroque illusionism of Bernini into Bavaria, and for combining this with the local tradition of realistic woodcarving.

element. Perhaps the most significant of such marriages from the point of view of patronage was that between Anna Maria Luisa, the daughter of Grand Duke Cosimo III of Tuscany, and Johann Wilhelm von Pfalz Neuburg, the Elector Palatine and a member of the Wittelsbach family.

Johann Wilhelm succeeded to the Palatinate in 1690 after it had been devastated by the troops of Louis XIV of France, but by his death in 1716 Düsseldorf, his capital, had been transformed into one of the artistic centres of Europe. Small military victories and a great deal of adroit political manoeuvering gave Johann Wilhelm an influence in European affairs totally out of proportion to the size and importance of the Palatinate, and to a certain extent this was assisted by both the marriage of his sister Eleonore Magdalena Theresia to the emperor Leopold I, and the whole question of the succession to the grand duchy of Tuscany. Gabriel Grupello's equestrian monument to him in Düsseldorf (1703–11) proudly reflects his political achievements. It is difficult, if not impossible, to try to separate the collecting activities of Johann Wilhelm from those of Anna Maria Luisa, and her influence has been often underestimated. As joint patrons of the arts they were lavish, and the wide range of their taste is most remarkable at such an early date.

Anna Maria Luisa brought with her to Düsseldorf, as part of her dowry, Raphael's *Holy Family of the Casa Canigiani*, but this remained at first somewhat isolated in the collection, for, after their visit to Holland in 1696, she and her husband developed a strong enthusiasm for the Dutch painters, in particular Jan Weenix and Adriaen van der Werff. The latter refused the post of court painter at Düsseldorf, but agreed to work exclusively for the elector for six months of the year, and the precious enamellike finish of his paintings was very greatly admired. However, Johann Wilhelm's agents in Holland and Flanders were outstandingly successful in their purchases of works by the great early 17th-century masters, and by his death the elector had assembled some seventeen paintings by Van Dyck and forty by Rubens.

176

The elector gave substantial commissions to a number of Italian artists, most notably the Neapolitan Luca Giordano, but his efforts to encourage Italian artists to settle in Düsseldorf were less successful, and both Antonio Balestra and the Venetian pastellist Rosalba Carriera refused. However, when the latter's brother-in-law Gianantonio Pellegrini left England in 1712 he accepted Johann Wilhelm's invitation. The splendid fresco of the Fall of Phaethon, which he painted over one of the staircases in Johann Wilhelm's castle at Bensberg survives in situ, while his great allegorical cycle glorifying the elector was later transferred to Schleissheim. After Johann Wilhelm's death, Anna Maria Luisa returned to Florence, and the brilliant court finally ceased to exist when the new elector, Karl Philipp, transferred the capital to Mannheim in 1720. The majority of the collections remained in Düsseldorf until the line of Pfalz-Neuburg went extinct, when they reverted to the senior branch of the Wittelsbachs who transferred them to Munich.

Art and patronage in northern Germany

The poor sandy soil of Brandenburg had long proved an obstacle to the economic growth of the area, but by the second half of the 17th century Brandenburg was emerging fast as one of the most dynamic forces in Germany. Although Friedrich Wilhelm II, the Great Elector, who reigned 1640–88, was more interested in the development of his state's resources than in patronage of the arts, he tried to persuade the painter Michael Willmann to settle in Brandenburg. Willmann was active there in 1657–60, but eventually he embraced the Catholic faith and decided to

150

BUST OF DUKE KARL I
OF BRUNSWICK

c. 1770 marble
Bartolomeo Cavaceppi 1716–99
over life-size
Herzog Anton-Ulrich-Museum, Brunswick

Karl I of Braunschweig-Wolfenbüttel, the grandson of Duke Anton Ulrich, added further works to the collection left by his forbear. Karl I was the brother-in-law of Frederick the Great, having married Philippine Charlotte of Prussia, and the classicising taste revealed by this bust is in part due to his influence and in part to that of his own son, Karl Wilhelm Ferdinand, who had visited Rome in the 1760s.

settle instead in the Cistercian abbey of Lubiąż in Silesia. With Johann Arnold Nering the Great Elector was much more successful, for after his training in architecture and mathematics Nering returned to Berlin, where he was appointed surveyor general of works in 1691 by the Great Elector's successor. Elector Friedrich III (later King Friedrich I of Prussia) commissioned from Nering the palace of Oranienburg (1689–95) and the Arsenal (begun 1695), while for his consort Sophie Charlotte, the sister of George I of England, Nering began the great palace of Charlottenburg. Unfortunately, his career was cut short by his untimely death in 1695 at the age of thirty-six, and he was replaced by the much more gifted sculptor and architect Andreas Schlüter, who had arrived from Warsaw the previous year.

Prussian Baroque reached its greatest heights in the hands of Schlüter, and the superb series of keystones he carved for the Arsenal have a simple intensity which makes them deeply moving. The bronze equestrian

154 monument to the Great Elector was begun by Schlüter in 1696 and cast in 1700, while the four slaves which decorate the pedestal were cast in 1708. In 1699 Schlüter was appointed surveyor general of the palace and made responsible for the rebuilding of the Schloss in Berlin, and there his dynamic use of a giant order for the central projection of the main façade gave the building a fully Baroque vigour. Damaged in the Second World War, the palace was finally demolished in 1950. It was much to be regretted, however, that Schlüter's skill as a designer was not matched by his building ability, and after repeated instances of damage due to faulty construction, culminating in the collapse of the Münzturm, a water tower which he had begun to build in 1702, he was dismissed. Friedrich I of Prussia died in 1713 and in the aggressively homespun court of his thrifty and militaristic successor, Friedrich Wilhelm I, there was no place for Schlüter. In 1714 he left for St Petersburg and died there in the same year, while in Prussia the arts temporarily stagnated.

The building activity of the other major Protestant ruler in North

167 Germany to show any interest in the arts, Duke Anton-Ulrich of Braunschweig-Wolfenbüttel, was on a less lavish scale, and to reduce costs his palace at Salzdahlum was timber framed. Included in the design was a long gallery, lit by high-level windows, and other smaller galleries and cabinets specifically designed for the exhibition of the great collection of paintings which Anton Ulrich had assembled. The great importance of Anton Ulrich lies in his activity as a collector rather than as a builder, and

177 the finest paintings were all there by 1710, including *Judith and Holofernes* by Rubens. At his death in 1714 he requested his heirs never to break up the collection and today it forms the basis of the Herzog Anton-Ulrich-Museum at Brunswick.

The Schönborn family as patrons

Lothar Franz von Schönborn was one of the most remarkable patrons of the early 18th century in Germany and the effective founder of the Schönborn family fortunes. Unlike his contemporaries already discussed, he was both an active builder and an insatiable collector. Lothar Franz was elected prince bishop of Bamberg in 1693 and archbishop elector of Mainz two years later, thus starting a half century of domination of Franconia and the middle Rhine by the family. His nephew Friedrich Karl was appointed imperial chancellor in 1705 which necessitated residence in Vienna, but subsequently he obtained permission to live outside Austria and reigned as prince bishop of Würzburg during the years 1729–46. Another nephew, Johann Philipp Franz von Schönborn, had previously reigned in Würzburg as prince bishop until 1724, while a

151
CENTRAL BLOCK
OF SCHLOSS POMMERSFELDEN
1711–18
Johann Dientzenhofer 1663–1726
Built for the elector Lothar Franz von Schönborn, Schloss Weissenstein at Pommersfelden near Nuremberg was one of the first great German Baroque country houses. Johann Dientzenhofer was responsible for the overall layout, and the exterior of the central block is mostly his work. Lukas von Hildebrandt was called in from Vienna to redesign the staircase inside, and Maximilian von Welsch came from Mainz to build the stables which close the court (1714–17).

third nephew, Franz Georg, became archbishop elector of Trier. Damian Hugo, the fourth and last ecclesiastical nephew, was prince bishop of Speyer and responsible for the construction of Schloss Bruchsal. The building activity of Lothar Franz was centred on Schloss Weissenstein at Pommersfelden, where Johann Dientzenhofer was responsible for the main blocks in 1711–18. However, problems arose over the staircase hall, which was too large as a result of the personal intervention of the elector in the planning, and Lukas von Hildebrandt was called in from Vienna. The three stories of arcades inserted by Hildebrandt round the interior was an ingenious solution to the problem as well as improving the communications within the palace.

Lothar Franz's taste in paintings is clearly revealed in his famous letter of 10th October 1708 where, in an execrable mixture of French and German, he acknowledged his unrepentant love of semi-erotic nudes. The subject matter of the paintings he bought or commissioned was of little interest to him so long as they contained female nudes. Often the exact subject was left to the painter to decide. The majority of these are still at Pommersfelden, or were until recently. The huge demand for such pictures from German and Austrian collectors gives much of Italian Late Baroque painting its characteristic and peculiar flavour. Other major works acquired by Lothar Franz include Dürer's *Man of Sorrows* which is still in the palace, and his *Portrait of Muffel*, now in Berlin.

The younger members of the Schönborn family were less forceful, but they had the taste and judgment to recognise the genius of the architect Balthasar Neumann and then to give him both a free hand and almost unlimited funds. After an initial period of study and travel. Neumann returned to Würzburg in 1720, when he and Johann Dientzenhofer were appointed by Johann Philipp Franz surveyors of the gigantic new Residenz. Two years later he became responsible for all building operations in the bishoprics of Würzburg and Bamberg, though in 1723 he had to submit to the advice of the French architects Robert de Cotte and Germain Boffrand. Unfortunately, just as Neumann gained the confidence of Johann Philipp Franz, the prince bishop died, and under his thrifty successor Christoph Franz von Hutten work was suspended. The accession of Friedrich Karl von Schönborn as prince bishop transformed the situation, but although the building work on the Residenz was pressed forward with great energy, Neumann was forced to accept Lukas von Hildebrandt as his collaborator, with special responsibility for the decoration. Today the uniform sombre tones of the building are most misleading, for originally the silver-grey stone was contrasted against a deep yellow ground, while the sculpture in the balustrades was painted a brilliant white and the coats of arms were gilded. Even before the Residenz was structurally complete in 1738, Neumann was called upon to collaborate again with Hildebrandt in the building of Friedrich Karl's summer seat, Schloss Werneck (1734–45). After 1733 Neumann held the post of superintendent at Trier under Franz Georg von Schönborn, and was responsible for the remarkable rebuilding of the Abbey Church of St Paulinus there, while in addition he worked as architect to Damian Hugo von Schönborn at Speyer, where from 1728 he built the staircase and flanking state rooms (since destroyed) of Schloss Bruchsal.

For the decoration of the Kaisersaal in the Würzburg Residenz, the prince bishop Karl Philipp von Greifenklau turned to the greatest fresco painter in Europe and, after great difficulties, in 1750 succeeded in engaging Giambattista Tiepolo. Here, the superb frescoes depicting *Apollo conducting Frederick Barbarossa's Bride Beatrice of Burgundy* are combined

152
THE OLD TOWN HALL
1744–56
Jakob Michael Küchel 1703–69
Bamberg

Jakob Michael Küchel designed the Old Town Hall of Bamberg on an island site approached by bridges, and the road passes through an archway. The rich rocaille carving decorating the balcony and the cartouche above was executed by Franz Mutschelle, and with the Crucifixion group by Leonhard Goldwitzer (1715) it forms a charming Rococo ensemble. Küchel worked under Neumann as a court architect at Bamberg, and was one of his most able assistants.

153

THE STAIRCASE OF
THE RESIDENZ

1737–50
Balthasar Neumann 1687–1753
Würzburg

The Residenz at Würzburg was begun in
1719, but the original plans were
substantially altered during construction.
Neumann began the staircase in 1737 for
the prince bishop Friedrich Carl von
Schönborn, whose successor, the prince
bishop Karl Philipp von Greiffenklau, in
1750 commissioned Giambattista Tiepolo
to decorate the vault with a vast fresco,
*The Four Continents of the World paying
Homage to the Prince Bishop.*

154

MONUMENT TO THE GREAT
ELECTOR OF BRANDENBURG

1696–1709
Andreas Schlüter 1662/3?–1714
bronze
over life-size
Courtyard of Schloss Charlottenburg,
West Berlin

The equestrian figure of the Great Elector,
Friedrich Wilhelm II, was cast in 1700. The
group of four slaves round the base were
cast in 1708, and the group placed in
position on the Lange Brücke near the
Schloss in Berlin in the following year.
It was moved to its present position after
the Second World War. The powerful
Baroque vigour with which Schlüter
endowed the horse and rider is developed
further in the agitated slaves below.

155

THE WALLPAVILLON
OF THE ZWINGER

begun 1716
Mathaes Daniel Pöppelmann 1662–1736
Dresden

Pöppelmann began the construction of the
Zwinger for Augustus the Strong, elector
of Saxony and king of Poland, in 1709 as a
setting for court fêtes. The wings were to
be in effect an orangery, while the pavilions
were to serve as grandstands for the
entertainments. The richly festive
architecture is in complete harmony with
this function, and the Wallpavillon is the
climax of the whole composition.

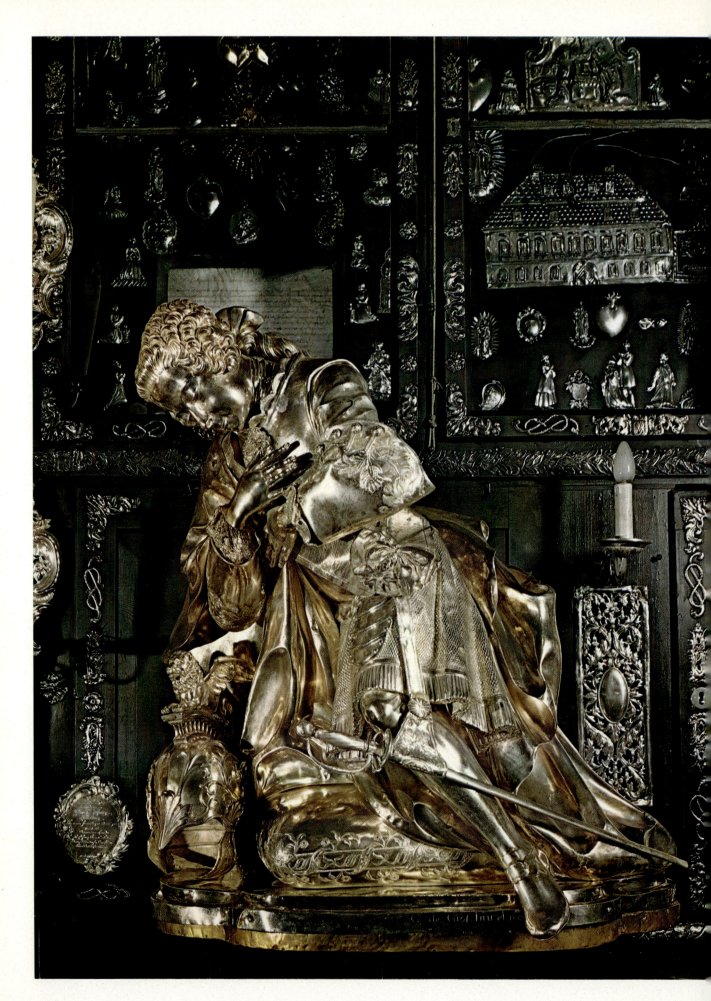

with Antonio Bossi's stucco decorations and giant columns cut from a rich red marble, making it one of the most splendid Baroque ensembles in all Germany. The success of this room led Karl Philipp von Greifenklau to assign the vault over the staircase also to Tiepolo, where in 1752 he painted *The Four Continents of the World paying Homage to the Prince Bishop*. Tiepolo always gave his best with such anachronistic and absolutist themes, and this vast fresco is perhaps the most significant expression of the 'ancien régime' in southern Germany. Adam Friedrich von Seinsheim, who became prince bishop of Würzburg in 1755 and of Bamberg four years later, was closely related to the Schönborns, and on a less lavish scale carried on their traditions of patronage. In particular he enjoyed the witty parodies of classical sculpture created by Ferdinand Dietz for the parks of his country houses, and the decoration of that at Veitshöchheim has an almost infectious vigour and gaiety. Nevertheless, the Festsaal and chapel of Schloss Sünching near Regensburg, decorated in 1761, are totally different in character, and the frescoes of Matthäus Günther contrasted with delicate white sculpture by Ignaz Günther and the stuccoes of Franz Xaver Feichtmayr make these two of the most important Rococo interiors in Germany.

Baroque and Rococo in Bavaria and the middle Rhine

Further south, in Bavaria, secular artistic activity in the first quarter of the 18th century revolved around the elector Max Emmanuel, the head of the Wittelsbach family. Max Emmanuel had succeeded in 1679 at the age of seventeen, and between 1685 and 1690 he fought under Prince Eugene of Savoy against the Turks. The culmination of his collaboration with the Austrians came in 1691, when he was appointed regent of the Spanish Netherlands, and the ten years he spent there were his most important as a collector. Max Emmanuel's biggest coup came in 1698, when he purchased 105 paintings from Gisbert van Ceulen, including ten by Rubens, thirteen by Van Dyck and Murillo's *Beggar Boys playing Dice*. The majority of these are now in Munich or Schleissheim. Ever politically capricious, Max Emmanuel sided with Louis XIV against the Austrians in the War of Spanish Succession, and returned to Munich in 1702. After his defeat by Marlborough at Blenheim, Max Emmanuel went into exile in Brussels and France until his electorate was restored to him by the Austrians after the Peace of Rastatt in 1714. Between his return to Munich in 1715 and his death in 1726 Max Emmanuel was intensely active as a patron of the arts, but now he concentrated on the building and decoration of his palaces.

Around the turn of the century Bavarian architecture was dominated by two Italo-Swiss, Enrico Zuccalli and Giovanni Antonio Viscardi, and the former had been responsible for the remodelling of Schleissheim (begun 1694) and the decoration of three suites in the Munich Residenz. But just as Max Emmanuel's political allegiance turned to France around 1700, so did his artistic interests. His protégé Joseph Effner was sent to study in Paris under Germain Boffrand, and in 1715 was appointed court architect in Munich. This appointment was followed by a flood of commissions from Max Emmanuel, first of all for the rebuilding of Schloss Dachau and then, in the park of the Nymphenburg Palace, for the delightful and subtle Pagodenburg and the Badenburg. Effner introduced into Bavaria the French 'Régence' style of decoration, but by the death of Max Emmanuel in 1726 he had developed a much freer and more dynamic decorative vocabulary.

At the succession of Karl Albrecht as elector of Bavaria, Effner was replaced as court architect by François Cuvilliés, who was responsible for the fullest development of the 'French Manner' of Rococo decoration in

157

164

156
VOTIVE STATUE
OF THE CROWN PRINCE
MAXIMILIAN JOSEPH
OF BAVARIA
1737
Wilhelm de Groff c. 1680–1742
silver
h. 37 in (94 cm)
Pilgrimage church of Altötting, Bavaria
Made as a votive offering for the Crown Prince Maximilian's recovery from an illness, this statue of him kneeling before the Virgin is extremely naturalistic. However, it illustrates well that special blend of elegant worldliness and deep devotion which was characteristic of the first half of the 18th century.

157
ALLEGORY OF AUTUMN
1765–68
Ferdinand Dietz 1708–77
sandstone
approximately life-size
Garden of Schloss Veitshöchheim,
near Würzburg

Ferdinand Dietz executed the majority of the garden sculpture at Veitshöchheim in the years 1765–68, but owing to weathering much of it, including this group, has had to be replaced by copies. The strong features of the figures verge on the grotesque and they have a wild rumbustious vigour. The element of parody of the classical world is emphasised by Bacchus's goat eating the grapes at the base of the group.

158

THE STAIRCASE
OF SCHLOSS BRÜHL

designed 1740
Balthasar Neumann 1687–1753

Schloss Brühl was reconstructed from 1725 by Johann Conrad Schlaun for Clemens August, the archbishop elector of Cologne, but in 1728 he was replaced by Cuvilliés. The design of the staircase created difficulties and in 1740 Balthasar Neumann was called in. The huge spacious staircase he created extends through the full height of the building and is crowned by a fresco painted by Carlo Carlone in 1750. The rest of the decoration, including the immensely rich stucco work by Artario, was not completed until 1764.

159

POPE CLEMENT'S VISION
OF THE HOLY TRINITY

1735
Giambattista Tiepolo 1696–1770
oil on canvas
192 × 101 in (488 × 256 cm)
Alte Pinakothek, Munich

This enormous altarpiece was commissioned from Giambattista Tiepolo by Clemens August, archbishop elector of Cologne and son of Max Emmanuel of Bavaria, for the high altar of the Church of the Congregation of Notre Dame at Nymphenburg. This is one of two major works commissioned from Tiepolo by Clemens August. The second, his *Adoration of the Kings* painted for the abbey of Schwarzach, is also in the Alte Pinakothek.

Bavaria. His decorations of 1730–37 for the Reichen Zimmer in the Munich Residenz are the earliest fully Rococo decorations in Germany, and there are important changes in the decorative details which separate this flowering of Bavarian Rococo from the Rococo decorations produced in France itself. These are the introduction of large amounts of naturalistic detail in contrast to the almost abstract stylisation of French Rococo decorations of the period. The climax of this new style is reached in the Amalienburg, built by Cuvilliés for the electress Maria Amalia in 1734–39, **165** where the stuccoes and woodcarvings by Johann Baptist Zimmermann and his collaborators are of unparalleled delicacy and refinement. Instead of employing the normal white and gold colour scheme, Cuvilliés decorated the main saloon in silver, pale blue and white, while other smaller rooms are decorated in two shades of yellow and silver.

Cuvilliés also worked for Karl Albrecht's younger brother Clemens August, the archbishop elector of Cologne, at Schloss Brühl near Bonn, where he was responsible for Falkenlust, a hunting lodge in the park. Clemens August (born in 1700) rapidly emerged as a considerable political figure, having become prince bishop of Münster and Paderborn in 1719, archbishop elector of Cologne in 1723, bishop of Hildesheim in 1724 and of Osnabrück in 1728 and grand master of the Teutonic Knights in 1732. However, his political power reached its peak on 12th February 1742, when he crowned his brother Karl Albrecht Holy Roman Emperor at Frankfurt am Main, but the latter was never emperor in more than name. Clemens August began the construction of Schloss Brühl in 1725, following the plans of Johann Conrad Schlaun, but in 1740 Balthasar Neumann took over control and the brilliant design of the staircase is **158** due to him. Cuvilliés was active there from 1728, but he has left less of a mark on the building itself than on the gardens. Throughout his career Clemens August remained a keen patron of Italian artists, despite his close political alignment with France, and the Italian painters who worked for him were all of exceptional ability. The ceilings painted by Carlo Carlone for Schloss Brühl (c. 1750) are amongst the greatest Baroque ceiling paintings in Germany, and from soon after 1730 Clemens August commissioned a series of altarpieces for the churches under his patronage from painters such as Giambattista Tiepolo, Giovanni Battista Pittoni and **159** Giovanni Battista Piazzetta.

During the last decades of the 18th century another member of the Wittelsbach family, Duke Karl August von Zweibrücken, distinguished himself as a collector. When his collection is compared to those of Johann Wilhelm of the Palatinate and Max Emmanuel of Bavaria, it is evident that a distinct change in taste has occurred. The huge purchases were almost entirely of Dutch and Flemish paintings. At the death of Karl August the collection devolved upon the elector of Bavaria, and around 1800 the Düsseldorf and Zweibrücken collections, together with that from the Residenz in Mannheim, were amalgamated with the Munich collection to form the central royal gallery in Munich, the basis of the Alte Pinakothek today.

Art and patronage in Upper Saxony

The foundations for the brilliant flowering of art in Upper Saxony during the first half of the 18th century were laid with the replanning of sectors of Dresden, first by Wilhelm Dilich and later by Caspar von Klengel, for the electors Johann Georg I, II and III during the 17th century. Klengel's most important contribution followed the destruction of Dresden by the great fire of 1685, when he laid out the sector afresh as the Neustadt. Baroque sculpture had also reached Dresden by 1690 in the work of the Heermann brothers and the Süssner family, and the stage was set for the transformation of Dresden into a European centre of culture. Augustus the Strong succeeded as elector of Saxony in 1694 and, having changed to the Catholic faith, was elected king of Poland in 1698. The artistic scene changed equally rapidly. Klengel died in 1691, and in the same year the architect Mathaes Daniel Pöppelmann arrived in Dresden to join the sculptor Balthasar Permoser, who had been summoned **160** to Dresden from Italy in 1689. Unfortunately, the economic conditions were not propitious at that time, as Augustus the Strong invaded Livonia in 1700 and was soundly defeated by the young Charles XII of Sweden at the Battle of Klissov in 1702. Augustus temporarily lost the crown of Poland to a Swedish nominee, and it was not until Charles XII was himself heavily defeated by Peter the Great of Russia at Poltava in 1709, that Augustus regained Poland and was able to begin a massive programme of building.

Pöppelmann and Permoser formed a brilliant partnership, and the design and execution of the Zwinger in Dresden from 1709 is remarkable **155** for the perfect integration of the dynamic vitality of Permoser's sculpture with the richly picturesque architecture. Intended as a parade ground for festivals, the Zwinger is an open courtyard surrounded by low wings and elaborate pavilions, originally built into the city's fortifications. The Kronentor (the southern gate) was completed in 1713. The Wallpavillon provides the climax of the composition and was built in 1716, but the enclosure was not finally completed until 1847–49. Augustus continued to provide major commissions, and in 1720 his attention turned to Schloss Pillnitz on the banks of the Elbe outside Dresden. Here Pöppelmann alone was responsible for the superb Wasserpalais, where the style is

160
JUPITER SEATED ON HIS EAGLE
1690–95
Balthasar Permoser 1651–1732
ivory
6·75 in (17 cm)
Grünes Gewölbe, Dresden
Formerly in the collection of Count Brühl in Dresden, this superb ivory group passed into the Grüne Gewölbe in 1765, and is the finial of a larger decorative column further ornamented with silver reliefs. The dynamism and vigour of the group reveal Permoser's deep understanding of the fundamentals of Italian Baroque sculpture, learnt when he was a pupil of Foggini in Florence.

strongly oriental, and for the Bergpalais. Shortly afterwards, Pöppelmann was commissioned to build an extension to the Holländisches Palais in Dresden, which was renamed the Japanisches Palais after its porcelain decorations designed by Zacharias Longuelune, and finally in 1728 he rebuilt the Augustusbrücke across the Elbe. All this building activity by the Catholic king inspired a reply from the Protestant civic authorities in the form of a church which would be the symbol of Lutheran power in the city. The Frauenkirche, begun in 1722, was not finished until 1743, after the death of the architect Georg Bähr. Until its total destruction in the Second World War, the Frauenkirche dominated the skyline of Dresden and was by far the most important Protestant 18th-century church in Germany. The Catholic Hofkirche was not begun by Gaetano Chiaveri until 1737, but, with its delicate openwork tower and profusion of sculpture by Lorenzo Mattielli, it initiated a revival of Baroque architecture in Dresden.

Augustus the Strong displayed a taste for paintings closely comparable at first to that of Lothar Franz von Schönborn, and the majority of the paintings he commissioned or acquired during the first two decades have the same strong emphasis on the female nude. However, he had visited Venice several times when crown prince and had formed a particular attachment to the pastels of Rosalba Carriera, of which he assembled a huge collection. Venetian artists who worked in Dresden included Gaspare Diziani, who was active there as a scene painter in 1717–20, and Sebastiano Ricci and Antonio Pellegrini, who painted altarpieces for the Catholic church. In 1723 Le Plat, an agent of Augustus the Strong, acquired twenty-one fine paintings for the elector from the collection of Countess Vršovcová in Prague, including Rubens's copy after Michelangelo's *Leda*. As far as Dutch and Flemish painting was concerned, Augustus conformed to the normal taste of the period and was most interested in the large figure pictures by Rubens and Van Dyck, as well as the precisely executed paintings of Gerrit Dou and Caspar Netscher.

The applied arts also received enthusiastic support from Augustus the Strong, and in 1709 Johann Friedrich Böttger succeeded in producing, apparently for the first time in Europe, true porcelain. During the remaining ten years of his life Böttger made great strides in porcelain technology in the factory at Meissen, but the most significant development took place when, in 1731, Augustus the Strong appointed the sculptor 169 Johann Joachim Kändler to the factory. The decoration of the Japanisches Palais was planned to include over 25,000 pieces of porcelain, with life-size figures of the Apostles and a porcelain throne. Kändler's groups of figures and animals became the rage, and during the course of the century dozens of porcelain factories sprang up across Europe in rivalry. Parallel with Kändler's activity was that of the goldsmith Johann Melchior 179 Dinglinger, whose superb extravaganzas in gold and precious materials are still preserved in Dresden.

By the death of Augustus the Strong in 1733, both Dinglinger and Permoser were already dead, and Pöppelmann died in 1736. The heroic period of Saxon architecture and sculpture was almost over, but Augustus III made up for this in the scale of his collecting. The War of Austrian Succession (1740–48) did relatively little damage to Saxony and Poland, but the financial pressures placed on the contestants helped the collecting activity of Augustus III greatly. In 1741, Johann Gottfried Riedl bought on his behalf 268 paintings from the Valdštein collection at Duchov. In the following year the art connoisseur Count Francesco Algarotti began working for Augustus III and produced a plan for extending the collection

161
THE SIGN OF
THE ART DEALER GERSAINT
1720
Jean-Antoine Watteau 1684–1721
oil on canvas
71·75 × 121 in (182 × 307·8 cm)
Charlottenburg, West Berlin
Originally executed as the shop sign of the Paris art dealer Gersaint, the painting hung in the archway of the shop entrance for only a few weeks before it was purchased. In 1744 the Prussian Ambassador in Paris, Count Rothenburg, acquired it on behalf of Frederick the Great. From about 1750 it was hung in the music room at Charlottenburg, cut into two pictures, and in 1760 it was further damaged by the swords of Russian and Austrian soldiers. However, it was reassembled and returned to Charlottenburg in 1930.

162
THE DESK OF PRINCE-BISHOP
ADAM FRIEDRICH VON
SEINSHEIM
1760
probably by B. Herrmann
veneered in walnut with gilt bronze mounts
Konversationsaal, Neue Residenz, Bamberg
This elegant roll-top desk carries at one end the arms of Count Adam Friedrich von Seinsheim, and at the other the monogram AFS. Adam Friedrich reigned as prince-bishop of Bamberg from 1757 until 1779, and carried on the traditions of lavish patronage of the Schönborn family, to which he was closely related by birth. However, this is one of the rare pieces of furniture known to have been made for him.

163

THE MIRROR CABINET

1751/52
wood, almost completely covered with mirrors
h. 100 in (250 cm)
Herzog Anton–Ulrich-Museum, Brunswick

The large and imposing *Prunkkabinett*,
which was often used to house collections
of small but precious objects, remained
thoughout the 17th and 18th centuries a
very popular piece of furniture for rich
interiors in Germany. An immense amount
of ingenuity was lavished on these pieces,
and the famous Mirror Cabinet by Sang
and Körblein in Brunswick is no exception.

164 *above*

THE FESTSAAL

1761
François de Cuvilliés 1695–1768
Schloss Sünching, near Regensburg

One of the most splendid Rococo interiors in Bavaria, the
Festsaal of Schloss Sünching was by tradition designed by
Cuvilliés for Count Adam Friedrich von Seinsheim, prince bishop
of Würzburg and Bamberg, and his brother Count Joseph Franz
Maria. Matthäus Günther frescoed the ceiling, the brilliant
stucco decorations were executed by F. X. Feichtmayr and Jakob
Rauch, Ignaz Günther carved the putti round the room, and
Desmarées executed the state portraits of the brothers over the
fireplaces.

165 *left*
THE SPIEGELSAAL IN THE AMALIENBURG

1734—39
François de Cuvilliés 1695—1768
Munich

The Amalienburg, in the park of Schloss Nymphenburg, was built in 1734—39 for the electress Maria Amalia as a small pleasure house, but the quality of the decoration makes it one of the masterpieces of the German Rococo. The superb naturalistic stucco decorations were executed by Johann Baptist Zimmermann, while the woodcarving is by Joachim Dietrich.

166
THE INTERIOR OF THE RESIDENZ THEATRE

1751—53
François de Cuvilliés 1695—1768
Munich

The Residenz Theatre in Munich is the most beautiful of the late works of Cuvilliés, and one of his most splendid Rococo ensembles. It was dismantled during the war and subsequently reassembled on a new site within the Residenz. However, despite heavy restoration the wood carvings of Johann Baptist Straub are of exceptional vivacity.

167
BUST OF DUKE ANTON ULRICH OF BRAUNSCHWEIG-WOLFENBÜTTEL

1705—10
Balthasar Permoser 1651—1732
alabaster
31·5 in (80 cm)
Herzog Anton-Ulrich-Museum, Brunswick

Duke Anton Ulrich assembled together at his residence of Salzdahlum one of the most remarkable collections of paintings to be formed during the 18th century in northern Germany. His preference in paintings lay with the Old Masters, but for sculpture he turned to Balthasar Permoser in Dresden. One of the best groups of ivories by Permoser, after those in Dresden, is still to be found in Brunswick.

168

HARLEQUIN AND COLOMBINE

c. 1760, Franz Anton Bustelli 1723–63
porcelain, h. 7 in (18 cm), Bayerisches Nationalmuseum, Munich

The Nymphenburg porcelain factory was established under the patronage of the elector Max III Joseph of Bavaria in Schloss Neudeck. In 1761 the factory moved to Nymphenburg, where it still operates. Bustelli was modeller at the Neudeck–Nymphenburg factory from 1754, and the figures he executed there are amongst the most delicate expressions of the Rococo.

169

SCARAMOUCHE AND COLOMBINE

1741, Johann Joachim Kändler 1706–75
porcelain, h. 6·75 in (17·2 cm), Kunstgewerbemuseum, West Berlin

Augustus the Strong established the first porcelain factory in Europe at Meissen in 1710, and the sculptor J. J. Kändler was called to it in 1731. Kändler developed the modelling of figures and tablewares to a level which has been rarely matched since, and his small porcelain groups started a rage which rapidly spread across Europe.

170
PORTRAIT OF
FREDERICK THE GREAT
1763
Johann Georg Ziesenis 1716–76
oil on canvas
Kurpfälzisches Museum, Heidelberg

This portrait is derived from an oil sketch for which the Prussian king sat in June 1763, and in the view of some scholars it is the only credible portrait of him. The Peace of Hubertsburg, signed on 15th February 1763, ended the Seven Years' War, and confirmed Frederick the Great as the ruler of Silesia after he had repeatedly defeated the armies of Austria and Russia.

171
GIRL RESTING
1752
François Boucher 1703–70
oil on canvas
23·25 × 28·75 in (59 × 73 cm)
Alte Pinakothek, Munich

The charming model is most probably Miss Louise O'Murphy, one of the mistresses of Louis XV, and the delightful, if thinly veiled, eroticism is characteristic of much of the work of Boucher. In 1765 he was appointed *peintre du roi* and enjoyed the patronage of Mme de Pompadour. His gay elegant style and bright luminous palette were highly influential throughout Europe. This painting formed part of the collection assembled by Duke Karl August von Zweibrücken during the last decades of the 18th century.

systematically on a strictly scholarly basis, with purchases of the finest examples of all schools except primitives. That year Riedl scored another conspicuous success when he bought eighty-four paintings from the imperial collection in Prague, including the important series of works by Domenico Fetti now in Dresden, and in the following year a further twenty-three were added from the same source. In 1744 Augustus III achieved his greatest coup to date when he acquired one hundred selected paintings from the collection of the duke of Modena, including the five major works by Correggio which are now amongst the glories of the Dresden collection. A second fabulous acquisition was made in 1749 when, after long negotiations with the empress Maria Theresa, a further sixty-nine pictures from the Prague collection were bought, including Andrea del Sarto's *Marriage of St Catherine*. However, the most famous purchase **195** was that of the *Sistine Madonna* by Raphael from the convent of San **191** Sisto in Piacenza in 1754 for a gigantic sum.

Augustus III's real love was always for the old masters, and the paintings commissioned by Algarotti on his behalf in Venice from Jacopo Amigoni, Piazzetta, Pittoni, Tiepolo and others, met with little enthusiasm, though Bernardo Bellotto, the nephew of Canaletto, arrived in Dresden in 1747 and his views were a tremendous success. As far as Dutch and Flemish paintings were concerned, tastes had changed since the purchases of Augustus the Strong, and interest first centred on the Italianate Dutch landscape painters, especially Nicolaes Berchem and Cornelis Poelenburgh. Later it was the turn of the more naturalistic landscape painters, and by 1750 over a dozen major works by Jacob van Ruisdael had been assembled, including *The Jewish Cemetery*. Augustus the Strong had **192** acquired four important Rembrandts before 1720, but the remaining twelve in the Dresden collection were acquired at this time. Parallel with the change in taste in Dutch and Flemish paintings was the shift in emphasis from the Venetian to the Roman school and the 'rediscovery' of Claude and Poussin, and by 1765 the taste for the Rococo had been so completely displaced by classicism that the paintings commissioned by Algarotti in Venice were all auctioned in Amsterdam.

The collecting activity of Augustus III's all-powerful minister Count Brühl at times almost rivalled that of his master, and at his death the collection was sold by his heirs to Catherine the Great of Russia and now forms part of the Hermitage collection in Leningrad. Equally lavish, however, was his patronage of the Meissen factory, and the 2,200 pieces of the Swan Service, created for him by Kändler in 1737–41, are now scattered throughout the world.

In September 1756 Frederick the Great of Prussia invaded Saxony, thus starting the Seven Years War which shattered the court of Augustus III, who himself died in 1763 shortly after the return of peace. The great era of Saxony was over, but the collections remained almost intact.

Art under Frederick the Great
After the death of Friedrich Wilhelm I of Prussia, the 'Soldier King', much of the pent-up energy and frustration of Friedrich II (Frederick the Great) **170** erupted into a fury of building. Frederick the Great was fortunate that he already had an able architect to hand in Georg Wenzeslaus von Knobelsdorff, who had been sent by him to Italy to complete his studies. Knobelsdorff was an aristocrat, a personal friend to Frederick and a man who understood the whims of his royal master. After his return to Prussia in 1737, commissions were immediately heaped upon him. First came a new wing to be added to Schloss Monbijou (1740–42) to make it more suitable for the residence of the queen mother, and then the large new wing

for the Charlottenburg Palace, this time for Frederick himself. The king took a close interest in his buildings, forever making alterations and additions, and, even when he marched into Silesia in 1740 in the First Silesian War, he continued to write almost daily to Knobelsdorff asking for detailed progress reports and urging the work on.

In the new wing at Charlottenburg Prussian Rococo makes its first appearance on a large scale, and its distinctive character was due almost as much to Frederick as to Knobelsdorff. The Dining Room, completed in 1742, is decorated with coupled Corinthian pilasters in white scagliola against pink walls, which give it a refined elegance and lightness totally different from any of the interiors in Munich. However, the ceiling painting, *The Wedding Banquet of Peleus and Thetis* by the French painter Antoine Pesne, who had settled in Berlin at Frederick's invitation, is something of an anticlimax, and in the Golden Gallery Knobelsdorff dispensed with a ceiling painting entirely. Instead, the decoration of the walls is carried over the vault with gilt rocaille forms of an incredible delicacy and clarity.

Knobelsdorff also began the Berlin opera house in 1741, and there the use of a monumental temple façade with giant Corinthian columns is characteristic and reveals the impact of English Palladian architecture. The
172 famous palace of Sanssouci at Potsdam was begun by Knobelsdorff in 1745 at the height of the Second Silesian War, but the differences of opinion between the architect and Frederick over the latter's insistence on the omission of a basement, led to a rift between them and to Knobelsdorff's dismissal in the following year. The layout provides an interesting parallel to the Amalienburg in Munich with its central oval saloon, while
155 the design of the termini recall those by Permoser on the Zwinger. The decoration of the interior, begun by Johann August Nahl, was completed by Johann Michael Hoppenhaupt.

During the years following Frederick's marriage in 1734 and his establishment of a small independent court at Rheinsberg, his taste remained closely aligned with the French Rococo, and he purchased large numbers of paintings from Paris to decorate his new palaces. Above all he developed a passion for Watteau and bought about thirty paintings by this artist, accounting for almost half his total output. The majority of these remain
161 in Berlin, including Watteau's masterpiece *L'Enseigne de Gersaint* now in Charlottenburg, though a number of others were sold around 1800. After 1750 a change took place in Frederick's taste in both the architecture he commissioned and the paintings he purchased. The Neues Palais at Potsdam, designed in 1755 by Johann Gottfried Büring and Heinrich Ludwig Manger, was not actually built until 1763–66 after the end of the Seven Years War. The model is clearly Vanbrugh's Castle Howard in England, but the effect of the huge palace is almost that of a stage set. Similarly a change in spirit separates Frederick's purchases of French Rococo paintings, which he genuinely appreciated, from his curious lack of interest in later purchases made under the influence of the Saxon court. He refused to pay the prices asked for the best Italian paintings, though he nevertheless succeeded in purchasing Correggio's *Leda* in 1755, and his shrewd agents bought Rembrandts as a 'second best'. Frederick's really heavy expenditure, however, was not on paintings but on classical sculpture, thus following the current trend towards classicism.

Minor aristocratic patrons

The heads of the two Franconian branches of the house of Hohenzollern were the margraves of Ansbach and Bayreuth, and, although these miniscule states were unable to rival the great patrons, they were neverthe-

172
SCHLOSS SANSSOUCI
1745–47
Georg Wenzeslaus von Knobelsdorff
1699–1754
Potsdam

Begun in 1745 at the height of the Second Silesian War, Schloss Sanssouci also marks the breach between Knobelsdorff and his patron Frederick the Great. The king, in opposition to Knobelsdorff, insisted on the omission of a basement, and in the following year dismissed him. The superb termini, which are reminiscent of those by Permoser for the Zwinger and add lightness to the design, were carved by Johann August Nahl.

173
THE ELECTOR PALATINE
KARL PHILIPP THEODOR
1757, oil on canvas
Johann Georg Ziesenis 1716–76
18 × 12·5 in (46 × 31·8 cm)
Bayerisches Nationalmuseum, Munich

Son of the Pfalzgraf Johann Christian von Sulzach, Karl Philipp Theodor succeeded Karl Philipp von Pfalz-Neuburg as Elector Palatine in 1743, and at the death of Max III Joseph in 1777 he succeeded as elector and duke of Bavaria. This brought together into one collection the paintings assembled in Düsseldorf by the Elector Palatine Johann Wilhelm, those collected by Karl Philipp at Mannheim and the collections of Karl Philipp Theodor himself and of the dukes of Bavaria.

less very active. The Residenz at Ansbach was rebuilt by Gabriel de Gabrieli for the margrave Wilhelm Friedrich in 1713–14 after a disastrous fire, and the margrave Karl Wilhelm Friedrich later placed the decoration in the hands of Leopoldo Retti. The splendid stuccoes by Diego Carlone, and the frescoes in the Festsaal by Carlo Carlone, reflect the influence of Wilhelm Friedrich's widow Christine Charlotte, the daughter of Duke Friedrich Karl of Württemberg. Karl Wilhelm Friedrich's own apartments (begun 1735), however, are some of the earliest surviving Rococo decorations in Germany and reveal the impact of Cuvilliés.

The margrave Friedrich of Bayreuth and his wife Wilhelmine were less successful in their efforts, except for the opera house, where the exterior of 1745–49 by Joseph St Pierre is very proper and classical. The interior, on the other hand, was designed in 1748 by Giuseppe Galli Bibiena with an unrepentant Italian Baroque exuberance. The Neue Schloss at Bayreuth, completed shortly before the outbreak of the Seven Years War, is impressive from a distance, but the interminable suites of rooms inside have a provincial coarseness, and much of the painted decoration is downright amateur.

The bombing of Mannheim, the capital of the Elector Palatine after 1720, destroyed a large percentage of the work of the brilliant sculptor Paul Egell, who had settled there in 1721 as court sculptor. Mannheim was the centre of his activity until his death in 1752, although he supplied sculpture for churches as far north as Hildesheim, and his expressive stylisation and elongated forms made a great impression on the young Ignaz Günther when he visited Mannheim in 1751. The opera house was designed by Alessandro Galli Bibiena in 1737, but after earning an important place in musical history it was burnt out in 1795. Most of the elector Johann Wilhelm's collection remained in Düsseldorf during the remainder of the 18th century, except for a brief time during the Seven Years War, when it was removed for safety to Mannheim. It is again indicative of the change in taste in the second quarter of the century that the large Rubenses and late Baroque paintings had been left by Karl Philipp in Düsseldorf, when the Dutch cabinet paintings were taken to Mannheim. In the middle of the century Karl Philipp, and later Karl **173** Theodor purchased examples of works by painters such as Jan Brueghel, Dou, Frans van Mieris the Elder, Netscher and Jan van Huysum, which reflected current French tastes, and of Rembrandt and his school.

Relatively close to Mannheim in southern Germany, the palace of Ludwigsburg had a shaky start in 1704. Commissioned by Duke Eberhard Ludwig of Württemberg, the Fürstenbau was considerably altered after 1714, when Donato Frisoni was promoted to the post of architect. It is the largest palace in Germany, and the building work and decoration took decades to complete: the southern block closing the main courtyard was not built until 1724–33. Carlo Carlone frescoed the vault of the Hofkirche in 1719–20, and later returned in the early 1730s with his brother, the stuccoist Diego Carlone. Jointly they were responsible for the decoration of the splendid vestibule in 1735. The dukes of Württemberg were active as collectors, and in 1736 120 paintings belonging to Count Gotter in Vienna were purchased en bloc, including Memling's *Bathsheba*, and these now form the basis of the Staatsgalerie in Stuttgart.

Further north, in Kassel, the landgrave Karl of Hesse-Kassel had begun the park and palace of Wilhelmshöhe in 1701, and in doing so initiated one of the most spectacular examples of town planning in 18th-century Germany. From the giant figure of the Farnese Hercules on top of an obelisk crowning the hill, cascades lead down to the curved body of the palace;

the downhill sweep continues through the wooded park and right into the city. Of the paintings collected by the predecessors of the landgrave Wilhelm VIII, who succeeded Karl, almost nothing survived, but since he had been educated at the court of his god-father William II of Orange, this Protestant prince had a tremendous knowledge and appreciation of Dutch and Flemish painting.

Tintoretto and Titian were ostensibly the best represented artists in the collection of Duke Anton-Ulrich of Brunswick, according to the 1744 inventory, closely followed by the Dutch and Flemish masters. His great-grandson Karl Wilhelm Ferdinand came into contact with the influential writer on antique art Johann Joachim Winckelmann in Rome, when he was still crown prince, and Pompeo Batoni's portrait of him shows the prince in a classical setting with his arm resting on a Greek vase, but nevertheless his purchases for the Brunswick collection were almost all Dutch. The Dutch and Flemish schools also predominated in the collections formed by the Frankfurt banker Johann Friedrich Städel in the period 1750–90, the basis of the present Städelsches Kunstinstitut in Frankfurt, and that formed in Leipzig by Gottfried Winkler, who died in 1795 leaving 1,300 paintings, including ten Rembrandts.

It was not until the last decades of the century that interest began to be aroused in German and Italian primitives, and most collectors before this date treated them as curiosities which formed an historically interesting part of a collection. Count Joseph von Truchess-Zeil-Wurzach was one of the earliest collectors to consider them seriously, and the majority of his German primitives were assembled before 1790. The collection was auctioned in London in 1803, but Hans Multscher's altarpiece of 1437 eventually became part of the Berlin collection, while Hans Strigel the Younger's *St John the Baptist, St Catherine and St John the Evangelist* is now in Stuttgart.

18th-century churches

As is to be expected the vast majority of important churches and monasteries built during the 17th and 18th centuries in Germany were in the Catholic areas, and the efforts of almost all the architects of Protestant churches were totally undermined by their determination to make them different from Catholic ones at all costs. The Frauenkirche in Dresden was the only important exception to this rule.

In the area of the Middle Rhine and Franconia the influence of the great princely families in the patronage of the religious foundations is vital, and the series of pilgrimage and abbey churches built by Balthasar Neumann in that area bears witness to it. Gössweinstein, Heusenstamm and, above all, Vierzehnheiligen all still survive in more or less their original condition. Neumann's last great abbey church, that of Neresheim (built for the Benedictines in 1745–92), is further south near Dillingen, and in it Neumann's centralised plans reach their climax. The details were altered after his death in 1753, and the growing influence of classicism is most clearly revealed in the frescoes by Martin Knoller, completed in 1775.

In Bavaria the influence of the ruling family was a great deal less, and thus the influence of the court style of Cuvilliés can be seen in relatively few churches. Furthermore, the magnificent Baroque interiors created by the brothers Egid Quirin and Cosmas Damian Asam at Weltenburg (1717–21) and St John Nepomuk, Munich (1733–35) have no parallels in the secular architecture of Bavaria. The Asam brothers were trained in Rome, and bringing back to Bavaria the theatrical illusionism of Bernini, they added to it the strong taste for realism represented by the local

174
THE INTERIOR
OF ST JOHANNES NEPOMUK
1733–46
Egid Quirin Asam 1692–1750 and
Cosmas Damian Asam 1686–1739
Munich

Begun in 1733 as the private chapel of the Asam brothers, the structure was completed and blessed at the end of 1734, but the decoration of the interior took much longer and was not completed until 1746, when the chapel was consecrated. The very tall narrow shape was dictated by the constricted site, but the Asam brothers took advantage of it to create an intensely dramatic effect focused upon the floating figure of St John Nepomuk, lit from concealed windows at each side.

175

PORTRAIT OF HIMSELF WITH SASKIA

c. 1634
Rembrandt van Rijn 1606–69
oil on canvas
63·5 × 51·5 in (161 × 131 cm)
Gemäldegalerie, Dresden

In 1634 Rembrandt married Saskia van Uylenborch, who brought with her a substantial dowry, and the mid-1630s were the years of his greatest material prosperity. This famous self-portrait with his young wife reveals, in its flamboyance and almost excessive opulence, the robust optimism of the times. The painting was acquired in 1739 in Paris through Le Leu, but it did not arrive in Dresden until after the War of Austrian Succession, in August 1751.

176

THE RAPE OF THE DAUGHTERS OF LEUCIPPUS

1617–20
Peter Paul Rubens 1577–1640
oil on canvas
87·5 × 82·25 in (222 × 209 cm)
Alte Pinakothek, Munich

Purchased by the Elector Palatine, Johann Wilhelm, for the Düsseldorf collection, this major Rubens entered the Bavarian Royal Collection in about 1800. The exuberant composition and immense vitality illustrate the role of Rubens as the most important exponent of Baroque painting north of the Alps, while the realism is enhanced by the contrast between the sun-burnt Dioscuri and the soft pale flesh-tones of Hilaeira and Phoebe.

177

JUDITH WITH THE HEAD OF HOLOFERNES

1632–35
Peter Paul Rubens 1577–1640
oil on panel
46 × 42·5 in (117 × 108 cm)
Herzog Anton-Ulrich-Museum, Brunswick

Duke Anton Ulrich of Braunschweig-Wolfenbüttel built up his collection at Salzdahlum in the decades around 1700, and *Judith with the Head of Holofernes* had entered the collection by 1710. The fierce dramatic nature of the subject is enhanced by the harsh light from the torch carried by the old serving-maid, a technique which Rubens had learnt from Caravaggio during his activity in Rome. At the express wish of Anton Ulrich his collection has remained intact in Brunswick ever since his death.

traditions of wood-carving. These traditions are brought together in the groups of St George and the Dragon over the high altar at Weltenburg and the Assumption of the Virgin at nearby Rohr. **149**

The Asams continued to employ their Italianate Baroque style throughout their careers, while the 'Bavarian Manner' of the Rococo developed separately from both their style and the 'French Manner' or court style. Here the greatest exponents were the brothers Dominikus and Johann Baptist Zimmermann, and their patrons were mainly the artistically independent abbots of southern Bavaria and Swabia. The pilgrimage church of Steinhausen was commissioned in 1727 by the abbot of Schuss- **185** enried, who also employed Dominikus Zimmermann to build the ravishing Rococo library for this abbey. The contrast between the gilt or **178** silvered rocaille decorations against white or coloured grounds, characteristic of the 'French Manner' of the Rococo, and the naturalistic stucco decorations tinted in delicate colours and only occasionally heightened with gold, characteristic of the 'Bavarian Manner' as evolved by the Zimmermanns, could not be greater. Dominikus Zimmermann's later abbey church at Günzburg (1736-41) is less successful, while the heavy gilding and vigorous rocaille structures of Die Wies, built 1745-54, **180** show a certain rapprochement with the court style. What is also remarkable about Die Wies is that the entire cost of the church was raised in a few years almost wholly from the contributions of simple pilgrims. The south German pilgrimage churches such as Steinhausen and Die Wies were built for the people through the efforts of the people alone, and they represent a fundamentally popular trend of religious fervour. On the Lake of Constance the pilgrimage church of Birnau was commissioned by **186** the abbot of Salem from Peter Thumb in 1745, and the joyous interior flooded with light reaches its climax in the high altar with its sculpture by Joseph Anton Feuchtmayer. Here the Rococo decoration is again in the 'Bavarian Manner' and has recently been restored to its former brilliance.

The most prolific of the south German architects was Johann Michael Fischer, who was born in the upper Palatinate and was wholly or partly responsible for over seventy churches in southern Germany. His most important patrons were the monastic orders such as the Benedictines (for whom he built Zwiefalten, Ottobeuren and Rott-am-Inn) the August- **187, 189** inians (Diessen) and the Premonstratensians (Osterhoven), though he built Berg-am-Laim in 1738-51 for Clemens August of Cologne. The strongly undulating interiors of his earlier churches such as Osterhoven give way to an increasing centralisation, comparable to that of Neumann, until his late masterpiece of Rott-am-Inn. There the central octagonal **187** space, with its vast shallow vault frescoed by Matthäus Günther, dominates the entire composition. Fischer always employed first-rate sculptors, painters and stuccoists in his churches, and the ecstatic frescoes by Franz Joseph Spiegler at Zwiefalten and those by Johann Jakob Zeiller at Ottobeuren are amongst the most distinguished examples of German 18th-century monumental painting. The superb stuccoes and sculpture were executed by Johann Michael Feichtmayr, alone and in collaboration with Johann Joseph Christian respectively, in both these churches, while Feichtmayr was also responsible for the rather more restrained stucco decoration at Rott-am-Inn. The sculpture in this church is by the greatest south German sculptor of the 18th century, Ignaz Günther, and in their refined elegance his languid figures are the epitome of the last phase of the Rococo.

Peter Cannon-Brookes

178

THE INTERIOR OF THE ABBEY LIBRARY AT SCHUSSENRIED

1754-61
Dominikus Zimmermann 1685-1766

Zimmermann's abbey library at Schussenried in south Württemberg is one of the Rococo jewels of Germany. The room is divided into two levels by the gallery, and below this white stucco figures by J. J. Schwarzmann are contrasted against the brightly coloured columns. The composition is united in the great fresco by F. G. Hermann, painted in 1757, depicting a complex allegory of Wisdom. Throughout, the emphasis is on lightness and movement, and with the exception of the columns hardly a single straight line of any importance is to be seen.

179 *below*

THE BIRTHDAY OF THE GRAND MOGHUL OF DELHI

1701–09
Johann Melchior Dinglinger 1664–1731
gold, enamel, gems and pearls
Grünes Gewölbe, Dresden

The jewelled creations of Dinglinger to a great extent parallel the porcelain decorations of Kändler, and provide some of the best illustrations of the brilliance of the court of Saxony under Augustus the Strong. Dinglinger reinterpreted the hardstone and enamelled *objets de vertu* of the Renaissance in the Baroque idiom, and his large set pieces, such as this one, are of unsurpassed splendour.

180 *centre*

THE PILGRIMAGE CHURCH OF DIE WIES

1745–54
Dominikus Zimmermann 1685–1766

Commissioned by the abbot of Steingaden in 1745, Die Wies was built to house a miraculous figure of Christ which was attracting large numbers of pilgrims. The clergy house is linked to the body of the church by the tower, while the façade is wrapped round part of the rotunda. This decorative use of architectural elements is emphasised by the abstract shapes of the windows and the coloured bands breaking up the wall surfaces.

181

CYLINDRICAL BUREAU

1773, David Roentgen 1743–1807
wood, with inlays of figured walnut, cedarwood, boxwood and coloured woods
h. 35·75 in (91 cm)
The Kurfürstenzimmer of the Residenz Munich

Roentgen specialised in high-quality furniture with pictorial veneers, and during the last decades of the 18th century he had the reputation of being the finest cabinet-maker in Europe. Included in the veneers on the bureau is the inscription 'Almanach 1773', which identifies the piece as having been made in Neuwied at Roentgen's father's workshop, taken over by David Roentgen in the previous year.

182 *right*

BELLONA

c. 1772
Ignaz Günther 1725–75
limewood
78 in (198 cm)
Bayerisches Nationalmuseum, Munich

Günther's statue of the Goddess of War was made for the palace of Count Johann Caspar de La Rosée in Munich, and the languid grace is characteristic of his increasing interest in Mannerist qualities. *Bellona* has a strong individuality, which is in contrast to the majority of Rococo sculpture in Germany, and this is enhanced by the brilliant characterisation of fabric, such as is applied by Günther to the skirt of the goddess.

183 *centre right*

THE DEATH OF CLEOPATRA

1673
Caspar Netscher 1635/36–84
oil on canvas
21 × 17·25 in (53·5 × 44 cm)
Staatliche Kunsthalle, Karlsruhe

Purchased by the margravine Caroline of Baden-Durlach from the collection of the Comte de Vence in Paris in 1761, this painting was considered by her the pearl of her collection, and there exists a copy, executed by her in pastel, dated 1764. Caroline of Baden-Durlach closely imitated contemporary Parisian taste, and her love of such glossy, highly finished Dutch cabinet paintings is characteristic.

184 *centre bottom*

THE HONEY-LICKING PUTTO

c. 1750, stucco
Joseph Anton Feuchtmayer 1696–1770
over life-size, Pilgrimage Church, Birnau

Decorating the altar dedicated to St Bernard in the pilgrimage church of Birnau on the shores of Lake Constance, this splendid robust putto carries in one hand a beehive in humorous allusion to the symbol of St Bernard of Clairvaux, while he licks the honey from his fingers. The vitality and homely realism is characteristic of Rococo sculpture in Swabia, and is in complete contrast to the refinement of the sculpture executed for the Bavarian court or the great pilgrimage churches of Franconia.

185

THE INTERIOR OF THE PILGRIMAGE CHURCH OF STEINHAUSEN *detail*

1728–31
Dominikus Zimmermann 1685–1766

In 1727 Dominikus Zimmermann received the commission to rebuild the pilgrimage church of Steinhausen, which belonged to the Premonstratensian abbey of Schussenried in Swabia. However, because of faulty estimating the building cost four times as much as originally intended and work stopped in 1731. By this time all the stucco decorations, by Dominikus Zimmermann, were complete, as well as the superb airy frescoes by his brother Johann Baptist.

THE INTERIOR OF THE
PILGRIMAGE CHURCH OF BIRNAU

1746–58
designed by Peter Thumb 1681–1766

Peter Thumb began the pilgrimage church of Birnau on the
northern shore of Lake Constance in 1746 to house a miracle-
working Madonna belonging to the monks of Salem, and
although the structure was complete in 1750 the decoration
continued until 1758. Thumb's light constructional technique
enabled him to keep the entire space clear of supporting columns,
and the effect is one of airiness and light. The richly decorated
balustrade, which is carried round the entire church interior,
reflects contemporary library designs.

187 *above*

THE SAINTS OF THE
BENEDICTINE ORDER IN GLORY

1767
Matthäus Günther 1705–88
fresco
Rott-am-Inn, Bavaria

The church of Rott-am-Inn was built by J. M. Fischer in
1759–63, but the decoration was not complete until 1767. The
series of ceiling paintings is dominated by the central dome. Here
the Trinity in glory is located at the centre, with the Virgin
below. Beams of light link her to St Benedict and St Scholastica
and thence to the assembled throng of Benedictine saints, while
below her St Michael slays the dragon of the apocalyptic vision.

188 *left*
CHOIR STALLS
1757–66
Johann Joseph Christian 1706–77
walnut, partly gilded
Abbey Church, Ottobeuren

For the execution of the choir stalls at
Ottobeuren J. J. Christian collaborated
with the carpenter and woodcarver Martin
Hermann of Villingen. The carving is
more restrained than that decorating the
choir stalls at Zwiefalten (completed by
them in 1756), and in Christian's figures
there is a greater spirituality. The scenes
represented are drawn from the Old
Testament and parallel those taken from
the Life of St Benedict which decorate the
choir stalls opposite.

189
THE INTERIOR OF THE ABBEY
CHURCH OF OTTOBEUREN

begun 1737
Johann Michael Fischer 1692–1766

The rebuilding of the great imperial
Benedictine abbey church of Ottobeuren
was begun in 1737, but relatively little had
been achieved by 1748, when it was taken
over by J. M. Fischer, and the building as
seen today is almost entirely due to him.
Johann Jakob Zeiller's frescoes
complement the brilliant stucco
decorations and elegant sculpture by
Johann Michael Feichtmayr. The
decoration was completed in 1767.

190
HEAD OF AN ABBOT'S CROZIER

1755
Joseph Deutschmann 1717–87
ivory
15·25 in (39 cm)
Bayerisches Nationalmuseum, Munich

From the abbey of Niederaltaich in Lower
Bavaria, this superb example of Rococo
ivory carving is dateable to *c.* 1755.
Deutschmann was a native of the Tyrol
and took over the workshop of J. M. Götz
in Passau in 1742, where this crozier was
carved. Shields are held by two putti, one
wearing an abbot's mitre, while the
decoration also includes the symbols of
the cardinal virtues.

191 *above*

THE SISTINE MADONNA

1513
Raffaello Sanzio (Raphael) 1483–1520
oil on canvas
104·25 × 77·25 in (265 × 196 cm)
Gemäldegalerie, Dresden

Originally painted to be hung above the
bier of Pope Julius II, the Sistine Madonna
is unusual in that it is the only known
painting by Raphael on canvas and that it
appears to be entirely by the artist's own
hand. St Cecilia and St Sixtus kneel
before the Virgin, and St Sixtus is depicted
with the features of Pope Julius II,
including the beard he grew between 1510
and his death in 1513. The painting was
sent almost immediately to Piacenza where
it remained on the High Altar of S Sisto
until purchased by Augustus III of
Saxony in 1754.

192 *left*

THE JEWISH CEMETERY

after 1670
Jacob van Ruisdael 1628/29–82
oil on canvas
33 × 37·5 in (84 × 95 cm)
Gemäldegalerie, Dresden

This view of the Jewish cemetery near Ouderkerk, purchased by the elector Augustus III of Saxony for the Dresden collection shortly before 1754, is one of the masterpieces of Jacob van Ruisdael. The sombre colouring and massive trees are characteristic of the heroic period of Dutch landscape painting, which came into favour with collectors in the middle of the 18th century. Augustus III acquired more than a dozen major works by Ruisdael.

193 *centre*

THE ADORATION OF THE SHEPHERDS

1530, Antonio Allegri da Correggio 1494 or 1489–1534
oil on panel, 100·75 × 74 in (256 × 188 cm)
Gemäldegalerie, Dresden

Alberto Pratoneri of Reggio Emilia commissioned the painting from Correggio in 1522, but it was probably not completed until 1530, when the Pratoneri Chapel in San Prospero in Reggio was finished and the altarpiece installed. In 1640 it was forcibly removed by Duke Francesco I of Modena and installed in his collection there, and with four other major works by Correggio it was sold to Augustus III of Saxony in 1746.

194

LADY READING A LETTER AT AN OPEN WINDOW

c. 1658
Jan Vermeer 1632–75
oil on canvas
33·75 × 25·4 in (83 × 64·5 cm)
Gemäldegalerie, Dresden

Bought in Paris in 1742 by De Brais, the Legation Secretary of Saxony, on behalf of Augustus III, this painting, like so many others by Vermeer, remained incorrectly attributed until the 19th century. Although signed faintly, it was engraved as a putative work of Govaert Flinck in 1783, while the other work by Vermeer in Dresden, *At the Procuress's*, was attributed to Vermeer of Utrecht.

195 *far left*

MYSTICAL MARRIAGE OF ST CATHERINE

1512, Andrea del Sarto 1486–1531
oil on canvas, 65·75 × 48 in (167 × 122 cm)
Gemäldegalerie, Dresden

First recorded in the collection of the Duke of Buckingham, this painting is listed in the inventory of that collection drawn up in Antwerp before 1650. It was in Prague by 1749, in which year it was included amongst the sixty-nine selected paintings sold by the empress Maria Theresa to Augustus III of Saxony.

The 19th century was a time of immense artistic activity in Germany, yet little of it is remembered with enthusiasm today. The vast architectural schemes, large moralising paintings and tedious feats of craftsmanship seem poor successors to the glorious creations of the Baroque. Everywhere one sees pedantry replacing the spontaneity and ingenuity of previous generations.

However, the situation is not as bleak as it might at first appear. Although official art, that bugbear of the 19th century, was much in evidence, many fine works by original talents were also produced alongside it. Furthermore, this crippling academicism was not fully felt until 1830, and before that time there is much in the fine arts that reflects the startling new developments that were taking place. For at the end of the 18th century there was a great upsurge of creative activity in Germany that was to affect the cultural development of Europe profoundly. Just as Kant and his followers opened up a new direction in philosophy, so writers like Goethe and Schiller achieved an international reputation for German literature, while Beethoven and other musicians to a large extent revolutionised musical composition. There were no figures of quite this stature in the fine arts, yet many artists were inspired with a similar enthusiasm and came to look on their work as having an almost prophetic character. **13, 201** This was certainly the case with Asmus Jakob Carstens, Philipp Otto Runge, and the Nazarenes, a group of artists who sought to restore the 'purity' of 15th-century art, and who, even if they did not lead to the type of breakthrough that other groups, such as the French Impressionists, were to achieve, were still representative of a revolutionary trend.

Before the French Revolution, Germany was a conglomeration of small states, as it had been since the Middle Ages, and it was not until near the end of the 19th century, in 1870, that it became unified as one country. At the beginning of the 19th century, however, Napoleon's invasions brought about a drastic revision of the German states. In 1806 he brought to a close the nine-hundred-year-old Holy Roman Empire, finally separating Austrian interests from those of Germany. He also halted the growth of Prussia, thereby winning the support of many southern German states. Eventually, however, the whole of Germany united against him in the nationalistic War of Liberation, only to be disappointed by the results. For at the Congress of Vienna in 1815, Germany was again divided into several states and remained disunited until 1870, when Prussia effectively took over the rest of Germany.

Neoclassicism in Berlin

The art of this period, therefore, flourished in several distinct centres, each one having its own period of particular distinction. In the late 18th century Prussia was undoubtedly the most rapidly expanding and successful state. Berlin, its capital, was beginning to reap the benefits of its sudden rise of status under the enlightened rule of Frederick the Great (1740–86). His successors, Friedrich Wilhelm II and Friedrich Wilhelm III, commissioned architects to decorate the city according to its new importance. They were fortunate in having architects of the highest merit at their command who, taking the French Neoclassical manner, turned it into something new – dry and precise, yet at the same time admirable and impressive. Karl Gotthard Langhans made the first tentative steps in this direction with his Brandenburg Gate (now the unfortunate symbol of a divided Germany) built 1789-93. He was followed by the more original Friedrich Gilly, who unfortunately died before he could put any of his schemes into operation. From the plans he left behind for the monument of Frederick the Great (1797) – a Doric temple on a geometric sub-

196

GERMANIA AND ITALIA

1811 – 28
Friedrich Overbeck 1789 – 1896
oil on canvas
37 × 41 in (94 × 104 cm)
Neue Pinakothek, Munich

This picture was, in its original form, one of the most personal statements of German Romanticism, giving expression to the spiritual and artistic ideals of Overbeck. The project was, however, put aside for many years after the death of the artist's close friend, Franz Pforr, to whom the picture was to have been presented. The final version, completed for the dealer Wenner, is an allegory on the union of German and Italian art. Overbeck, as a German artist working in Rome, felt that he had achieved such a combination.

structure—one can see a surprisingly early example of functional thinking in architecture.

It was left to his successor Karl Friedrich Schinkel to determine the course of German architecture. The style, grace and severity of his buildings established a precedent that was still having its effects on architects at the time of the Third Reich. Schinkel's real architectural career began in 1815, when he was named state architect by Friedrich Wilhelm III. In 1816 he designed the Neue Wache, in which his use of Doric columns does not obscure his concern with the basic proportions of the building. Similarly his Schauspielhaus of 1818–21 shows a subordination of classical elements to clear design, particularly in the way that the columns on the side walls are reduced to simple rectangles. His master-piece was the Alte Museum (1823-28), in which his impeccable sense of proportion made the frontal façade of columns so memorable. With these and similar buildings he set as definitive a style for central Berlin as Nash did for London and Haussmann was to do for Paris.

In this atmosphere the sculptors Gottfried Schadow and his pupil Christian Rauch produced works of great elegance. Both artists centred their activity on the Prussian court, making a large number of portraits; but after Rauch had made a visit to Rome, where he studied under the Neoclassical Danish sculptor Bertel Thorvaldsen, their alliance turned into rivalry. There was an element of lifelessness in Rauch's work that typified a new direction in Neoclassicism, but, with his more meticulous manner, he succeeded in gradually monopolising the royal favour, and Schadow, in true 18th-century style, passed off the situation with a 'mot' saying that his reputation had *in Rauch aufgegangen* (gone up in smoke).

Berlin was also a flourishing centre for the applied arts. In the royal factories many of the products were based on the designs of Schinkel and other 'fine artists', but there were also independent designers who made significant contributions. Among these, the furniture designer David Roentgen evolved a simple refined use of forms, in which the highly elaborate inlays of 18th-century furniture were abandoned for the simple contrasts of metal and dark wood. The straightened legs of his chairs and tables show the influence of English designs, unusual in Germany at that time, and through the continued tradition of his work-shop this simplicity long remained a characteristic of Berlin furniture.

Developments in the rest of Germany

Other German monarchs were also concentrating on aggrandising their cities. Throughout southern Germany, where the Baroque had had its greatest effect, Neoclassicism left its mark to a lesser degree than in the north, although in Würzburg there was a certain amount of remodelling in the classical 'directoire' style that was prevalent in Paris in the late 1790s. Further south, in Munich, capital of the new kingdom of Bavaria created by Napoleon as part of the Confederation of the Rhine, King Maximilian I was commissioning many new buildings in the first two decades of the 19th century. But as Munich had been a centre for the German Baroque, the rebuilding tended to be around, rather than inside, the centre of the city. Mainly the work of Karl von Fischer and Leo von Klenze, these schemes were on the whole more grandiose and less taste-ful than those made for Berlin. Fischer's Karolinenplatz and Klenze's Königsplatz were, however, a mere prelude to the greater projects of the post-Napoleonic Bavarian king, Ludwig I.

Above all, it was the French Neoclassical style that prevailed throughout Germany. In Baden, another of the new sovereign states created by Napoleon, the grand duke made use of the French-trained architect

197

198

198
DOUBLE STATUE OF PRINCESSES LUISE AND FRIEDERIKE OF PRUSSIA
1794–97
Gottfried Schadow 1764–1850
marble
h. 5 ft 7.75 in (1.72 m)
Staatliche Museen, East Berlin

This is one of the early portraits of members of the Prussian royal family made for King Frederick William II by Schadow. Like many other early Neoclassical sculptors, Schadow retained much Rococo charm in his work, which is enhanced here by the attractiveness of the two princesses he is portraying. It was this tenderness, evident even in his portraits of men, that caused him to lose ground in court circles to the more classical manner of Rauch.

197

ALTES MUSEUM
1824–28
Karl Friedrich Schinkel 1781–1841
Berlin

This was one of the many buildings erected by Schinkel in Berlin after his appointment as state architect to Frederick William III of Prussia in 1815. It is, perhaps, the most distinguished of the innumerable museums that sprang up throughout Europe at this time in response to the growing demand for the public exhibition of works of art. Its severe but beautifully balanced façade makes it one of the most memorable works of Neoclassical architecture.

Friedrich Weinbrenner. In the relatively small town of Karlsruhe, capital of the grand duchy, Weinbrenner was given a free hand and in the first quarter of the 19th century he created, on a small scale, a perfect Neoclassical town, in which open centralised planning replaced the spatial intricacies of the Baroque. The most successful feature of Weinbrenner's scheme is the Marktplatz, which forms the centre. The French influence affected the applied arts too, and the porcelain factories of Dresden and Meissen turned from producing independent designs to copying the latest Paris fashions. Thus, even before the processes of industrialisation began to set in, German decorative arts were undergoing a gradual reduction in originality.

Idealist painters

If painting has so far been left out of this account, it is because its problems were so radically different from those of the other arts. Monarchs, old and new, certainly had their court painters, but these were rarely first-rate artists. In addition, an estrangement between painter and public was felt particularly strongly at this time. Romantic theorists, such as the poet and philosopher Friedrich Schiller, had cast the artist, not in the role of craftsman, or even of gentleman, but of prophet. Like the Neoclassical poet Friedrich Hölderlin, the major painters of the period had proclaimed their freedom and struck out against the conventions of their time. They often paid dearly for such independence, for many, by failing to woo the right patrons, lost the means to put their grandiose schemes into practice. Thus, for instance, Asmus Jacob Carstens proudly **213** followed his own ideals, creating his designs in isolation in Rome, and contemptuous of institutions and the demands of patrons. When reminded of his obligations to the Berlin Academy, which had made his visit to Rome financially possible, he gave a reply that typified the outlook of the new generation: 'I do not belong to the Berlin Academy, but to mankind which has the right to demand from me the highest possible cultivation of my talents'. Bowing to no benefactor, he lacked a patron to finance his ambitious schemes which, as a result, only exist now in fragments and sketches.

Carstens's assertion of individuality was, like Hölderlin's in poetry, directed through an idealistic belief in the perfection of classical antiquity, but later painters were to apply this spirit to many different problems. Rome became a centre of German idealist painters for nearly a century, representing with its artistic tradition a place where painters could devote themselves to the expression of their own artistic belief, and where the patrons would be more sympathetic to such objectives. Joseph Anton Koch transferred Carstens's ideas to landscapes, which he painted in a 'heroic' manner. Other artists associated the high intentions of painting with religious motives, seeking to re-establish the supposed piety of medieval painters and craftsmen. This feeling was most strongly expressed by a group of painters who went so far as to imitate medieval clothing in their own dress and to grow their hair long. Because of this they were nicknamed the 'Nazarenes', and this term of derision was later used to describe their art. The two leaders of this group, Franz Pforr and Friedrich Overbeck, arrived in Rome from Vienna with a few **196** friends in 1810. They set up a form of monastic existence together to help create a religious atmosphere for their painting, and were soon joined by other German artists, of whom the most important were Peter von Cornelius and Julius Schnorr von Carolsfeld. At first they were ridiculed, but they then found a patron, the Prussian consul-general Jakob Salomon Bartholdy, who commissioned them to decorate a room in his house in

Rome. In these murals (now in the Nationalgalerie in East Berlin), Cornelius, Overbeck, Philipp Veit and Wilhelm Schadow looked to the 15th-century painting of Germany and Italy for simplicity of style and for the technique of fresco painting. Their work was so well received that, when the young crown prince Ludwig of Bavaria came to Rome in 1818 in search of artists to work in Munich, he naturally turned to the Nazarene

204 painters. He succeeded in luring Peter Cornelius to his capital, where this artist dominated official painting for a quarter of a century.

While this strongly idealistic art was developing in Rome, art patrons were desperately trying to raise standards in Germany itself. The most notable example of this was the Weimar Prize Competition (1801–05), established by Goethe and his friend the Swiss painter Heinrich Meyer. This attempted, in a series of annual competitions based on subjects from classical antiquity, to establish an improved standard of taste among the young painters of Germany. However, the narrow concern of the two sponsors with classicism caused them to overlook all the artists of real talent, such as Runge and Cornelius, who entered the competition, and their endeavours did nothing more than encourage arid pedantry.

The outdatedness of such patronage is clearly demonstrated by the fact that at the same time in nearby Dresden, the great masters of German Romantic painting, Phillip Otto Runge and Caspar David Friedrich,

201 were realising their ideals independently. Runge, in his allegories and his personifications of natural forces, sought to embody a pantheistic unity between man and nature. Like Carstens, he dreamed of creating monumental schemes, yet all that became of his vision of a 'cathedral of art' were four engravings of the *Tageszeiten* (phases of the day), designs for murals which were never executed. Unable to make a living, he returned to his native Hamburg, where he was supported by his brother and a few faithful friends. It was they who preserved his work from destruction and, when it had become appreciated, presented it to the Kunsthalle in Hamburg.

202 Friedrich obtained a greater degree of success than Runge, finally becoming a professor at the Dresden Academy in 1824. Like Constable in England, he devoted his life to the study of nature, but he was more subjective in his interpretations, basing his ideas as much on the remembered impression of a landscape as on the immediately observed record. In this way he hoped to capture the feeling of a landscape, giving it a greater relevance to the moods and perceptions of man than previous landscape painters had done.

Art for the glorification of the monarchies

Art and politics are often closely linked in Germany. The reaction against Napoleon's occupation of Germany brought about the concept of a united Germany which artists and writers equated with the supposedly ideal society of the Middle Ages. Medieval art became the fashion, and even the Neoclassical artist Schinkel designed Gothic monuments. Alongside these came the connoisseurs, who began the collections of Gothic art that are the backbone of medieval collections in German museums today. The most famous, that of the Boisserée brothers of Heidelberg (who even managed to interest the classically-orientated Goethe in this art), is now in the Alte Pinakothek in Munich, while the collections of Wallraf and Richartz and of August Kestner are in the Wallraf-Richartz Museum in Cologne and the Kestner Museum in Hannover respectively. Nothing can better illustrate the enthusiasm for the Middle Ages generated at this time than the decision to complete Cologne

199 Cathedral according to the original 13th-century plans for its construction –a project which took nearly sixty years to carry out, and absorbed the

199

THE SPIRE OF COLOGNE CATHEDRAL

1824–80
F. A. Ahlert 1788–1833, E. F. Zwirner 1802–61 and Richard Voigtel 1829–1902

The completion of Cologne Cathedral according to the original 13th-century plans was one of the most remarkable architectural achievements of the 19th century in Germany. It represented the high point of the careers of the famous Gothic enthusiasts, the Boisserée brothers. For most of the architects employed on the scheme, however, it represented an irksome and interminable task, and few of them produced any important works of their own.

200

INTERIOR WITH THE ARTIST'S SISTER

1847
Adolf von Menzel, 1815–1905
oil on canvas
18 × 12·5 in (46 × 32 cm)
Neue Pinakothek, Munich

Menzel thought his most important works to be the large reconstructions of life at the court of Frederick the Great of Prussia that he painted for members of the Prussian government and civil service. Nevertheless, he is best known today for his spirited and unconventional records of everyday life. This early study of his sister in their parent's house was never intended as a finished painting. It remained in the artist's family, and was donated to the *Neue Pinakothek* after his death.

201

THE HÜLSENBECK CHILDREN

1805–06
Philip Otto Runge 1777–1810
oil on canvas
4 ft 3 in × 4 ft 7 in (130·5 × 140·5 cm)
Kunsthalle, Hamburg

Despite Runge's preoccupation with art theory, his most successful finished works are usually portraits of family and friends, which often have a symbolic meaning behind them. In this work, painted for his friend Hülsenbeck, there is an association between the growing children and the sunflowers that is reminiscent of the plant symbolism of his more allegorical works. However, there is nothing pedantic about his unsentimental observation of the children or his feeling for the landscape.

202
THE CROSS IN THE MOUNTAINS
1808, Caspar David Friedrich 1774–1840
oil on canvas
45 × 43·5 in (115 × 110 cm)
Gemäldegalerie, Dresden

Friedrich's apparently artless landscapes have strong symbolic associations and express the spiritual life of man through the moods of nature. This picture is a work of religious intention, painted for the private chapel of Count Thun's castle at Tetschen. Abandoning the traditional form of such scenes, Friedrich has turned the cross away from the spectator towards the landscape – the main subject of the picture – in which the rising sun is a reminder of the hope of resurrection.

203
THE ISHTAR GATE
6th century BC, enamelled bricks, Staatliche Museen, East Berlin

In the 19th century, the Berlin Museum not only collected objects from all over the world, but also attempted to reconstruct some of the larger fragments of antiquity acquired. Seen indoors, this neo-Babylonian gate seems even more overpowering than it would have done in its original setting. Its former potency lay more in the quasi-magical protective emblems that adorn it.

204
THE LAST JUDGMENT
1836–39
Peter von Cornelius 1783–1867
fresco
92 ft 10 in × 37 ft 1 in (28·3 × 11·3 m)
Ludwigskirche, Munich

This is the largest of the many works that Cornelius painted in Munich for the Bavarian king, Ludwig I. Harking unashamedly back to Michelangelo's great *Last Judgment* in the Sistine Chapel at Rome, it reveals the seriousness with which Cornelius took his role as the reviver of Christian art. However, Ludwig refused to allow him to decorate the whole of the Ludwigskirche in this manner, and this disappointment contributed to Cornelius's decision to leave Munich for Berlin.

working lives of three architects, F. A. Ahlert, E. F. Zwirner and R. Voigtel.

However, this mood of idealism was soon dispelled, for with the settlement of Germany that took place after Napoleon's defeat at Waterloo in 1815 the monarchies of Germany became firmly entrenched and reactionary. They took over the interest in medievalism, but turned it to their own particular use. This was particularly so in Bavaria, where Ludwig the son of Maximilian I tried to establish himself as the artistic mentor of Germany. He sought to bring about a whole new era of art by assembling the best talents in Germany and making them work for the greater glory of the Bavarian monarchy.

In this way, as has already been said, he lured Cornelius from Rome to Munich, where the artist was responsible for the decorations in both Klenze's Glyptothek, built 1822-25, and the Ludwigskirche (1838-42), which he painted in a high-minded and didactic manner – his great mural of the Last Judgment in the choir of the Ludwigskirche attempts to fuse the artistic ideals of classical Greece and Christianity. Schnorr, another Nazarene painter, came to Munich a little later, and decorated a wing of the royal palace with scenes from the *Nibelungenlied*, the German medieval saga that became as popular in Germany as the Arthurian legends did in England. However, neither of these artists was quite flattering enough to Ludwig's idea of monarchy, and he preferred the younger Wilhelm Kaulbach, who painted murals representing the most glorious moments from Bavarian history.

King Ludwig was no less ambitious in the field of architecture. He demanded of his favourite architect, Friedrich Gärtner, a 'new style', which was obligingly produced. However, this new style does not appear to us to be as original as Ludwig thought. Many of the buildings that were erected in it in Munich are, in fact, copies of Italian Renaissance buildings; examples are the Feldherrnhalle (1841-44), which is a copy of the 14th-century Loggia dei Lanzi in Florence, and the Residenz, designed by Klenze, which was inspired by the Pitti Palace, also in Florence. In other buildings, such as the Ludwigskirche, one can see how the style was concocted from a mixture of Renaissance and Romanesque architecture. In Germany this style was generally known as the *Rundbogenstil* (round-arched style) and was extremely popular in the second quarter of the century.

In his attempt to create an 'art city', King Ludwig did not neglect any aspect of artistic production. As well as employing architects, sculptors and painters on an unprecedented scale, he also fostered the applied arts, reviving the use of stained glass, establishing porcelain factories and, perhaps most important of all, encouraging the growing interest in producing illustrated books. The press of Johann Nepomuk Strixner had made Munich one of the centres of the new process of lithography in the first part of the century, and now an equal interest was shown in that of wood engraving, leading to such sumptuous works as the 1840 edition of the *Nibelungenlied*.

Despite this, however, it is probably as a collector that King Ludwig is most favourably remembered today. Not only did he enrich the royal collection, but he also established museums in which his works could be seen by the public. The most famous of these, the Alte Pinakothek, still owes much of its character to the works that he provided for it, in particular the collection of early German paintings that he acquired from the Boisserée brothers. He also owned a fine collection of sculptures, including the famous friezes from the 5th-century BC Temple of Aphaia at Aegina in Greece. The latter were housed in the Glyptothek, the sculpture

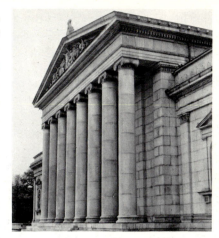

205

THE GLYPTOTHEK
1816–30
Leo von Klenze 1784–1864
Munich

The Glyptothek was designed to house the antique sculptures that had been collected between the years 1805 and 1816 by Ludwig I when he was still crown prince. The most important of these were the reliefs from the temple at Aegina, bought by Ludwig in 1812, and subsequently restored by the Neoclassical sculptor Bertel Thorvaldsen. The building is suitably, but rather pedantically, Ionic. Its best feature, the interior coffered vaulting, was unfortunately destroyed during the last war.

206

THE LUDWIGSKIRCHE
1829–40
Friedrich von Gärtner 1792–1847, Munich

Friedrich von Gärtner was the architect most closely associated with King Ludwig I's ambitious building schemes. He became the master of a style which, being half Florentine Renaissance and half Romanesque, pleased the king because of its religious and cultural associations. The Ludwigskirche, characteristically named after the king, is one of the focal points of the Ludwigstrasse, the long street leading into the centre of Munich.

gallery which was in fact specially designed for them by Leo von Klenze.

All the monarchies of Germany were impressed by Ludwig's example, and made their own attempts at fostering the arts. In Berlin Friedrich Wilhelm III, the patron of the architect Schinkel, was also an avid collector Under the guidance of the art historian Friedrich Waagen, he obtained many famous works of art, including the collection of the Englishman Solly, which contained one of Raphael's early masterpieces, now known as the Solly Madonna.

Art and the middle classes

However, it was not only monarchs who supported this kind of art. Members of the bourgeoisie also provided patronage through *Kunstvereine* (art unions), in which they pooled their resources together every year to buy a work by one of the academy successes. This was then raffled to one of the members of the society, the others contenting themselves with engravings of the subject. How the lucky winners managed to fit some of these vast creations into a house of normal size is not recorded.

Fortunately, painting in Germany was not confined to the high-minded art approved by the academies. Other types of painting also flourished, for the small town burgher, if he bought pictures (as opposed to winning them from an art union), preferred portraits of his family or scenes of his native countryside to pretentious allegories. This type of art, known as 'Biedermeier' (a phrase originally descriptive of Austrian society at this time), is the German equivalent of the 'low art' of Victorian England – the sentimental animals of Landseer and the crowded scenes of Frith. At its best this art has a refreshing sense of simplicity and honesty, whereas at its worst it indulges in sentimentality. The Biedermeier style became common throughout the whole of northern Europe, but probably had its greatest impact in Austria, with painters like Ferdinand Georg Waldmüller.

Amongst German painters, it is often difficult to separate the Biedermeier artists from those who were interested in 'high' art. Karl Blechen, who was made much of in the literary circles of Berlin, turned his skill to depicting light with dramatic effect, and his idyllic scenes have little to do with peasant life. Carl Rottmann, the leading landscape talent of Munich, always had leanings towards a classical form of landscape, and this tendency was intensified when King Ludwig commissioned him to produce frescoes of scenes from Italy and Greece. Amongst figure painters, Moritz von Schwind – best remembered now for his fairy-tale subjects – always hankered after the high manner and leapt at chances to produce such works as the murals which he painted for count Ullstein in the latter's castle at Eisenach. Similarly, Ludwig Richter of Dresden would often turn from his scenes of everyday life to historical subjects. The only
218 artist who managed to stay completely free of high art was Carl Spitzweg, one of the few Munich artists who was not patronised by King Ludwig. Self-trained as an artist (after starting life as a chemist), he depicted small-town characters with gentle humour. He was at the same time a popular artist, so that those people who bought his works also enjoyed his drawings for the comic newspaper *Fliegende Blätter*.

Perhaps Biedermeier found its fullest expression in book illustration. Wood-engraving, popularised by English artists, gave the illustrated book to a new public. Not only did artists like Schwind and Richter produce much of their best work in this form, but academic artists too were able to use their sense of design to good effect. Alfred Rethel, whose historical
207 paintings are rather tedious, achieved great vigour in *Another Dance of Death*, an allegory based on the revolution of 1848. These six woodcuts

207

THE TRIUMPH OF DEATH

1851
Alfred Rethel 1816–59
wood engraving

Alfred Rethel was one of the Düsseldorf academy's most brilliant pupils. He executed many large historical murals in the Rhineland, but his greatest works are his book illustrations. In 1849 his series of engravings, *Another Dance of Death*, inspired by the events of the 1848 revolution, brought him international fame. Unlike much revivalist work, Rethel's designs have a terse and intensely felt immediacy.

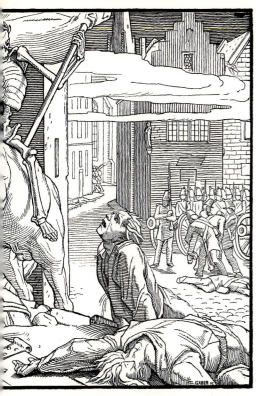

208

THE GREAT ALTAR OF ZEUS
FROM PERGAMON

197–159 BC
marble
Staatliche Museen, East Berlin

The Pergamon Altar was one of the major acquisitions of the Museum in Berlin in the late 19th century, and the thoroughness with which it was reconstructed shows the new educational aspect of museums that came to the fore at that time. The frieze of this famous Hellenistic altar, of which the section shown here depicts Athena defeating the Giants, is one of the finest examples of realistic Hellenic art at its climax.

have close affinities with the work of Dürer and with the famous *Dance of Death* series by Hans Holbein the Younger.

Just as the most attractive art of the early part of the century was not 'official', so in the applied arts it was not the royal factories that produced the best work. Germany was still a highly traditional society with pre-industrial conditions existing in most parts, and while design in royal porcelain factories such as those of Dresden had declined since the 18th century, individual craftsmanship was still valued and local crafts still flourished. In interior design the Biedermeier period is usually represented by simple, unpretentious decoration, especially in the north of Germany, and the development of domestic appliances like the round sewing-table common in the south. Particularly fine examples of local craftsmanship are to be found in outlying areas. In Hamburg, for example, this can be seen in the decoration of a house for an important local figure, Dr Abendroth.

During the 1830s, however, industrialisation began to affect most applied arts, and it was only in the traditional folk crafts, such as paper-cutting (a technique sometimes used by Runge) and wood-carving, that manual techniques remained unaffected. As with most European countries, the process of industrialisation brought about an initial decline in the standards of goods produced, and it was only gradually realised that different standards had to be applied to mass-produced articles.

It was towards the middle of the century that things really began to change. The revolution of 1848, if it did not bring about the world revolution that Marx and Engels hoped for, at least shook German society and emphasised that industrialisation was taking place. In the eyes of Europe, Prussia, with its industrial expansion, replaced Bavaria and its 'art city' capital as the focal point of Germany. Even in patronage, however, the king of Prussia was now leading, and it is significant that Cornelius spent his last years in Berlin. The Neoclassicism which characterised Schinkel's Berlin now became associated with the new imperialism that was to reach its climax in 1870, when the Prussian king became the Kaiser of Germany.

The growth of the Berlin museums

Like the king of Bavaria, Kaiser Wilhelm (Wilhelm II of Prussia) is perhaps best remembered for the art collected during his reign rather than for that which he commissioned. His museum in Berlin has been renamed after its greatest director, Wilhelm von Bode, but it must be remembered that if the king did not supervise the details of collecting, he did give the museum his sympathetic support. The museums of Berlin have a different emphasis from those of Munich, and represent the more scientific spirit of a later age. While King Ludwig's collections were arranged to suit the taste of the connoisseur, the Berlin museums were seen primarily as places where information could be gained about different historical periods and civilisations. Like a large inventory of mankind, they stretch out behind Schinkel's Alte Museum on a special 'museum island' and contain not merely the loot of Europe but of the whole world. Vast relics from ancient Greece were brought there, including the Great Altar from Pergamon in Asia Minor. This victory monument, restored in **208** the Staatliche Museen, (East Berlin), is surrounded by friezes, the smaller portraying the story of Telephus, the legendary founder of Pergamon, and the other depicting a battle of gods and giants. The Pergamon Altar quite dwarfs the Aegina Marbles of King Ludwig of Bavaria or the Elgin Marbles in the British Museum. The Hellenistic market-place of Miletus, another Greek city of Asia Minor, was also transported to

Berlin and restored in the museums there. Whole town walls, including
203 the famous Ishtar Gate decorated with bulls and dragons in enamelled
tiles, came from Babylon. The contents of entire tombs (including the
209 famous bust of Queen Nefertiti, now in West Berlin) were brought from
Egypt. The art of so-called primitive peoples, in particular from the
Pacific where the Germans, late in the field of colonisation, had made
themselves an empire in Micronesia, also began to enter the Berlin
museums towards the end of the 19th century. Most of this was collected
from a scientific rather than an aesthetic point of view, yet ironically it
was these collections that were to have the greatest interest for the 20th
century – and the greatest effect on its artists.

King Ludwig II of Bavaria

Munich remained a respected art centre during the later part of the
century, yet the line of monarchs who had created this 'art city' was
drawing to a bizarre conclusion in Ludwig II. Despite the altered condition
of the monarchy, especially after the unification of Germany in 1870, this
king was determined that the role of cultural arbiter should not slip from
his hands. A passionate Wagner enthusiast, he summoned the composer to
his court as soon as he ascended the throne in 1864, and helped to bring
about the stupendous festivals of Wagner's operas at Bayreuth. However,
Ludwig must at times have been an embarrassment even to that grandiose
composer, for he tried to make the most fanciful elements of Wagner's
world a tenet of everyday life. Debarred from effective political power,
he surrounded himself with representations of those myths based on the
medieval past, and dreamed of being an absolute monarch. A misogynist
and a recluse, he built himself a series of castles in which he could retire
from any semblance of reality. One of these, Linderhof (1870–86),
sentimentally reconstructed the architectural glory of the Bavarian
Baroque, while another, Herrenchiemsee (begun in 1878 and never
completed), imitated Versailles, the palace of his hero, the absolute
monarch Louis XIV of France. The rich Rococo interiors of Linderhof,
designed by Franz von Seitz, director of the Munich State Theatre,
themselves resemble stage-sets. Ludwig's favourite castle, however, was
212 Neuschwanstein (1869–81), a Romanesque fantasia on Wagnerian themes,
culminating in the amazing *Singersaal* (minstrels' hall). Here, mural
decorations, designed by Dr Hyazinth Holland, show grandiose scenes
from Wagnerian legend - Tannhäuser, Lohengrin, Tristan and Isolde. It
was at Neuschwanstein that the Bavarian monarch spent his final years,
in isolation and madness.

The arts at the end of the century

There were changes in the field of painting in the latter part of the
century, for painters were now increasingly working on their own. But
there was no revolution equivalent to that of the French Impressionists,
and too often artists of great ability seem to have failed to follow through
the implications of their discoveries. One of the best of these was the
200 Berlin painter Adolf Menzel. In the early stages of his career he painted
spirited naturalistic works, but later on, patronised by the court circles of
Prussia, he turned to historical subjects reflecting the nationalistic pride of
Prussia, many of his pictures being based on the Prussian hero, King
Frederick the Great. In such works Menzel's naturalism tends to become
little more than a means of giving the scenes a lively interest, and it is
significant that in these later years the artist should have dismissed French
Impressionism as 'lazy art' and considered his own early work to be
little more than sketches. A naturalist painter whose work was closer to
that of Gustave Courbet, the first great Realist in 19th-century painting,

209
QUEEN NEFERTITI
c. 1370 BC
limestone
h. 19 in (48 cm)
Staatliche Museen, West Berlin

The bust of Queen Nefertiti is one of the
most beautiful works to be discovered as a
result of the growth of archaeological
activity within the last century. It was
found by German excavators in the royal
tombs at Tell-el-Amarna and taken
thence to Berlin. This portrait of the
enigmatic consort of the revolutionary
king, Akhenaten, has subsequently become
world-famous as a symbol both of
Egyptian art and feminine grace.

was the Munich artist Wilhelm Leibl. He worked for a time in Paris (where he was a friend of Courbet) and, on his return to Germany, made studies of peasant life, such as his *Three Women in Church*. However, **220** even these are overlayed by a certain historicism, not least in the meticulous detail, reminiscent of the work of the 16th-century artist Holbein, with which he overlayed his work.

Ideal art still persisted, although German idealist painters were now turning from the didacticism of Cornelius and the Nazarenes to more private worlds. Rome still remained their spiritual centre, but more for the classical beauty of its artistic traditions than for its religious heritage, for these idealists were humanists rather than religious enthusiasts like the Nazarenes. Such artists could now no longer depend on royal patronage and were supported instead by a few enlightened enthusiasts. Count Adolph Schack was such a collector, and his gallery in Munich remains the best place to see examples of this type of work. It was Schack who enabled Anselm Feuerbach, the most dignified of these 'intellectual' painters, to **210** continue working in Rome, and who bought the bizarre, almost surrealist paintings of Arnold Böcklin, creator of idealised landscapes peopled with symbolic forms, battling men and mythological creatures. He also supported Hans von Marées, a painter of a rather different class. This **219** artist, a close associate of the sculptor Adolf Hildebrandt and the critic Conrad Fiedler, evolved a private world of idealised figures in which he sought the mystic supremacy of pure form. The quality of his paintings as well as his technique has led him to be compared with Cézanne.

Hildebrandt, ten years Marées's junior, was the first major German sculptor since Schadow. Like Marées, he was deeply concerned with the question of form, an interest that led him to write the book *Das Problem der Form* (The Problem of Form) in 1893. However, his sculptures are far from being overweighed by theory. Even his early classicising works, **215** like the *Water-carrying Youth* of 1884 have vibrant proportions. Later on, when he received public commissions such as the Wittelsbach Fountain in Munich, he was able to avoid the tediousness of most of the large nationalistic constructions of his time by means of his fine sense of spacing and economic use of decoration.

In architecture, too, theory was beginning to reassert itself. Gottfried Semper, the most outstanding architect of the middle years of the century, was a noted theorist and, although he worked for monarchs at Dresden (where he designed the Gemäldegalerie and opera house), he was no court servant. On the contrary he was a revolutionary who had to flee the country in 1848. Towards the end of the century, there was little to parallel the magnificent Neoclassical buildings that had been erected by a previous generation. The new German emperors Wilhelm I and Friedrich I failed to make their capital, Berlin, a centre of late 19th-century architecture in the way that Napoleon III had done in Paris, and it was not until the 20th century that German architecture rose again to its previous high standard.

It is paradoxical that many works which were less esteemed when they were produced in the 19th century now so often appear to us to be the more important – paintings by less successful artists, the lesser-known pictures of famous artists, the productions of traditional craftsmanship and objects collected for scientific curiosity. All these areas provided the source material to be used by 20th-century artists in their great innovations in the use of form and colour, but, historically important as they are, they also deserve to be looked at for their intrinsic value.

William Vaughan

210

PLATO'S SYMPOSIUM
1869
Anselm Feuerbach 1829 – 80
oil on canvas
9 ft 8 in × 19 ft 7·5 in (2·95 × 5·98 m)
Staatliche Kunsthalle, Karlsruhe

Feuerbach, like his contemporary Leighton in England, was a stern pursuer of the ideal in art. In the case of both artists, their reconstructions of classical scenes are too tasteful to be really moving. On the other hand, Feuerbach has an admirable sense of design, a quality that lent much dignity to his portraits.

211

THE THRONE ROOM

1825–33, Leo von Klenze 1784–1864
Residenz, Munich

In his later years, working under King Ludwig I of Bavaria,
Klenze gradually turned away from the Greek revivalism of
buildings like the Glyptothek (**205**). In the throne room of the
Residenz he chose, appropriately enough, to express regal
splendour through a combination of Roman and High
Renaissance architecture. Such a change of manner was typical of
the gradual submerging of Neoclassicism in the highly ornate
architectural styles of the mid-century.

212 *below*

NEUSCHWANSTEIN CASTLE

1869–81, Eduard Riedel 1813–85 and
Georg Dollman 1830–95, Bavaria

This is the most fantastic of the castles built for King Ludwig II
of Bavaria to satisfy his taste for the exotic. The interior, with its
sumptuous decorations and murals, is based on the mythology of
Wagner's operas. The exterior is based on the Romanesque
architecture of the Wartburg, the famous 11th-century castle in
Thuringia. Perched on a precarious peak, it is also a feat of
modern engineering.

213

NIGHT WITH HER CHILDREN SLEEP AND DEATH

1795
Asmus Jacob Carstens 1754–98
pencil
36 × 46 in (91 × 116 cm)
Schlossmuseum, Weimar

During the last years of his life in Rome,
Carstens prepared many designs for large
monumental schemes that were never to be
commissioned or executed. He often drew
his subjects from Greek mythology, but
the treatment is more reminiscent of
artists of the High Renaissance, especially
Michelangelo. His emulation of this artist
led him to shun any compromises in his
own work and to live the life of a self-
styled genius.

214

THE VISION OF ST BERNARD

late 15th century
Pietro di Cristoforo Vannucci, called Perugino 1450–1523
oil on wood, 68·1 × 67 in (173 × 170 cm)
Alte Pinakothek, Munich

Like Fra Angelico, Perugino was an Italian 15th-century painter who was highly popular with German revivalist artists of the 19th century. The teacher of Raphael, he was felt to have been responsible for many of the virtues of that artist's early style. This altarpiece was one of King Ludwig's finest acquisitions. He bought it from the Capponi family in 1829.

215

A YOUTH

1884, Adolf von Hildebrandt 1847–1921
marble, 60·75 in (175 cm)
Staatliche Museen, East Berlin

Hildebrandt was a highly intellectual artist whose main interest, like that of his friends the art critic Conrad Fiedler and the artist Hans von Marées, was form. In works like this statue of a youth he managed to achieve a striking classic simplicity that shows little sign of the great amount of mental energy that he spent in its conception.

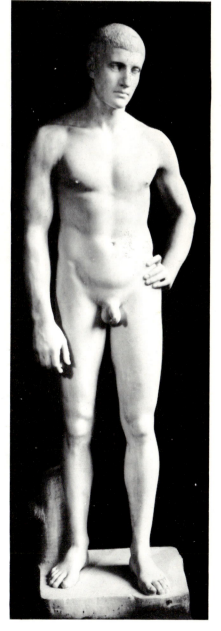

216
PASTOR RAUTENBERG
AND HIS FAMILY

1833, Karl Julius Milde, 1803–75
watercolour, 17·9 × 18 in (45·6 × 45·7 cm)
Kunsthalle, Hamburg

The extreme north of Germany has always
been remote from the customs and
traditions of the rest of the country,
having more in common with Denmark
and the Scandinavian countries. In the
19th century local artists evolved an
unpretentious naturalism that has been
compared with that of English landscape
painters. Milde, after studying in Dresden,
Munich and Rome, chose to return to the
north, where he painted many works of
touching honesty.

217
PARADE ON THE OPERNPLATZ
detail

1824–29, Franz Krüger 1797–1857
oil on canvas
8 ft 2 in × 12 ft 3·25 in (2·49 × 3·74 m)
Staatliche Museen, West Berlin

Krüger faithfully depicted the appearance
of the Berlin of his time. This picture, one
of his largest works, was painted for the
grand duke Nicholas of Russia, who is
shown parading his cuirassiers in the
Opernplatz on the occasion of his marriage
to Charlotte, daughter of Frederick
William III of Prussia, in 1824. It hung in
the Winterpalace at St Petersburg for many
years, but was presented by the Tsar to the
Kaiser before the First World War.

218 *left*

THE POOR POET

1839, Carl Spitzweg 1808–85
oil on canvas
14 × 17 in (36 × 44 cm)
Neue Pinakothek, Munich

Spitzweg, a self-trained artist, devoted most of his artistic career to portraying small-town characters who are the epitome of Biedermeier society. He observed his subjects with humour rather than insight. Here the theme of the artist struggling against poverty, a subject that had been portrayed so bitterly by Hogarth and other satirists, is the object of gentle amusement rather than sympathy.

219 *left*

THE HESPERIDES *detail*

1884–85
Hans von Marées 1837–87
oil on canvas
complete panel 15 ft 10 in × 11 ft 2 in (4·82 × 3·40 m)
Bayerische Staatsgemäldesammlungen, Munich

This depiction of a paradisical subject is typical of Marées's mature painting. Not only did the artist intend the subject to be idyllic, but he also tried to represent an ideal of physical beauty in the arrangement of the figures. For Marées, beauty was almost a religion, and he deliberately designed this work as a triptych, making it reminiscent of an altarpiece. As with many of his pictures, the quality of the painting is slightly marred by being overworked.

220

THREE WOMEN IN CHURCH

1878–81, Wilhelm Leibl 1844–1900
oil on canvas, 44 × 30 in (113 × 77 cm), Kunsthalle, Hamburg

This picture is the masterpiece of Leibl's 'Holbein' period, the decade in which he returned to the meticulous style of German 16th-century artists after his return from Paris in 1870. Unlike the Nazarenes' cult of medievalism, there is nothing pedantic about Leibl's return to the art of the past, for he used its influence only as a direction, retaining an honesty of approach. Despite his desire to represent uncritically what he saw, he displays an innate sense of composition and unwittingly characterises the people he portrays.

In Germany more than in any other European country of comparable size, politics have affected the course of patronage. This is made very evident by the events of the present century, during which not only enlightened museum directors and collectors, but also creative artists were opposed by reactionary or evil regimes. However, the earlier part of the century was also a period of intense creativity in German art, and for the first time for many centuries Germany developed, in the Expressionists, a strong, original, national school of international significance.

The Berlin Impressionists

Impressionism, like the other important art movements to originate abroad, came late to Germany. Although the forward-looking artists of Berlin showed themselves more ready to accept the new movement than the artists of other German cities, the Establishment of the capital was as antagonistic towards it as had been that of Paris a generation earlier. History painting, the depiction of anecdotal scenes and academic salon painting in all its other forms, remained the taste of the majority until well after the turn of the century. Such works as the lavish descriptions of the Prussian army and of the war of 1870 by Anton von Werner, president of the Berlin Academy, were felt to match the national spirit.

231 Several of the more advanced of Berlin's artists, led by the Impressionists, registered their protest against the reactionary forces which dominated the artistic life of the city when, in 1892, they resigned from the official Berlin Artists' Association. This followed the closure of an officially-sponsored exhibition of the work of Edvard Munch, the Norwegian painter who, in his depictions of subtle psychological relationships, made use of expressionistic techniques of colour and line. Disturbed and scandalised by the unusual paintings, the official worthies had closed the exhibition after only two days.

The breakaway group of progressive Berlin artists in 1896 became known as the 'Berlin Secession', which held its first exhibition in 1899. The exhibition was an immediate success, and overnight the Berlin Impressionists became a force to be reckoned with. The three leading Impressionists were Max Liebermann, Lovis Corinth and Max Slevogt. Liebermann, the leader of the Secession and a man greatly liked in Berlin for his wit and sardonic comments about life in general, cultivated what was in fact a form of Realism enlivened by Impressionist brushwork. Corinth also resolutely continued to indulge in literary motifs until the end of his life, although his brushwork was freer than Liebermann's and

225 his colours less tied to the more sombre values. Slevogt, who, like Corinth, came from Munich, felt a natural affinity with Rococo. He was nevertheless the closest of the three to the original French Impressionist style, and his landscapes show a real feeling for light and movement.

Under the leadership of Liebermann the Berlin Secession was quick to recognise the talent of other German painters working in different styles. They introduced the Berlin public to the work of the most important modern artists from at home and abroad, such as Van Gogh, Cézanne, Toulouse-Lautrec and Hodler, artists who were virtually unknown in the country at that time.

Attitudes to modern art

Among the first to recognise the greatness of the Impressionists was Hugo von Tschudi, director of the Nationalgalerie in Berlin. From 1896 onwards he encouraged wealthy collectors to present to the gallery fine examples of recent French painting by such artists as Daumier and Courbet, Manet, Renoir and Monet. That such masterpieces should have been given official approval so late is a mark of how far German taste

Expressing the Modern World

c. 1900 to the present day

221

SELF-PORTRAIT WITH MODEL
c. 1907
Ernst Ludwig Kirchner 1880–1938
oil on canvas
59·1 × 39·5 in (150·5 × 100·5 cm)
Kunsthalle, Hamburg

Probably repainted later than 1907, this shows Kirchner's early style at its best with its bright colour-harmonies and its negation of space. The painting was among the works confiscated by the Nazis during their campaign against 'degenerate' art, but it returned to Hamburg after the war.

had lagged behind that of other European countries. Moreover, Tschudi's liking for the Impressionists met with much opposition, particularly from the court and the Kaiser, who considered that an interest in French art was close to treason, and he was eventually dismissed from his post in 1909. This is the first example in Germany of political interference in artistic matters during the present century.

Although Germany had been a united country since 1870, it was still in many respects a federal collection of states with many provincial centres, each with a proud tradition and a determination that the capital should not become supreme in all matters. Because of this, even the smallest provincial centre was keen to found a museum. By 1900 most of the directors of such provincial museums were showing an aversion for traditional, academic painting and a decided preference for contemporary work. Lichtwark at Hamburg, Wörmann at Dresden and Hagelstange in Cologne began to acquire contemporary work and managed to find enough wealthy people to help finance their activities. Because of people like these, Germany possessed the most spectacular array of contemporary work anywhere and had bought important examples of works by Cézanne, Gauguin, Van Gogh and the Neo-Impressionists at never-to-be-repeated prices. Most of these were removed by the Nazis, either to Switzerland or to Goering's private collection, and all the provincial museums had great difficulty after the war in attempting to fill the lacunae left by the politicians.

The growing knowledge of modern art promoted by such liberal museum officials early in the century also led to the appearance of a new kind of collector in Germany: the man who is interested in modern German art as a whole and avant-garde work in particular. He became the equivalent of the wealthy patron in the Renaissance, and saw his role as much in the founding of museums as in the building up of large collections for his own personal aggrandisement. One of the most important of these was Karl Ernst Osthaus who paid for a museum in the Rhineland, the Folkwang Museum, and commissioned Henri van de Velde, one of the most advanced architects of the day, to design it. Opened in 1902, it immediately laid the foundations for one of the most important collections of modern art in Europe.

An interest in and appreciation for contemporary art also manifested itself in the art schools and academies. Artists were given professorships not because they could turn out competent history paintings but because they had ideas of their own. This in itself must be regarded as an important kind of patronage, for artists who might otherwise not have sold enough work to live from were paid handsomely as teachers. There was in fact more interest in modern art in Germany at the beginning of the 20th century than anywhere else in Europe, and the marked difference between the strides forward made in the provinces and the relatively reactionary situation in Berlin is proof of the restricting influence of officialdom.

Jugendstil and art in industry

The importance to patronage of provincial centres with jealously guarded traditions is shown by events in Darmstadt, until 1918 the capital of the grand duchy of Hesse. The grand duke Ernst Ludwig was a man of liberal views with an overriding interest in the arts. He had been fascinated by the development of Art Nouveau, the movement in decorative arts which arose in Europe in the 1890s, the German version of which was known as Jugendstil. In sympathy with its theories, particularly its new approach to building and interior design, he brought a number of distinguished artists to Darmstadt, paid them, gave them land, and asked

222

WINE GLASS

Louis Comfort Tiffany 1848–1933
Hessisches Landesmuseum, Darmstadt

Ernst Ludwig, the grand duke of Hesse who founded the Artists' Colony in his capital, Darmstadt, was also a collector of Art Nouveau objects, furniture and graphic art. This piece by the leading American Art Nouveau glass maker, Tiffany, is one of a large number of such pieces which the grand duke's son presented to the Darmstadt Museum in 1960. It is the nucleus of perhaps the best collection of Art Nouveau work in Germany, a collection which continues to expand.

them to build an artists' colony and exhibition halls where they could put their work on show. The Mathildenhöhe, a hill with a commanding view over the city, was the site selected for the scheme. The houses the artists built for themselves, the exhibition hall and the Wedding Tower, **240** built by Joseph Maria Olbrich, one of the most successful builders of his generation, to commemorate the marriage of the grand duke, are some of the finest examples of Art Nouveau architecture anywhere, and the personal collection of objects and furniture that Ernst Ludwig brought together is one of the most representative in the world. Most of it, from Tiffany Glass to chairs and desks by Van de Velde, can now be seen in the **222, 223** Landesmuseum at Darmstadt.

Other provincial courts conferred patronage in different ways. Weimar, capital of Thuringia, was noted for the interest of its court in the social

223
WRITING DESK
Henri van de Velde 1863–1957
wood
Hessisches Landesmuseum, Darmstadt

Although Van de Velde was a Belgian, it was in Germany that he exercised the strongest influence. His own style was derived from the curving rhythms and plant-like decorations of Art Nouveau, but in his intellectual approach to the problems of design, he was above all concerned with the social role of art. He developed radical ideas about education, which he was able to put into practice in the school of design founded by him in Weimar and named the Bauhaus.

application of arts and crafts. In 1901, Henry van de Velde was called to the city to be artistic designer to industry, for it was felt that the machine had been mass-producing ugly objects for far too long, and that it was time an artist of real merit applied his thoughts and energies to the problem. Van de Velde founded an art school in Weimar in 1908 under official patronage, and this school was the first in the world to propose a working partnership between artist and engineer. Later, as the Bauhaus, it was to change the face of architecture and design all over the world.

An understanding of the importance of co-operation between artists and engineers was well advanced in Germany, and this is one of the reasons for the rapid progress of German architecture in the 1920s. One of the most influential figures in this respect was Hermann Muthesius, who, in 1907, succeeded in founding the *Deutsche Werkbund*, an official organisation which, through publications and exhibitions, was intended to bring art and technology together. The Werkbund was a great success. Many large firms were persuaded to employ artists as designers (in 1907 a very advanced idea indeed), so that the functional and visual qualities of their products should improve. The AEG (general electricity company) in Berlin brought Peter Behrens, previously a member of the artists' colony at Darmstadt, to advise it on all design matters. Behrens in fact designed everything for AEG, from the large turbine sheds, through all its products **224** to its advertising and letter-heads. Behrens's appointment marks a new stage in the history of patronage since, for the first time, industry was commissioning an artist to produce objects for specific and highly specialised purposes.

The Brücke
German painting in the 19th century had been dull, for the most part pale

imitations of foreign originals. The Expressionist movement changed this situation. Founded in Dresden in 1905 by a group of young artists, Ernst Ludwig Kirchner, Erich Heckel, Karl Schmidt-Rottluff and Fritz Bleyl, who called themselves *Die Brücke* (the Bridge), the movement expanded and had repercussions throughout the country.

The artists of the Brücke gradually broke away from an imitation of Van Gogh and other Post-Impressionist artists, brightened their colour still further and emphasised the freedom of their brushwork. They did this is an attempt to paint such intangible subjects as their own emotions, and used aspects of nature for their motifs, but only as forms through which their spirituality might manifest itself. Like the Fauves in France, they also opened their minds to the influence of primitive art, which they had seen in the ethnological museum in Dresden, and they also brought a new attitude to Gothic art which had been considered to be a low form of art for many years. Paintings like Grünewald's Isenheim Altarpiece at Colmar became key works for the Expressionist generation. Two new recruits to the Brücke in 1906 were Max Pechstein, the only member of the group to have had formal art lessons, and the much older Emil Nolde, whose brilliant colours and daring brushwork thrilled the young artists.

In order to increase communal funds and to stimulate public interest in what they were doing, the Brücke had the idea of bringing out annual portfolios of their graphic work, to be presented to 'passive' members of the group who paid a modest annual fee. These have become some of the most highly prized examples of modern graphic art.

In 1907 the group finally found a dealer willing to give them wall space, and an exhibition of their work was held at the Salon Richter, one of Dresden's best galleries. The owner was not rewarded for his courage, however, for the exhibition was received with hostility. In the same year Nolde decided to leave the group and return to his native north Germany. Pechstein went to Berlin in 1908 and decided to settle there permanently, although he remained a member of the Brücke. In Berlin Pechstein founded the 'New Secession', a group of advanced artists whose work had been rejected by the Berlin Secession for its 1910 exhibition. The Berlin Secession, once a protest movement against officially accepted art, had itself become conservative and wary of advanced tendencies. All the Brücke artists from Dresden were invited to show at the New Secession's exhibition which ran concurrently with that of the Berlin Secession. The most modern exhibition that the capital had ever seen, it received some good notices in the press, mainly from people who rightly saw these young artists as the direct heirs of Van Gogh and Gauguin.

The artists of the Brücke (except for Pechstein) did not, however, long remain associated with the New Secession, because they were not convinced by most of the other work shown there and felt that it was damaging to be seen together with inferior talents. They all decided to leave Dresden and settle permanently in Berlin as Pechstein had done, for they felt that in the capital, by now more courageous in its taste, they would gain both more recognition and more money than in the provinces. By 1911 Berlin had become a cultural centre of considerable importance. The progressive dealers had begun to acquire reputations abroad and there was a rich and varied intellectual life centred, as in Paris, on the cafés. The first dealer to take up the cause of the Brücke in Berlin was Fritz Gurlitt, who organised a small show in 1911. In the same year there were Brücke exhibitions in Danzig, Lübeck and the Folkwang Museum in Hagen.

It was in Berlin that all the artists of the Brücke reached a climax in their careers, but it was also there that they began to grow away from

224

AEG TURBINE HALL
1909
Peter Behrens 1868–1940
West Berlin

Peter Behrens was undoubtedly the most important figure in pre-war German architecture. He was associated with the *Werkbund*, the organisation founded to encourage cooperation between artists, designers and industry and was in 1907 made director of design to the great electrical combine, the AEG. He designed everything from letterheads to industrial buildings. The turbine erecting shop was Behrens's first major achievement. It is still in its original state and used for its original purpose.

221,
227, 229

230

228

225

VIEW OF THE ALSTER
NEAR HAMBURG

1904
Max Slevogt 1868–1932
oil on canvas
National-Galerie, East Berlin

The German Impressionists, led by
Slevogt, Liebermann and Corinth, were
centred on Berlin where, in the 1890s, they
founded and dominated the breakaway
group of artists known as the Secession.
The German artists were never so
completely interested in light as their
French masters, nor did they succeed in
banishing literary subjects entirely from
their work. Slevogt came closest to French
Impressionism, but nowhere approached
the clarity of light characteristic of the
French version of Impressionism.

226

MEDITERRANEAN COAST

Alexei Jawlensky 1864–1941
oil on canvas
Galerie Stange, Munich

Like Kandinsky, Jawlensky was born in
Russia and came to Munich to study art
in 1896. He was the first of the Munich
artists to establish contacts with French
contemporaries, and the French influence
is particularly clear in this picture. Later he
concentrated on portraits, where his
individual style, a synthesis of Russian and
French elements, emerged.

227
PAINTERS OF THE BRÜCKE
1925
Ernst Ludwig Kirchner 1880–1938
oil on canvas
65·75 × 49·75 in (167 × 125 cm)
Wallraf-Richartz Museum, Cologne

Kirchner painted this group portrait from memory during his self-imposed exile in Switzerland. It shows, from left to right, the painters Müller, Kirchner, Heckel and Schmidt-Rottluff. Nolde and Pechstein, as well as Bleyl, a founder member of the Brücke, are omitted. This painting, which celebrates one of the most important groups of German artists to emerge in this century, was auctioned by the Nazis in Switzerland in 1937. It returned to Germany in 1951.

228
FLOWER GARDEN
c. 1904
Emil Nolde 1867–1956
oil on canvas
35·25 × 29 in (89·5 × 74 cm)
Wallraf-Richartz Museum, Cologne

This, one of Nolde's finest flower studies, dates from the period just before he joined the Brücke. Like most of the advanced artists of his generation, Nolde was defamed by the Nazis and his work was removed from all public collections. This painting was presented to the Wallraf-Richartz Museum by a private collector in 1946.

229
LANDSCAPE WITH FIELDS
1911
Karl Schmidt-Rottluff, born 1884
oil on canvas
34·5 × 37·75 in (88 × 96 cm)
Wilhelm-Lehmbruck Museum, Duisburg

The painting was first exhibited at the New Secession's exhibition in Berlin and was acquired by the Duisburg Museum in 1952 at an auction in Stuttgart. After the war all the German museums attempted to regain works lost during the Nazi cultural actions. This is one of the many paintings which returned to Germany, although not to its former home, as it originally belonged to the Folkwang Museum in Essen.

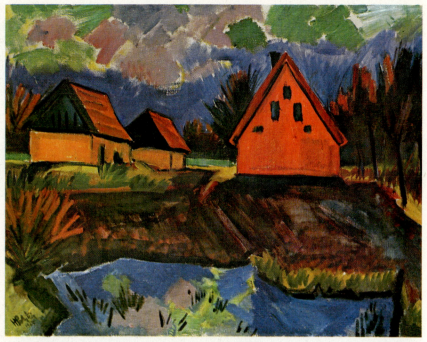

230 *top*

RED HOUSES

Max Pechstein 1881–1953
oil on canvas
Landesgalerie, Hannover

Pechstein joined the Brücke artists' group
in 1906 and was the only trained painter
among them. At first his painting stayed
close to French Fauvist models but later
his colours became even brighter, with
clashing harmonies and harsh contrasts.
Pechstein was never as radical a painter as
his fellow Brücke artists Kirchner and
Schmidt-Rottluff, and his work was,
perhaps for this reason, more popular than
theirs. He was the first member of the
Brücke to gain fame and was for years held
to be the archetypal Expressionist artist.

231

VILLAGE STREET
NEAR THE BEACH AT AASGARD

c. 1902
Edvard Munch 1863–1944
oil on canvas
Neue Staatsgalerie, Munich

Although born in Norway, Munch lived
for many years in Germany, where he was
eventually recognised as an artist of huge
significance. He was among the first
painters to explore the subject-potential of
states of mind and succeeded in endowing
even the most conventional subject with
emotional tension. In this he exerted an
enormous influence on the course of
Expressionism.

232

TIGER

1912
Franz Marc 1880–1916
oil on canvas
43 × 39 in (109 × 99 cm)
Koehler Collection, West Berlin

Franz Marc, one of the founders of the Blaue Reiter, was interested almost exclusively in animal subjects and, using a formal language derived from Cubo-Futurism, he attempted to depict his own mystical version of the animal world. This, one of his most famous paintings, attempts to depict the energies of the tiger, its unique qualities, in terms of its external appearance. Marc was on the threshold of an abstract style when he was killed during the First World War.

233

TUNISIAN LANDSCAPE

1914
August Macke 1887–1914
oil on canvas
17·7 × 21·7 in (45 × 55 cm)
Hessisches Landesmuseum, Darmstadt

Macke's enthusiasm for brilliant colour and the stylisations of Cubism and Futurism led him towards his own style, which combined elements of all these. In 1914 Macke went to Tunis with Paul Klee, and the picture was painted there. This trip brightened Macke's colours still further, but before a truly original style could emerge he was killed in action during the First World War.

each other. In Dresden each had suppressed his individuality in favour of an intentionally communal style, but in the capital the coherence of the group was weakened. Pechstein, who was generally recognised as the one real talent of the Brücke and its true leader, left the group in 1912 after disagreements with the self-sufficient and ambitious Kirchner. A year later the other members decided that it was time to end their association and thereafter never exhibited as a group again.

The Brücke painters were also associated with *Der Sturm* (Storm), a project organised by Herwarth Walden, a remarkable patron of the arts. *Der Sturm*, founded in 1910, comprised a publishing-house and journal to which many Expressionist writers contributed, a small theatre and an art gallery where works of the principal German and European Expressionists, Cubists, Futurists and Constructivists were shown. In 1913 the Berlin Secession had planned to hold an 'autumn salon' in Berlin, but when it did not take place Herwarth Walden immediately saw his chance and organised the first German Autumn Salon himself. He travelled all over Europe inviting the avant-garde of each country to exhibit. The result was 366 paintings and pieces of sculpture by ninety artists from fifteen countries – certainly the most comprehensive exhibition of its kind ever held, and mainly composed of Cubist and Futurist works.

The Blaue Reiter

Munich, had, since the very beginning of the century, been a centre for advanced art. Vassily Kandinsky and Alexei Jawlensky were among a 247, 226 group of young artists who arrived there from Russia in the 1890s and who were to be extremely influential. The Phalanx, a progressive artists' group, was founded in 1901, and in 1909 Kandinsky and Jawlensky helped to form the New Artists' Association of Munich. This group broke up in 1911, the result of an inner split which was in fact present from the beginning, as painters like Kandinsky and Jawlensky were simply too progressive even for the other members. Kandinsky, having begun his career as a painter with frankly academic exercises, had learned a great deal from Jugendstil and the Post-Impressionists. His colours having become increasingly bright and his subject matter less and less clear, he was in fact on the threshold of a breakthrough to abstract painting. When the Association's exhibition jury rejected works by Kandinsky, the latter, together with Franz Marc (who had joined the 232 Association only a few months previously), Gabriele Münter (Kandinsky's mistress and an artist in her own right) and Alfred Kubin resigned.

In December 1911 Marc and Kandinsky organised the first exhibition of the Blaue Reiter. This organisation was not strictly speaking a group of artists, but was the name of a magazine about modern art, music and literature which Kandinsky and Marc had been working on for some months. The first and only issue contained articles by Marc and Kandinsky, pieces on primitive art and on modern music and even reproductions of scores by Arnold Schoenberg, the 'inventor' of twelve-tone music.

The Blaue Reiter exhibitions were to be seen as part of the activities of the editorial board (Kandinsky and Marc), and the first exhibition was very international in character. The second, held in 1912, included works by Paul Klee and brought the Brücke and the Blaue Reiter together for the first time in an exhibition. The advanced artists from Berlin and Munich quickly realised that they had not been working alone, but had been independently striving towards something like a common goal. For the first time Germany was the possessor of a vital and important modern movement which was making a great contribution to the history of art.

The artists of the Brücke and the Blaue Reiter shared the same basic aim:

to express truths which lie deeper than the surface appearance of nature. Both movements were also, at root, expressions of artistic protest—against the suffocating restrictions of contemporary society and for the freedom of the individual spirit. But the two movements differed in their basic character, the works of the Brücke artists being violent products of primitive emotion, while those of the Blaue Reiter—an essentially intellectual movement—were refined by a quality of spirituality.

Developments after the First World War

Many Expressionist artists, above all poets and writers, foresaw the 1914-18 war and were filled with foreboding. Two leading members of the Blaue Reiter—Franz Marc and August Macke—were killed in action, and their deaths seemed to mark the eclipse of the movement. The war changed the face of Europe for ever; a generation was decimated and a way of life destroyed. When the war ended in 1918 many hoped that the new society would be better: more egalitarian, more humane.

232, 233

In Germany the reforming zeal led to attempts at social revolution. Bavaria briefly became a Soviet republic under the Independent Socialists, and in Berlin there was a spate of ugly demonstrations ruthlessly put down by Prussian officers. Although the revolution soon foundered, the German empire gave way before democracy, and in 1919 the Weimar Republic was established. Many artists and intellectuals joined the newly-formed Communist Party. They felt that Expressionism was part of the same society which it indirectly criticised. It was, above all, an intensely personal form of expression, tied to the artist's own individual conception of the world. What was needed was a form of art directly serving society.

The *Novembergruppe*, a self-styled 'union of radical artists' was founded in 1918 in Berlin, one of the initiators being Max Pechstein. Artists in other cities formed similar groups with the object of bringing art and society closer together. Two of the Novembergruppe's most prominent members were George Grosz and John Heartfield, who invented the technique of photo-montage: cutting up photographs and rearranging them, often to make a political point. Heartfield's compositions were scathing and powerful and often obscene in their attacks on jingoists, capitalists and political exploitation. Heartfield and Grosz also co-operated in the founding of the Dada movement in Berlin. This anti-art movement, which already existed in other cities in Europe, took on a different, notably political character in Berlin.

Socially-committed artists adopted a new dry technique to portray often unpalatable subjects with a type of realism which was seen as objective. In fact G. F. Hartlaub, director of the Mannheim Kunsthalle, in 1923 adopted the term *Neue Sachlichkeit* (new objectivity) for such artists, who included the painters Max Beckmann and Otto Dix, as well as Grosz and Heartfield.

243

Although the most advanced artists rejected Expressionism after the war, the style was beginning to meet with wide public success. The art market boomed, mainly because there was a series of financial crises which made money, shares and securities quite worthless, while works of art were seen as a more secure form of capital. Galleries were opened in Berlin by French dealers (Bernheim, Vollard, Kahnweiler) as well as by Germans (Flechtheim, Nierendorf, Möller). Paul Cassirer, who had been a champion of the Impressionists, began to show the Expressionists, whom he had at first rejected. Both the Nationalgalerie in Berlin and the provincial museums began to buy contemporary art in quantity. Ludwig Justi, who succeeded Hugo von Tschudi as director of the Berlin Nationalgalerie, had continued his predecessor's liberal and informed policy, and pictures by Kokoschka, Heckel and Macke were among the advanced

234
EINSTEIN TOWER
1920—21
Erich Mendelsohn, born 1887
Potsdam

This building was both a monument to Albert Einstein, and a laboratory and observatory. Mendelsohn began sketches for the tower in 1919, although earlier drawings indicate that he was thinking along similar lines even before he was commissioned. His design was in fact impracticable in many ways and he found it necessary to alter details on the building site. The tower is nevertheless one of the key buildings of modern architecture. After the war it fell into disrepair and has recently been renovated by the East German government.

235
STEEL TUBE CHAIR
1925
Marcel Breuer, born 1902
Bauhaus-Archiv, Darmstadt

One of the major activities at the Bauhaus was furniture-design. Marcel Breuer, chief teacher in the design department, was one of the first artists to design in terms of modern materials, preferring shapes to ornament. The Darmstadt Bauhaus-Archiv was set up in the 1950s with the assistance of some of the old teachers and students of the Bauhaus. Another archive exists in Weimar.

works which found their way into the gallery during his term of office. In 1920, following the Kaiser's abdication in 1918, he took over one of the royal residences and used it to put all the most up-to-date painting on show: the Brücke, the Blaue Reiter and the work of the Bauhaus, after that splendid institution had begun to produce enough for exhibition, were all represented.

By contrast with other artists, architects found the immediate post-war period extremely difficult, for during the series of acute financial crises there was no money for building. They therefore indulged in extravagant theorising, dreaming up buildings which could never be built. Paradoxically, this period of pipe-dreaming and utopian theorising proved to be one of the most fruitful in the history of modern architecture. A significant example of architectural thinking of this time is a model by Mies van der Rohe for a skyscraper in Berlin, a glass structure uncannily like some of the most modern buildings of half a century later.

When in the late 1920s the funds for building began to flow again, most architects in fact executed buildings in a style far removed from the imaginative conceptions of their sketches. Some, however, realised buildings which can only be described as Expressionist: notable examples are Erich Mendelsohn's Einstein Tower (built at Potsdam in 1921) with its **234** curiously organic form, and Hans Poelzig's conversion in 1919 of the Busch Circus buildings in Berlin into a theatre for Max Reinhardt's Grosses Schauspielhaus. Poelzig achieved his object in a brilliantly imaginative way, creating a strange fantasy world of stalactite-like forms, a grotto into which the spectators came to escape from the outside world and be presented with an entirely new form of reality on the stage.

The Bauhaus

After the war of 1914-18 Van de Velde's school of design at Weimar took on a new significance for the history of art and design. Van de Velde had left the school in 1915 and Walter Gropius succeeded him. Gropius had been a junior in Behrens's practice in Berlin and had learned a great deal from AEG's designer about modern architecture and the importance of co-operation between artists and industry. Gropius had in fact made his name with the design for a factory and office building at the Werkbund exhibition of 1914. From 1919 the Weimar school was known as the Weimar State Bauhaus (building house), the name emphasising Gropius's convictions. His intention was that the school should henceforth train students specifically to produce designs for industry, for machine pro- **235** duction, and not teach any of the old techniques associated with 'fine art'. This was a radical conception of art education, for everything was to be taught from the standpoint of basic design. Industrialists, it was hoped, would be prepared to co-operate with Bauhaus-trained people.

The school, which was financed by the city of Weimar and the state of Thuringia, was itself the result of a rare sort of patronage, as artists received salaries and accommodation and were encouraged to do their own work. During the first few years of the school's existence, Vassily Kandinsky and Paul Klee were among those called to teach at Weimar. **247, 250** Others were the Expressionist painters Oskar Schlemmer, Lyonel Feininger and Georg Muche. Although, as Expressionists, all these **246** artists were apparently far removed from the rationalist and functionalist aesthetic which Gropius wished to propagate, they were the most brilliant artists of their generation, and Gropius saw that they, better than anyone else, could teach the basics of design and visual perception. The teaching methods evolved by Kandinsky and Klee, to name but two, have had an enormous influence on the development of art education.

Nazi art policy

In 1933 the Nazis, now in full command of the country, began their fight against what they called 'degenerate' art; in other words just that kind of art that Justi, whom they removed from his post, had been acquiring during the previous twenty-four years for the Berlin gallery.

Nazi policy demanded that accepted forms of thoroughly German art, together with paintings extolling the Nazi idea, take the place of Post-Impressionism and what had followed. Eberhard Hanfstaengl, Justi's successor at the Berlin Nationalgalerie, concentrated therefore on buying works from the Romantic period, by Caspar David Friedrich and Alfred Rethel for example. Hanfstaengl had already resigned before the Nazis carried their 'degenerate art' policy to its logical conclusion by removing politically dangerous works from all German museums in 1937.

The Bauhaus was also a victim of Nazi hostility. When the Nazis came to power in the Weimar region in 1925, the budget of the Bauhaus was cut and the school was forced to move away to Dessau. Dessau provided Gropius with the funds for a new school building, and his design for the Dessau Bauhaus, including the living accommodation for his staff, is one of his best works. In Dessau the school flourished, and Gropius handed over the directorship to Hannes Meyer, but by 1930 the Nazis were gaining hold all over Germany and Meyer, who did not hide his Communist sympathies, was dismissed. In 1932 the Bauhaus was expelled from Dessau, the Nazis there having got the whip hand. Mies van der Rohe, who had succeeded Meyer, attempted to carry the Bauhaus on as a private school in Berlin, but after a few months the Nazis caught up with it again, and all the staff were forced out because they were what the Nazis called 'cultural Bolsheviks'.

The effects of the Nazi art policy were also naturally felt by artists themselves. Without exception the most significant painters and sculptors, those who had engendered the modern movement in Germany, were banned as 'degenerate'. They were dismissed from all the artists' associations, their work was removed from galleries and they were forbidden to sell work. In a few cases the Nazis even forbade artists to continue painting, a bizarre order which emphasises the stupidity of the entire policy. In 1933 Max Liebermann, who was a Jew, resigned as president of the Prussian Academy of Arts, and Max Sauerlandt, director of the modern museum in Hamburg, was dismissed.

The Nazi attacks on 'degenerate art' began in earnest in 1937. An exhibition, which opened in Munich and then travelled throughout Germany, was intended to expose modern art by showing Expressionist works together with paintings by lunatics and 'primitive' Africans. Goering took advantage of the situation by claiming for his own collection fourteen 'degenerate' pictures, including paintings by Van Gogh, Cézanne and Marc. In 1939 most of the works that had been removed from museums were sold by public auction in Lucerne in Switzerland, with the result that works by all the most important modern German artists, as well as priceless pieces by the French Post-Impressionists, were scattered throughout the world. A number of works of art that were not disposed of in this way were secretly burned.

Then officially-approved art came into its own. A 'German Art Exhibition' was staged in Munich, in the 'House of German Art', founded by Hitler to be a shrine of nationalist art. Heroic gestures, battle scenes, portraits and erotic nudes bore witness to the Nazi idea of the German soul and the enduring spirit of Aryan culture, in pictures which call to mind the worst pomposities of 19th-century academic painting.

236

236

THE BAUHAUS
1926
Walter Gropius 1883–1969
Dessau

This picture shows part of the building which Gropius designed for his school of arts and crafts, the Bauhaus. It remains unaltered though in a dilapidated state. One of Gropius's most successful designs, the Dessau Bauhaus, was financed by the City Council after the school was asked to leave Weimar, the town of its foundation, and it included studios and living accommodation for the staff.

Many of the artists who had been defamed as degenerate were persecuted (some died in concentration camps); others went into enforced early retirement or escaped abroad. Beckmann, Kandinsky, Heartfield, Grosz, Mies van der Rohe and Gropius were among the latter, most of them taking refuge in America. The strength of post-war American art and architecture owes a great deal to the exiled Germans.

Seen as patrons (and perverse though this might sound this is what the Nazis ultimately were), the German cultural politicians from 1933 onwards absolutely determined the development of art in all its aspects and at all levels. All important buildings were commissioned and carried out in a style prescribed by the Nazi architects' association. Clearly defined rules were also laid down for painters, who had to work within them to be successful. A painter who received a commission to paint the Führer was assured of great wealth from the reproduction rights alone.

The art scene after the war

After the Second World War Germany experienced great difficulties in re-entering the cultural mainstream, for German artists had been isolated from the rest of the world for more than a decade. History itself had been re-written. It was difficult to find museum officials to take over from those approved by the Nazis, and it was even harder to attempt to replace those pictures removed by the degenerate art actions. Professors at art schools had once again to be replaced, and younger artists and architects needed encouragement.

From the point of view of patronage the most important post-war event in West Germany was the passing of a bill which laid down that a percentage of the money allowed for every new public building project was to be spent on art. Each building therefore was given a piece of sculpture or decoration, commissioned by the architect and usually carried out especially for that building. The effects of this bill were felt immediately: younger sculptors were earning enough money to live simply from such public projects, and the buildings themselves benefited.

Usually, public projects in Germany are not simply commissioned from a well-known architect. There is a tradition that an open competition should be held to choose the best design. Thus, many unknown architects become famous by winning a competition, and the architecture of the country is itself improved by the wealth and variety of new ideas.

Successful attempts were also made to bring young artists into contact with modern art, from which they had been cut off for so long. Perhaps the most important event to have a bearing on this was the first 'Documenta' exhibition, put on in Kassel in 1955, which brought together the best of pre-war German art and surveyed what was going on all over the world at that particular moment. Since then, the Documenta has been a regular, four-yearly event, showing the best of modern art. In importance it has become the equal of the Venice Biennale and is once again evidence of the strength of the provinces in German artistic matters. For Documenta is almost completely financed by the state of Hesse, the city of Kassel and a few large firms.

237 New museums have also been founded during the post-war period, and two of the most interesting are in the Ruhr, a district which has become an important cultural centre in Germany in the last ten years. The Wilhelm-Lehmbruck Museum in Duisburg shows the work of the early 20th-century sculptor Lehmbruck, but also includes one of the best collections of modern sculpture anywhere in Germany. All of these pieces were acquired since the war, partly in the form of gifts from the artists themselves, partly bought from funds provided by the town. For a relatively

237
SEATED YOUTH
1918
Wilhelm Lehmbruck 1881–1919
bronze
h. 41 in (104 cm)
Wilhelm-Lehmbruck Museum, Duisburg

Lehmbruck, one of the leading German sculptors in the years before the First World War, was a native of Duisburg, and it was long the ambition of that city to establish a museum in his honour. After the war the artist's widow presented her collection of his work to the city and Lehmbruck's son designed a splendid museum whose focal point is sculpture, both by Lehmbruck himself and by the most significant of other modern sculptors. The museum has been subsidised by city funds and by industry.

small place like Duisburg to have built up a collection of this kind is evidence of the vitality of cultural life in Germany at the moment.

The state collection of modern art housed in Düsseldorf is one of the best of its kind in Europe. Started in 1960 by its first director, Werner Schmalenbach, this very representative collection of 20th-century European and American art includes one of the world's largest collections of works by Klee. Düsseldorf is Germany's richest city, and this fact is reflected by the funds put at Schmalenbach's disposal. He was given enough to compete at auctions with American collectors and used the money wisely, buying representative works by Mondrian, Léger, Picasso and Rothko, for example, in very quick succession.

Throughout Germany, provincial museums have been rapidly improving their collections by judicious buying and bequest. Gabriele Münter gave her enormous collection of Blaue Reiter paintings (mainly by Kandinsky) to the Munich city art gallery, and a further selection of the most modern art was provided by a museum of modern art founded by the financier Günther Sachs.

The situation in East Germany after the war was to all intents and purposes a continuation of the hide-bound political art policy pursued by the Nazis, although the emphasis changed slightly here and there. Artists working in the modern avant-garde tradition were discouraged and those working in the approved 'Socialist-Realist' manner were furthered at every stage. The lack of any private galleries (they were banned along with all other private concerns) has had far-reaching effects on the state of art in the country. Few foreign exhibitions are staged by museums and they are exclusively of the approved art of other Socialist countries. Although other countries behind the iron curtain, notably Czechoslovakia and Poland, have tried to encourage modern art based on Western models, the Communist policy in East Germany has been strictly applied.

The economic situation has also prevented museums specialising in older types of painting and sculpture from making any new acquisitions, although museums like the Zwinger in Dresden remain among the most important in Europe.

German painting today

After the Nazi interruption German painters and sculptors found it difficult to produce work which had international validity and significance. Painters like Willi Baumeister and Ernst Wilhelm Nay either continued to develop modes that they had begun before the war or attempted to bring something of their own to a manner derived from the American Abstract Expressionist style. Contemporary artists like Lothar Quinte, Lenk and Pfahler are equally tied to American models and produce work which has a great deal in common with the 'hard-edge' style of Elsworth Kelly.

The Zero Group of Düsseldorf, composed of Heinz Mack, Piene and Gunther Uecker and now broken up, produced a form of kinetic art which was original and valid and deserved the international recognition the group was given. Other artists, notably Konrad Klapheck, have persisted in a form of surrealism which has pre-war roots.

So far, with the exception of the Zero Group, German artists have not made a big contribution to the development of post-war art. There is no doubt that the liberal museum policy, the improvement in the art schools and the superb economic conditions that all these factors represent, will bear fruit before very long, and that German artists will once again be among the foremost in Europe.

Frank Whitford

238
PORTRAIT OF A YOUNG MAN (ARMAND ROULIN)
1888
Vincent van Gogh 1853–90
oil on canvas
26 × 21·5 in (66 × 55 cm)
Folkwang Museum, Essen

This picture originally belonged to Karl Ernst Osthaus, possibly the most famous of all pre-war German collectors and one of the first to devote himself entirely to near-contemporary art. In 1922 his collection was brought to Essen. Although many Post-Impressionist works were removed from the museum by the Nazis in 1937, the war prevented them from confiscating everything, and all the Folkwang Van Goghs remained.

239 *top right*
THE NATIONAL MUSEUM
finished 1968
Ludwig Mies van der Rohe 1886–1969
West Berlin

After the war the original Berlin museum complex fell in the Soviet sector, although the larger part of the painting and sculpture collections was located in the western part of the city. The West Berlin Senate commissioned Mies van der Rohe to design a building to house the collections of works of the 19th and 20th centuries. The choice was appropriate, for Mies, although living in America since his exile, has close connections with Berlin and was in fact Director of the Bauhaus during its brief period in Berlin.

240
THE WEDDING TOWER
1905–08
Joseph Maria Olbrich 1867–1908
Mathildenhöhe, Darmstadt

The city of Darmstadt commissioned Olbrich to design this tower to commemorate the marriage of the grand duke Ernst Ludwig of Hesse and Princess Eleonore zu Solms-Hohensolms Lich in February 1905. It was Ernst Ludwig who invited Olbrich and six other architects and designers (Behrens among them) to Darmstadt in 1889 to set up an artist's colony which would devote itself to problems of art, architecture and design. Olbrich designed the exhibition hall and the Ernst-Ludwig House near the Wedding Tower, and part of this complex can be seen in the picture.

241 *left*

DREIKLANG

1919
Rudolf Belling, born 1886
mahogany
$35.75 \times 28.75 \times 31.5$ in $(91 \times 73 \times 80$ cm$)$
Wilhelm-Lehmbruck Museum, Duisburg

During the Expressionist period few German artists excelled in sculpture. An exception was Rudolf Belling who produced his own version of Futurism. This is his best-known work. The museum bought the sculpture direct from the artist in 1960. The August Thyssen steel concern, which has its headquarters not far from Duisburg, provided the money for the purchase and has been extremely generous since the museum's foundation. Most German provincial museums have enjoyed such industrial patronage since the end of the war.

242 *left*

READING MONKS

1932
Ernst Barlach 1870–1938
wood
h. 33 in (84 cm)
Nationalgalerie, West Berlin

Barlach, who was an Expressionist poet
and dramatist as well as a sculptor,
concentrated on wood-carving,
emphasising rhythms and large forms and
reducing detail to a minimum. A religious
man, he executed many commissions for
memorials during the Weimar Republic,
but lived to see his work banned from the
museums by the Nazis.

243 *bottom left*

PORTRAIT OF THE POET
MAX HERRMANN NEISSE *detail*

1925
George Grosz 1893–1959
oil on canvas
39·4 × 39·75 in (100 × 101 cm)
Städtische Kunsthalle, Mannheim

Grosz was the foremost exponent of that
type of painting known as *Neue
Sachlichkeit*, a style whose keynote is
sharp, heightened realism and an interest
in socially-engaged subjects. Gustav
Hartlaub, a former director of the
Mannheim Kunsthalle, organised the first
exhibition of such work, and bought
many examples of Grosz's work for his
museum, all of which were removed by
the Nazis. This splendid portrait was
re-acquired by the Mannheim Kunsthalle
after the war.

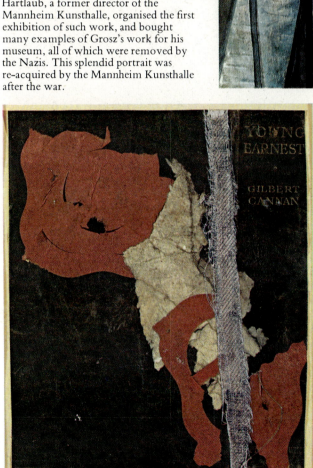

244

PORTRAIT OF A WOMAN

1942
Pablo Ruiz Picasso, born 1881
oil on wood
23·75 × 21·25 in (60·5 × 53·8 cm)
Folkwang Museum, Essen

After the war all the German museums were anxious to bring
their collections up to date, not only replacing those works
removed by the Nazis, but also filling gaps left by the Nazi period.
This splendid example of Picasso's portraiture came to Essen in
1957, and was paid for by a trust set up by the Waldthausen-
Platzhoff family. Many of the modern works that came to
Germany after the war were paid for either by such trust funds or
by industrial concerns.

245

YOUNG EARNEST

after 1941
Kurt Schwitters 1887–1948
collage on canvas (book cover) on cardboard
7·75 × 6·5 in (19·5 × 16·2 cm)
Kunstsammlung Nordrhein-Westfalen, Düsseldorf

This collage is an example of Schwitters's version of Dada, which
he called 'Merz'. Schwitters found refuge from Nazi persecution
in England in 1940, and this work was done during his English
exile. *Young Earnest* was first exhibited at the London Gallery's
Schwitters Exhibition in 1950, where it was bought by J. B.
Urvater of Brussels. It was bought from him in 1963.

246

THE CHURCH AT GELMERODA IX

1926
Lyonel Feininger 1871–1956
Folkwang Museum, Essen

Feininger, a German-American, was a successful newspaper
cartoonist before he turned to full-time painting in 1907. He
was associated with the Expressionist movement, in particular
with Herwarth Walden's *Der Sturm*, and was one of the
painters called to the Bauhaus in Weimar to teach there. This
study of the village church at Gelmeroda is one of a series of
thirteen, painted from 1913.

247

OUTSIDE THE TOWN

1908
Vassily Kandinsky 1866–1944
oil
Städtische Galerie, Munich

Although he was a Russian, Kandinsky was for many years an
influential figure on the German art-scene. Together with Franz
Marc, he founded the Blaue Reiter in Munich in 1911. This
picture, painted three years earlier, when the artist was living
with Gabriele Münter in the village of Murnau in Upper Bavaria,
shows Kandinsky's feeling for colour. In such early works
Kandinsky had not yet moved towards the abstraction which
characterised his later works.

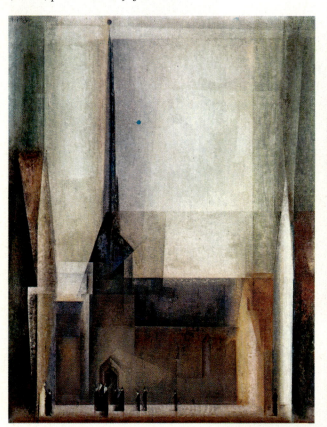

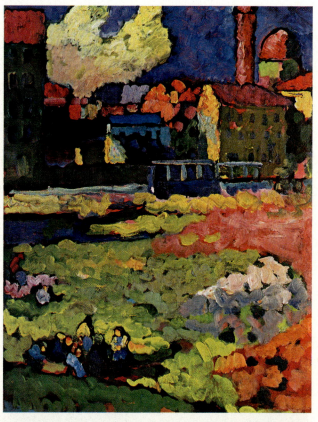

248
GIRL WITH A FAN

1902
Paul Gauguin 1848–1903
oil on canvas
Folkwang Museum, Essen

German collectors were early enthusiasts for Impressionism and Post-Impressionism, and brought many fine examples of this kind of work while their French counterparts were still rejecting artists like Gauguin as dangerous eccentrics. Karl Ernst Osthaus acquired an unparalleled selection of works by Van Gogh, Cézanne and Gauguin at a time when the prices were still low. In 1920 his pictures were transferred to the Folkwang Museum, where most of them, including this Gauguin, escaped the Nazi art auctions.

249
VERTICAL COMPOSITION WITH BLUE AND WHITE

1936, Piet Mondrian 1872–1944, oil on canvas
47·5 × 23·25 in (121·3 × 59 cm)
Kunstsammlung Nordrhein-Westfalen, Düsseldorf

This composition was first exhibited at the Museum of Modern Art, New York, in 1939 during Mondrian's American exile. It previously belonged to Walter P. Chryseler, Jr., and then to Harry Holtzman, both of New York. Werner Schmalenbach, Director of the Kunstsammlung Nordrhein-Westfalen, bought it for the collection in 1963, from the Sidney Janis Gallery, New York. It first went on German exhibition at the third 'Documenta' exhibition in Kassel in 1964.

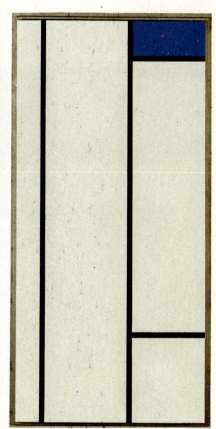

250 *far left*
ADVENTURERS-SHIP

1927
Paul Klee 1879–1940
oil on wood
Bayerische Staatsgemäldesammlung, Munich

Klee was born in Switzerland but later became a German citizen. He was associated with Kandinsky during the Blaue Reiter period, and later taught at the Bauhaus with the Russian, who exerted a powerful influence on him. This picture was painted while Klee was at the Bauhaus. It shows to advantage his whimsy, his feeling for line and colour and his tendency to render his subjects in terms of hieroglyph-like simplifications.

Museums and Monuments

An index of museums, churches, palaces and public buildings, listing some of the major treasures they contain.

Illustrations on this page

left

251 *St Veronica with the Holy Shroud*; Alte Pinakothek, Munich
252 Capital from the Church of St Michael, Hildesheim
253 *The Disturbed Sleeper*; porcelain group by F. A. Bustelli; Bayerisches Nationalmuseum, Munich

centre

254 *The Flood*; Hans Baldung Grien
255 The Residenz, Würzburg
256 Candlestick from the workshop of Bishop Bernward; Hildesheim Cathedral Treasury

right

257 St Stephen from the Worms Manuscript; Hessisches Landesmuseum, Darmstadt
258 *Self-portrait with a Red Scarf*; Max Beckmann; Staatsgalerie, Stuttgart
259 Renaissance buffet; Schloss Zeil, Allgäu

West Germany
with West Berlin

AACHEN, Northern Rhineland – Westphalia
1 **Cathedral** Begun *c.* 800. Palatine Chapel, outstanding example of Carolingian architecture. Gothic chancel 1355–1414; chapels 14th-15th C; outer roof of chapel 17th C; w steeple is modern. 9th C bronze doors; Henry II's ambo; Romanesque chandelier; Pala d'Oro; 11th C crucifix; gold Karlsschrein 1215. Extremely rich treasury: gold and silver reliquary head of Charlemagne *c.* 1350; gold cross of Lothair 990; Aachen Gospels (Rheims school, early 9th C).
2 **Suermondt Museum** German, Dutch and Flemish paintings 15th-17th C; German sculpture 13th-18th C.

AHRENSBURG, Schleswig-Holstein
3 **Castle** Beautiful Renaissance style, 1596. Interesting furnishings.

ALPIRSBACH, Baden-Württemberg
4 **Abbey Church** Important 11th-12th C Romanesque. Two-storey Gothic apse; tower 15th C. w door with 14th C carved tympanum; 12th C paintings. Restored Flamboyant Gothic cloisters.

ALTENMARKT, Bavaria
5 **Abbey Church** Baroque. Interiors by Asam brothers.

ALTÖTTING, Bavaria
6 **Stiftskirche** Flamboyant Gothic. Fine early 15th C gold horse.

AMBERG, Bavaria
7 **St Martin** Gothic, begun 1421. Stylistically perfect.
8 **Castle** 13th-14th C. Gothic chapel with 15th C stained glass.

ANDECHS, Bavaria
9 **Abbey Church** Remodelled in Baroque style 1751-55. Frescoes and stuccowork by J B Zimmermann. Statue of Virgin 1500.

ANDERNACH, Rhineland-Palatinate
10 **Pfarrkirche** Typical Rhineland Romanesque built 1206. Choir, with gallery of small columns, dates from 1120.
11 **Rheintor** Fortified gate, partly 12th C.

ANSBACH, Bavaria
12 **Residenz** 14th C; burned down 1710; rebuilt in Baroque style by Gabriel de Gabrieli 1713-32. Good symmetrical interiors. Porcelain collection; paintings by Veronese, Titian, Rubens; tapestries by Charles Le Brun.

AROLSEN, Hesse
13 **Castle** 1714-28. Modelled on Versailles. Interiors Baroque to 19th C.

ASCHAFFENBURG, Bavaria
14 **Abbey Church** Gothic; Romanesque w door; tower completed in 15th C. Romanesque cloisters. Numerous works of art: Cranach the Elder *Resurrection* 1520; Matthias Grünewald *The Dead Christ* 1525; 16th C reliquary by Hans Dirmsteyn.
15 **Johannisburg** Castle in Renaissance style, 1605-14. Hollow square plan; 4 towers. Picture gallery.
16 **Schönbusch Castle** Late 18th C Empire style. Superb ornamental gardens.
17 **Stadtmuseum** General collection including Riemenschneider's *St Joseph* and Rembrandt's *John the Baptist.*

AUB, Bavaria
18 **Pfarrkirche** Tilman Riemenschneider *Crucifixion.*

AUGSBURG, Bavaria
19 **Cathedral** Started 994-95; Romanesque pillared basilica. Extensions 1335 and 1431; double side aisles. Bronze doors *c.* 1015; early 12th C stained glass. 4 altars by Hans Holbein the Elder.
20 **St Anne** 1321. Flamboyant Gothic; Rococo interior. Fuggerkapelle by Burgkmair 1518; Cranach the Elder *Jesus the Friend of Little Children;* 15th C murals.
21 **St Ulrich and St Afra** Late Gothic by Valentin Kindlin and Burkhard Engelberg 1474-1500; 17th C alterations. Bronze Crucifixion 1607.
22 **Rathaus** Renaissance style by Elias Holl 1615-20.

23 **Schätzlerpalais** Especially Rococo banqueting hall. Houses art collections. Paintings of 12th-18th C: Cranach the Elder, Holbein the Elder, C Amberger, Tintoretto etc.
24 **Zeughaus** Early Baroque by Elias Holl 1602-07. Dynamic use of broken pediments, cornices and scrolls contrasts with Rathaus by the same architect.
25 **Maximilian-Museum** Local history and culture. Very good on 15th-16th C.

BADEN-BADEN, Baden-Württemberg
26 **Kurhaus** By F Weinbrenner 1821.
27 **Neues Schloss** Old fortress rebuilt in Renaissance style. Art and porcelain collections.
28 **Roman Baths** Ruins.

BADENWEILER, Baden-Württemberg
29 **Roman Baths** Well preserved.

BAMBERG, Bavaria
30 **Cathedral** Started by Emperor Heinrich the Holy in 1003. Romanesque with Gothic alterations in 13th C. 4 spires, double apse. 14th C choir stalls; *Bamberg Rider c.* 1230; tomb by Tilman Riemenschneider; Veit Stoss, St Mary's Altar 1523. Vestments. Chapterhouse by Balthasar Neumann 1730.
31 **Neue Residenz** Part early 17th C Renaissance style, part Baroque by Dientzenhofer 1695-1707. Superb interiors and furnishings. Houses Bayerische Gemäldesammlungen and Baroque section of Germanisches Museum.
32 **Landesbibliothek** MSS and early books: Livy Manuscript; Alcuin Bible (9th C); Bamberg Apocalypse of Henry II *c.* 1020.

BANZ, Bavaria
33 **Abbey Church** Baroque by J Dientzenhofer; completed 1719. Fascinating complex roof.

BAYREUTH, Bavaria
34 **Holy Trinity** Basilican form. Base of tower early Gothic; 14th-15th C choir.
35 **Markgräfliches Opernhaus** 1745. Built entirely of wood. Rococo interior by G Galli Bibiena.
36 **Neues Schloss** Built 1753-54, largely by remodelling existing buildings. Interiors Rococo and Louis XV; stuccowork by Pedrozzi. Houses art gallery and cultural-historical museum.

BEBENHAUSEN, Baden-Württemberg
37 **Former Cistercian Abbey** 13th C; extensively altered. Fortified (triple walls). Cloisters with fine fan vaulting and tracery.

BENEDIKTBEUERN, Bavaria
38 **Abbey Church** 1680-86. Frescoes by H G Asam. Chapel of St Anastasia. Delightful Rococo by Michael Fischer 1751-58.

BERCHTESGADEN, Bavaria
39 **Stiftskirche** Romanesque foundations; 14th C chancel; early 16th C nave. Interesting façade using stones of contrasting colours.
40 **Castle** (former priory) Romanesque cloisters with superb elaborate columns; Gothic dormitory; some Renaissance interiors. Italian 15th-16th C furniture; oriental art; good collection of late Gothic religious art: Yselin, Veit Stoss, Erhart, Riemenschneider etc.

BERG AM LAIM, Bavaria
41 **Church** Baroque by J M Fischer.

BERLIN (West)
42 **Reichstag** Rather ponderous Renaissance style, 1894.
43 **Schloss Charlottenburg** Begun 1695. E wing by Knobelsdorff. Rococo interiors, extensively restored. Contains works by Chardin; Watteau's *L'Enseigne de Gersaint;* porcelain; musical instruments. In courtyard equestrian monument to the Great Elector by Andreas Schlüter.
44 **Staatliche Museen der Stiftung Preussischer Kulturbesitz** Includes **Ägyptisches Museum** with famous bust of Nefertiti (1370 BC); **Antikensammlung** with Greek and Roman antiquities; **Museum für Völkerkunde** with good Central American collection; **Museum für Vor- und Frühgeschichte; Skulpturenabteilung** including the *Ravensburg Madonna* and Donatello's *Lazzi Madonna;* **Gemäldegalerie** with old masters of German, Flemish, Dutch, Italian, French and Spanish schools; **Kunstgewerbemuseum** containing Guelph Treasure.

45 **Galerie des 20 Jahrhunderts** Modern painting.

BIRNAU, Baden-Württemberg
46 **Wallfahrtskirche** Rococo by Peter Thumb 1746-50. Domed apse and chancel; pierced ceiling above nave. Sculptures and paintings by J A Feuchtmayer. 15th C Virgin and Child.

BLAUBEUREN, Baden-Württemberg
47 **Abbey Church** 15th C. Carved choir stalls by Jörg Syrlin the Younger; high altar by various 15th C Ulm masters.

BONN, Northern Rhineland-Westphalia
48 **Minster** 11th C crypt; towers and part of the chancel 12th C Romanesque; Gothic nave; beautiful 12th C cloisters.
49 **Poppelsdorf Castle** In combined French and Italian styles by Robert de Cotte 1715.
50 **University Buildings** (part of Elector's Castle) Also by Robert de Cotte.
51 **Rheinisches Landesmuseum** Neanderthal man and other prehistoric remains; Roman and Frankish exhibits; Dutch paintings 15th-18th C; Rhenish sculpture, paintings etc. to 20th C.
52 **Städtische Kunstsammlung Bonn** Paintings and sculpture of 18th-20th C. Especially work of Auguste Macke.

BORDESHOLM, Schleswig-Holstein
53 **Abbey Church** Gothic brick-built, 1132.

BRAUWEILER, Northern Rhineland-Westphalia
54 **Pfarrkirche** Romanesque murals.

BREISACH, Baden-Württemberg
55 **Minster** Original building 11th C. Romanesque basilica; Gothic chancel (1300-30); planned w tower never built; badly damaged 1945. High altar 1526; Gothic screen; *Last Judgment* frescoes by Martin Schongauer.

BREMEN
56 **Cathedral** Romanesque to Gothic. Romanesque crypt and lower part of exterior; Flamboyant Gothic fan vaulting in N aisle. 13th C bronze font; 16th C carvings and sculptures.
57 **Liebfrauenkirche** 1013-29. 13th C ogival vaulting.
58 **Roselius Haus** 16th C with contemporary furniture.
59 **Kunsthalle** Good 19th C and Impressionist section. Also Worpswede school; Japanese art.
60 **Überseemuseum** General museum with good ethnographic collection.

BRUCHSAL, Baden-Württemberg
61 **St Peter** Baroque by Balthasar Neumann.
62 **Castle** Baroque 1731; bombed but being rebuilt. Magnificent staircase by Balthasar Neumann 1731. Most paintings by Johann Zick.

BRÜHL, Northern Rhineland-Westphalia
63 **Castle** 1724-28. Baroque staircase by Balthasar Neumann 1744-65.

BRUNSWICK, Lower Saxony
64 **Cathedral** Romanesque with extensive Gothic additions. First church in Germany to be uniformly vaulted. Gothic aisles with some good Flamboyant-style twisted columns; octagonal towers linked by extended Gothic belfry porch (1275). Romanesque tombs, mid-12th C. Imerward Crucifix; 13th C murals.
65 **St Martin** Late 13th C. Similar in style to the cathedral. Romanesque font; 14th C sculptures.
66 **Altstadtrathaus** 1393-1468. Double galleries; stepped gables. One of finest stone town halls.
67 **Herzog Anton-Ulrich-Museum** Early paintings, prints, drawings, ceramics, ivories etc.

BÜCKEBURG, Lower Saxony
68 **Stadtkirche** 1611-15. Basic layout that of a late Gothic hall church, but with fantastic Mannerist decoration, particularly on façade.
69 **Castle** Renaissance façade and balcony of inner courtyard; 17th C gateway. Good Renaissance to Baroque interiors, especially Golden Hall.

BURGHAUSEN, Bavaria
70 **Castle** Largest fortress in Germany; ½ mile of Gothic fortifications; further defences built in 16th C. Gothic chapel. Collection of medieval painted panels.

BÜRRESHEIM, Rhineland-Palatinate
71 **Castle** N wing and tower 14th-15th C; s wing 17th C. 15th-18th C furniture, paintings etc.

CELLE, Lower Saxony
72 **Castle** 1292, enlarged 1521-46; modified 1670. Square plan with corner towers; Renaissance E façade. Chapel, late 16th C by Martin de Vos; bizarre interior. Baroque theatre.
CLOPPENBURG, Lower Saxony
73 **Museumdorf** 40 acres of 17th-18th C peasant houses from all over the area.
COBURG, Bavaria
74 **St Maurice** 14th-16th C late Gothic. Good sculpture and tombs.
75 **Schloss Ehrenburg** Destroyed by fire 1500; restored 1543; partly rebuilt in 19th C neo-Gothic style. Furniture and Gobelins tapestries.
76 **Veste** Original building 12th C; present one 16th C. Fine collections of furniture, silver, porcelain, glass and carriages. Cranach paintings; 300,000 engravings including work by Dürer and Rembrandt.
COCHEM, Rhineland-Palatinate
77 **Castle** 1207; destroyed 1689; rebuilt 1869-77 in 14th C style. Furniture.
COLOGNE, Northern Rhineland-Westphalia
78 **Cathedral** Begun 1248. One of the finest Gothic cathedrals in Germany; modelled on Beauvais and Amiens. Chancel and part of the nave medieval; nave and spires completed in 19th C following original plans. s transept bronze doors by Mataré; 13th and 14th C stained glass; Stefan Lochner's Adoration of the Magi Altar c. 1444. Good choir stalls, carvings, sculptures and paintings. Excellent treasure, especially 10th C Cross of Gero and 12th C Three Kings Shrine by Nicolas of Verdun.
79 **St Aposteln** Romanesque 1035-1220. Trefoil ground plan; sexpartite vaulting in nave instead of usual quadripartite.
80 **St Gereon** 11th-13th C. Roman foundations. Early example of Gothic. Remarkable ten-sided domed nave (1219-27) based on Soissons. Romanesque murals.
81 **St Maria im Kapitol** 1407. Sexpartite vaulting; 11th C carved doors; Renaissance rood-screen. Madonna of Limburg, 1300; fine crucifix c. 1310.
82 **St Pantaleon** 10th C Ottonian. Flamboyant rood-screen 1502-14.
83 **Altes Rathaus** 14th C Gothic and Italian Renaissance styles; 15th C tower.
84 **Dionysus Mosaic** 2nd C Roman.
85 **Praetorium** Remains of Roman palace 1st-4th C.
86 **Kunstgewerbemuseum** Decorative arts.
87 **Kunsthalle** New gallery opened 1967.
88 **Wallraf-Richartz Museum** Excellent general art collection. Particularly good on 14th-16th C Cologne masters and 15th-16th C German and Dutch painters; modern sculpture.
CONSTANCE, Baden-Württemberg
89 **Cathedral** 11th-17th C, but Romanesque in mood. Delightful spiral staircase in Flamboyant Gothic style.
90 **Rathaus** Renaissance style. Pleasant inner court with 16th C house.
91 **Rosgarten Museum** Former guildhall with good Gothic doorway. Prehistoric and Roman exhibits. Arts and crafts from Middle Ages to 19th C.
CORVEY, Northern Rhineland-Westphalia
92 **Benedictine Abbey** Founded 822. w façade remains (oldest parts 873-85). Carolingian 5-aisled entrance hall leading into square baptistry above.
CREGLINGEN,
93 **Herrgottskirche** Tilman Riemenschneider altar 1505.
DARMSTADT, Hesse
94 **Prinz-Georg-Palais** 18th C. Excellent porcelain collection. Also furniture, faïence.
95 **Hessisches Landesmuseum** General collection. Best on Dutch, Flemish and German old masters.
96 **Landesbibliothek** Contains *Hitda Codex,* early 11th C.
DETMOLD, Northern Rhineland-Westphalia
97 **Castle** Destroyed 16th C; rebuilt Renaissance style. Rectangular plan; corner towers with linking corbelled gallery. Porcelain; 17th C Brussels tapestries designed by Charles Le Brun.

DIESSEN AM AMMERSEE, Bavaria
98 **Abbey Church** Rebuilt in Baroque style by J M Fischer 1732-39. Excellent stuccowork.
DINKELSBÜHL, Bavaria
99 **St George** By Nicolaus Eseler the Elder 1448-92. Romanesque tower; late Gothic hall interior; piers rise to fine netted vaulting without a break. 15th C Trinity Altar; sculptures.
DONAUESCHINGEN, Baden-Württemberg
100 **Castle** Porcelain, tapestries etc.
101 **Fürstlich-Fürstenbergisches Museum** Old German to modern. 2 Grünewalds; *Wildenstein Altarpiece* by Master of Messkirch; works by Holbein the Elder etc.
DONAUSTAUF, Bavaria
102 **Walhalla** Neoclassical temple by Leo von Klenze built 1842 for Ludwig I with busts of famous Germans.
DONAUWÖRTH, Bavaria
103 **Heiligkreuzkirche** Baroque 1720. Wessobrunn stuccoes.
104 **Stadtkirche** Gothic. Good medieval frescoes and sculptures.
DORTMUND, Northern Rhineland-Westphalia
105 **St Mary** c. 1175. Romanesque basilica; Gothic chancel. Konrad von Soest Altar of Our Lady c. 1400.
106 **Museum für Kunst und Kulturgeschichte Dortmund** Includes early Westphalian sculpture.
107 **Ostwall Museum** Modern art, particularly German Expressionist.
DUISBURG, Northern Rhineland-Westphalia
108 **Municipal Art Museum** Modern paintings; also work of sculptor Wilhelm Lehmbruck.
DÜSSELDORF, Northern Rhineland-Westphalia
109 **St Lambert** 14th C Gothic hall church with interesting twisted belfry.
110 **Hofgarten** Statues include Maillol's *Harmony.* Houses **Kunstsammlung Nordrhein-Westfalen** with 20th C paintings. 24 Klees and works by Léger, Kandinsky, Picasso etc. Also Schneider collection with Meissen porcelain, Aubusson carpets, gold and silver.
111 **Jägerhof Castle** Largely rebuilt by Nicolas de Pigage 1752-63.
112 **Kunstmuseum** Mainly 19th-20th C German painters. Extensive ceramics collection.
EBENHAUSEN-SCHÄFTLARN Bavaria
113 **Abbey Church** Rococo by Cuvilliés, 1733.
EBERBACH, Hesse
114 **Cistercian Abbey** Church Romanesque; completed 1186. Gothic side aisle. Chapterhouse 1345; 14th C 2-aisled dormitory.
EBRACH, Bavaria
115 **Former Abbey** 12th-13th C; largely rebuilt by Balthasar Neumann in Baroque style. Church modelled on Cîteaux; Gothic with Baroque interior details. Contains Crucifixion by Rubens.
EICHSTÄTT, Bavaria
116 **Cathedral** Romanesque towers; Gothic interior; Baroque façade. 15th C carved Pappenheim Altarpiece. 15th C cloisters; mortuarium (15th C Gothic hall chapel).
117 **Willibald Castle** Fortifications 14th C. Rare example of early Baroque fortress (1593).
ELTZ, Rhineland-Palatinate
118 **Castle** Oldest parts 12th C; major alterations 16th C; fire 1920; restored. Beautiful Romantic building; interesting furnishings.
EMDEN, Lower Saxony
119 **Ostfriesisches Landesmuseum** Important collection of 16th-18th C arms and armour.
ERLANGEN, Bavaria
120 **Castle** 1704. Good painting collection.
ESSEN, Northern Rhineland-Westphalia
121 **Minster** 852. 10th C w chancel based on Aachen; Gothic hall-type nave. Important early 11th C Golden Madonna (one of the earliest 3-dimensional representations of the Madonna).
122 **Museum Folkwang** Particularly good on 19th-early 20th C painting with examples of the work of many of the great names of the period.

ESSEN-WERDEN, Northern Rhineland-Westphalia
123 **Abbey Church** 13th C late Romanesque. Rare pierced gallery in crypt. 11th C bronze crucifix.
ESSLINGEN, Baden-Württemberg
124 **Liebfrauenkirche** 1321-1516. Striking richly decorated Gothic church. Notable exterior sculpture.
ETTAL, Bavaria
125 **Abbey Church** Gothic; polygonal plan. Rebuilt Baroque by Enrico Zucalli and Joseph Schmutzer 1710-48. Ceiling by Johann Jakob Zeiller; Virgin by Pisano.
EXTERN STONES, Northern Rhineland-Westphalia. Rocks with a 12th C Romanesque bas-relief of the Descent from the Cross and 2 chapels (11th and 12th C) carved into them.
FLENSBURG, Schleswig-Holstein
127 **St Nicolas** 15th C brick Gothic.
128 **Nordertor** 1595. Brick with two gables. One of a number of town gates.
129 **Städtisches Museum** General collection; especially good on early local furniture.
FORCHHEIM, Bavaria
130 **Pfarrkirche** 14th C Gothic with Baroque onion spire. Contents include 8 15th C panels.
FRANKFURT AM MAIN, Hesse
131 **Cathedral** On foundations of 9th C Salvatorkirche; 13th-14th C 3-aisled Gothic hall church; important Gothic tower begun 1415; bombed 1943; restored and rededicated 1954. Marienpforte, with statue of Madonna 1350. 14th C choir stalls; frescoes in choir by a Cologne master 1427; important altars; Van Dyck *Deposition from the Cross;* cathedral treasure. Wahlkapelle 1411, originally library where electors chose emperor.
132 **Liebfrauenkirche** 15th C late Gothic but extensively rebuilt. Sculpture of the Adoration, 1430, on s portal; 16th C frescoes.
133 **Saalhofkapelle** 13th C. Only surviving part of Saalhof founded by Barbarossa and badly damaged in war.
134 **St Leonard** 15th-16th C Gothic hall church on remains of 13th C basilica. 13th C doorways by Master Engelbert.
135 **Römer** Group of reconstructed 15th C buildings.
136 **Städelsches Kunstinstitut** Comprehensive collection of paintings: early Dutch and German masters; Italian and French paintings; modern German artists.
137 **Städtische Museen** Include galleries of painting and sculpture; **Museum für Kunsthandwerk** with good collections of furniture, medieval religious art, MSS etc. from all parts of world; **Museum fur Vor- und Frühgeschichte** with prehistoric, Roman, early Mediterranean and oriental exhibits.
FRAUENCHIEMSEE, Bavaria
138 **Benedictine Convent** Superb 11th C portal. 13th C church rebuilt in 15th C.
FREIBURG IM BREISGAU, Baden-Württemberg
139 **Cathedral** One of the finest Gothic churches in Germany. Original structure Romanesque c. 1200; transept crossing and towers (with Gothic upper portions) remain; w front 1275-c. 1340; present fan-vaulted chancel (by Hans Parler) started 1354; superb octagonal tower with pierced spire; Renaissance-style s porch. Outstanding sculptures on exterior; 13th-14th C stained glass; 12th C crucifix by Böcklin, altar by Baldung Grien; altar panels by Hans Holbein the Younger; painting by Lucas Cranach the Elder.
140 **Augustiner Museum** Excellent collection of medieval art. One panel of Grünewald's *St Mary of the Snows* altarpiece c. 1520 from Aschaffenburg.
FREISING, Bavaria
141 **Cathedral** Romanesque basilica 1161-1205 with extensive interior alterations in Baroque period by the Asam brothers. Gothic choir stalls; Rubens *Virgin and Child.* Cloisters with stuccowork by J B Zimmermann.
FRITZLAR, Hesse
142 **Collegiate Church** Mainly 13th C but

incorporating elements of earlier church. Notable carved capitals in crypt (begun 1171).

FULDA, Hesse

143 **Cathedral** Redesigned Baroque by Johann Dientzenhofer 1704-12. Stuccowork.

144 **Petersberg Propsteikirche** Romanesque, rebuilt 15th c. Carolingian crypt; 9th c frescoes and 12th c reliefs.

145 **St Michael** 791-822; finished end 10th c. One of the oldest churches in the country. Extensively modelled on Old St Peter's.

146 **Abbot's Palace** Baroque by Dientzenhofer and Gallasini. Orangery by Maximilian von Welsch 1721-30. Flora vase 1728.

147 **Landesbibliothek** Important 7th-8th c codices.

FÜSSEN, Bavaria

148 **Castle** Medieval; rebuilt 16th c. Interesting Prince's Hall and Knight's Hall. 15th c paintings.

GELNHAUSEN, Hesse

149 **St Mary** Good example of 13th c Rhineland Romanesque.

150 **Imperial Palace** Late 12th c Romanesque ruins; fine decoration.

GIESSEN, Hesse

151 **Oberhessisches Museum** Includes treasures of Roman-German and early Franconian cultures. Also paintings and modern engravings.

GLÜCKSBURG, Schleswig-Holstein

152 **Castle** Renaissance 1582-87. Beautiful and well preserved; reminiscent of Chambord. Contains one of the best tapestry collections in Germany.

GOSLAR, Lower Saxony

153 **Imperial Palace** c. 1050; rebuilt after 1132 and again 1789; badly restored 1873. Retains 12th c chapel; 13th c tomb of Henry III.

154 **Rathaus** 15th c. Standard arcaded, gabled and balustraded building. Contains paintings, gold and silver plate.

HAGEN, Northern Rhineland-Westphalia

155 **Karl-Ernst Osthaus Museum** Paintings by Christian Rohlfs (1849-1938).

HAINA, Hesse,

156 **Abbey Church** Gothic hall church on Cistercian pattern. Romanesque chapels and Romanesque to Gothic cloisters.

HAMBURG

157 **St James** 13th-15th c Gothic hall church. Art treasures.

158 **St Michael** Interior and tower 1751-61; tempietto 1777-86. Good Baroque.

159 **Hamburger Kunsthalle** Paintings, drawings and engravings, 14th-20th c; modern (19th-20th c) sculpture; Greek and Roman coins.

160 **Museum für Kunst und Gewerbe** European sculpture and applied arts; Asiatic and ancient art, graphics etc.

HAMELN, Lower Saxony

161 **Collegiate Church** 11th c Romanesque basilica with later additions. Good carved columns in the transept.

HÄMELSCHENBURG, Lower Saxony

162 **Castle** Fine Renaissance 1588-1612. Built in shape of horseshoe.

HANNOVER, Lower Saxony

163 **Marktkirche** 14th c. 14th c stained glass; 15th c bronze font; 15th c Passion altarpiece.

164 **Herrenhäuser Gardens** 1666-1710. Outstanding.

165 **Kestner Museum** Egyptian, Greek, Etruscan, Roman art; ill. MSS; incunabula, applied art; prints and drawings of 15th-20th c.

166 **Niedersächsisches Landesmuseum** Prehistoric; modern sculptures; paintings from Italian Primitive to modern German.

HARBURG, Bavaria

167 **Castle** 13th c; rebuilt 18th c. Important collections of paintings, sculptures (Veit Stoss, Riemenschneider), Gobelins tapestries, books, illuminated MSS and engravings.

HEIDELBERG, Baden-Württemberg

168 **Church of the Holy Ghost** Basically Flamboyant Gothic hall church 1400-36.

169 **Castle** 14th-early 17th c; relatively little remains. Gothic library; important late Renaissance Ottheinrichsbau with 3-tier façade 1566; Friedrichsbau, Renaissance with Baroque elements; charming Elisabethentor 1615.

170 **Ritterhaus** 1592. Superb late Renaissance.

171 **Kurpfälzisches Museum** Sculpture including Tilman Riemenschneider's Twelve Apostles altarpiece 1509. Romantic art.

172 **Universitätsbibliothek** Books and MSS including the Manesse Codex c. 1300.

HEILBRONN, Baden-Württemberg

173 **St Kilian** 13th-15th c. Important Renaissance-style tower 1513. Altar carvings by Hans Seyfer.

174 **Rathaus** 1535-96. Gothic with Renaissance decoration.

HEILSBRONN, Bavaria

175 **Abbey Church** 12th-17th c. Notable works of art.

HERRENCHIEMSEE, Bavaria

176 **Castle** 1878-85. Built for Ludwig II; modelled on Versailles.

HERSFELD, Hesse

177 **Abbey ruins** Abbey church remodelled in Romanesque style and extended 11th-12th c. Good w apse and Romanesque towers.

HILDESHEIM, Lower Saxony

178 **Cathedral** Destroyed in Second World War; reconstruction modelled on original 11th c basilica. 11th c bronze column; Romanesque bronze doors; 11th c chandelier; 13th c font. Romanesque cloisters.

179 **St Gothard** 12th c Romanesque; square pillars support semicircular arches in nave.

180 **St Michael** Double-chancelled basilica 1001-33; badly damaged 1945, but reconstructed. Note the use of the square as a basic unit. Late Romanesque ceiling painted c. 1225.

181 **Palizaes-Museum** One of the best Egyptian collections in the world.

HIRSAU, Baden-Württemberg

182 **Abbey** Destroyed 1692. Romanesque Owl Tower, chapel (Flamboyant-style windows) and St Mary's chapel have survived. Church, Romanesque 1038-71; recently restored. Façade modelled on Strasbourg Cathedral.

HOHENZOLLERN, Baden-Württemberg

183 **Castle** Feudal fortress destroyed 1423; rebuilt 1493; and again 1850-67, except for 12th c St Michael's Chapel. Oldest stained-glass windows in Germany.

IGEL, Rhineland-Palatinate

184 **Igel Column** Well-preserved Roman reliefs.

INGOLSTADT, Bavaria

185 **Franciscan Church** Early Gothic 1380. Madonna 1502; 16th c frescoes, carvings.

186 **Liebfrauenmünster** 1425. One of biggest Gothic churches in Germany. Fine vaulting in chapels built 1509-24. Renaissance Annunciation window 1527; sculptures; paintings including a fine altarpiece by Hans Mielich 1572.

187 **Maria de Victoria** Important church decorated in Rococo style by Asam Brothers 1763.

188 **Neues Schloss** 1418 with later rebuildings. Some good interiors. Paintings.

189 **Rathaus** 4 Gothic buildings combined.

IPHOFEN, Bavaria

190 **Pfarrkirche** 1351 late Gothic. Tilman Riemenschneider's *St John* and other sculptures.

KALKAR, Northern Rhineland-Westphalia

191 **St Nicholas** 15th c Gothic hall church. Important religious carvings and paintings including Douvermann's *Seven Sorrows of the Virgin* 1520.

KARDEN, Rhineland-Palatinate

192 **St Castor** Romanesque to Gothic. Magi altarpiece 1420; St Castor shrine 1490.

KARLSRUHE, Baden-Württemberg

193 **Castle** Started 1715. Centre of radial system of avenues.

194 **Badisches Landesmuseum** Egyptian, Greek and Roman antiquities; European sculpture; historical objects.

195 **Staatliche Kunsthalle** German Primitives and old masters including a Grünewald Crucifixion. Also Dutch, Italian, French paintings 15th-20th c.

KASSEL, Hesse

196 **Wilhelmshöhe** Castle, Baroque. Superb park designed by the Italian Guerniero 1701-18. Baroque temples, grottoes, statues, fountains. Copy of *Farnese Hercules.*

197 **Hessisches Landesmuseum** Excellent collection of German old masters and Dutch 17th c works.

KELHEIM, Bavaria

198 **Befreiungshalle** Neoclassical rotunda with busts and trophies, built 1842-63 to commemorate liberation from Napoleon.

KIEDRICH, Hesse

199 **Pfarrkirche** Interesting organ (partly 14th c); 14th c Kiedrich Virgin; early 16th c choir stalls.

KIEL, Schleswig-Holstein

200 **Castle** Started c. 1280; badly damaged in Second World War.

201 **Kunsthalle** 19th-20th c paintings.

202 **Museum** Good Roman and early German sections.

KOBLENZ, Rhineland-Palatinate

203 **Liebfrauenkirche** Romanesque; 15th c Gothic choir; carved keystones; 17th c belfries.

204 **St Castor** 11th c. Façade modelled on that of Strasbourg Cathedral; bishops' tombs; paintings.

205 **Electoral Palace** 1780-86. Theatre 1787 modelled on that of Versailles.

206 **Rathaus** Oldest part 1580; rest Baroque by Sebastiani 1695-1700. Staircase ceiling by Carlo Pozzi.

KÖNIGSLUTTER, Lower Saxony

207 **Abbey Church** Romanesque basilica. Superb carved decoration. Romanesque cloisters; beautiful elaborate columns.

KULMBACH, Bavaria

208 **Plassenburg** Beautiful 12th c fortress; rebuilt 1569. Exquisite Renaissance inner court with tiered galleries and elaborate use of Renaissance decorative motifs.

209 **Luitpold Museum** Late 16th and early 17th c goldsmith's work.

LAACHERSEE, Rhineland-Palatinate

210 **Maria Laach Abbey Church** 12th c 2-choired Romanesque structure similar in design to Worms Cathedral. w choir 1156; atrium 1220-30; 13th c baldachin with decorative use of basalt.

LANDSBERG AM LECH, Bavaria

211 **Pfarrkirche** 1454. Multscher Madonna 1440.

212 **Bavarian Gate** 1425. One of the finest Gothic gates in Germany.

213 **Rathaus** 1699-1702. Façade (1719, good stuccowork) by Dominikus Zimmermann who also built or rebuilt several churches in the area.

LANDSHUT, Bavaria

214 **St Martin** Late Gothic by Hans Stetthaimer c. 1390-1432. Said to have highest (436 ft) brick tower in the world. Good slender octagonal piers. Important carved late Gothic Madonna (1518) by Hans Leinberger.

215 **Rathaus** 1380. Based on Frankfurt Römer. Renaissance decorative elements.

216 **Residenz** Begun 1536 by Sigmondo. Earliest Italian Renaissance palace in Germany. Classical façade 1780. Historical collection; paintings; 18th c furniture and objets d'art.

217 **Trausnitz Castle** 12th-13th c; rebuilt in Renaissance style 16th c; serious fire damage 1962.

LAUFEN, Bavaria

218 **Church** 1330-38. Oldest Gothic hall church in s Germany.

LIMBURG AN DER LAHN, Hesse

219 **Cathedral** 1213-42. Good example of Romanesque to Gothic transitional. Romanesque exterior; interior inspired by French Gothic (Laon Cathedral). Good capitals and galleries. 13th c murals.

220 **Castle** 13th-16th c. Religious art; 10th c Byzantine reliquary cross known as Limburger Staurothek.

LINDAU, Baden-Württemberg

221 **Abbey Church** Ceiling paintings by Appiani. Good frescoes.

222 **Cawazzenhaus** Elaborate Baroque 1729. 15th-16th c wood sculpture.

LINDENHARDT, Bavaria

223 **Church** Matthias Grünewald altar-paintings.

LINDERHOF, Bavaria

224 **Castle** Combination of Renaissance and

Baroque styles 1870-86. Interior copies Versailles; excellent park with grotto and fantastic pavilions.

LIPPOLDSBERG, Northern Rhineland-Westphalia
225 **Abbey Church** Mid 12th C. One of first vaulted Romanesque churches in N Germany.

LORSCH, Hesse
226 **Benedictine Monastery** 774. Mainly ruined, but retains fine Carolingian decorated gateway, probably modelled on one at Old St Peter's, Rome.

LÜBECK, Schleswig-Holstein
227 **Cathedral** Romanesque; founded 1173; choir 1251-91; 14th C towers. Bernt Notke triumphal cross 1477.
228 **St James** 12th C Gothic hall church with double side aisles; rebuilt 13th C. Fine 16th-17th C organ lofts. Gothic style equestrian figure known as the *Dachreiter*.
229 **St Mary** 1250-1330 Extremely fine French-influenced Gothic brick church; in turn served as model for many other German churches.
230 **Hospital zum Heiligen Geist** 1280. Superb example of medieval domestic architecture. Gothic hall church 1286. 13th-14th C murals.
231 **Behnhaus** Collection of mainly 18th-19th C art.
232 **St Annen-Museum** General collection, mainly N German. Includes work by Bernt Notke and a Passion altarpiece (1491) by Memling.

LÜDINGWORTH, Lower Saxony
233 **Church** Origins pre-Carolingian. Interesting 14th-18th C furnishings.

LUDWIGSBURG, Baden-Württemberg
234 **Castle** Largest (but rather dull) Baroque castle in Germany. By Nette and Frisoni 1704-33. Contains paintings; Baroque section of regional museum.
235 **Schloss Monrepos** 1767. Horseshoe-shaped Louis XV style pavilion.

LÜNEBURG, Lower Saxony
236 **Lüne Convent** 15th C. Gothic cloisters. Good late Gothic tapestries.
237 **Rathaus** 13th-18th C. Attractive façade with Renaissance-style statues in niches. Superb Gothic Prince's Hall (fine ceiling) and Renaissance Great Council Chamber 1566-84 (carvings by Albert of Soest). Paintings by Memling.

MAINZ, Hesse
238 **Cathedral** Romanesque basilica begun 975; nave and E end 1081-1137; w end and rib vaulting *c.* 1200-39. Apses, flanked by towers, at both ends. Rood-screen *c.* 1239; Gothic monuments; 15th C painting and sculpture; Rococo choir stalls. 15th C chapterhouse; Gothic cloisters.
239 **Gutenbergmuseum** Important museum of typography. Contains Gutenberg 42-line Bible.
240 **Zentralmuseum** History of the Rhineland and of art in the area. Contains famous Roman Jupiter Column.

MANNHEIM, Hesse
241 **Castle** 1720-60. One of largest Baroque palaces in Germany; extensively rebuilt. notable Rittersaal and Rococo library.
242 **Städtische Kunsthalle** 19th-20th C paintings and sculpture (Impressionists and Expressionists).
243 **Reiss-Museum** Historical exhibits and applied art. Frankenthal porcelain.

MARBURG, Hesse
244 **St Elisabeth** 1235-83. First Gothic hall church in Germany. Shows German characteristic of ending transept in apses. Gothic rood-screen. Important works of art: gold shrine of St Elisabeth *c.* 1250; Pietà 1360; 14th-15th C frescoes; 15th-16th C painting, sculpture and tombs.
245 **Castle** 13th-14th C. Note Gothic Knights' Hall and chapel.
246 **Universitätsmuseum für Kunst und Kulturgeschichte** Best items from St Elisabeth's.

MAULBRONN, Baden-Württemberg
247 **Monastery** Founded 1148. Outstanding collection of beautiful and well-preserved

Romanesque to late Gothic buildings. Church 1178. Romanesque rood-screen; 14th-15th C painting and sculpture.

MEERSBURG, Baden-Württemberg
248 **Fürstenhäusle** Said to be oldest castle in Germany. One tower 7th C; keep with stepped gables.

MERGENTHEIM, Baden-Württemberg
249 **Castle of the Teutonic Order** 1565; partly rebuilt late 18th C. Museum of relics of the order.

MICHELSTADT, Hesse
250 **Stadtkirche** 1461-1537. Important library.
251 **Kellerei** Given by Charlemagne to his biographer and architect Einhard.
252 **Rathaus** 1484. Supported on wooden posts instead of the more usual arcade.

MINDEN, Northern Rhineland-Westphalia
253 **Cathedral** Early Gothic (begun 1267); restored. Notable w façade and dome-like vaulting. Romanesque crucifix.

MITTENWALD, Bavaria
254 **Church** Baroque by Joseph Schmutzer 1738-49. Stuccowork; murals by Matthäus Günther.

MÖNCHEN-GLADBACH, Northern Rhineland-Westphalia
255 **Minster** Started 10th C; early Gothic choir by Gerhard von Riehl, architect of Cologne Cathedral.

MUNICH, Bavaria
256 **Frauenkirche** 15th C Flamboyant Gothic-style church in red brick, virtually destroyed 1944; rebuilt. Bulbous cupolas on towers. Late 14th C stained glass; 15th-16th C altarpieces (one by Johann Polack); early 16th C carved busts by Erasmus Grasser.
257 **Ludwigskirche** 1830-40. Neoclassical paintings by Cornelius, especially *The Last Judgment*.
258 **St Michael** 1583-97. Italian Renaissance style. Largest barrel-vaulted interior in Germany.
259 **Theatinerkirche** Renaissance to early Baroque by Barelli and Zuccalli 1663-90. Coarse Baroque façade by François Cuvilliés; better interior.
260 **Antiquarium** 1570. Good interiors in Rococo style by Effner and Cuvilliés; fine Rococo theatre by Cuvilliés 1751-53.
261 **Nymphenburg** Outstanding Baroque by Barelli and Viscardi; begun 1664; additions and alterations in late Baroque and Classical French styles. Early 18th C pavilions; important interiors (Rococo, French and Chinese styles) with fine panelling, frescoes, stuccowork, tapestries and paintings. Nymphenburg porcelain factory. Complex includes **Amalienburg** 1739 with marvellous Rococo interiors by Cuvilliés; **Pagodenburg** 1719, Chinese style.
262 **Residenz** Renaissance to Neoclassical.
263 **Alte Pinakothek** Venetian Renaissance style by Leo von Klenze 1826-36. Superlative collection of paintings 14th-18th C. Artists represented include Dürer, Altdorfer, Burgkmair, Cranach, Van der Weyden, Memling, Rembrandt, Rubens, Van Dyck, Fra Angelico, Botticelli, Raphael, Tintoretto, Titian, Claude Lorrain, Poussin, Boucher, El Greco etc.
264 **Bayerisches Nationalmuseum** Excellent fine arts collection; also prehistoric and Roman antiquities.
265 **Bayerische Staatsbibliothek** Incunabula; Otto III's illuminated Bible *c.* 1000.
266 **Glyptothek** Leo von Klenze 1816-30. Sculpture.
267 **Städtische Galerie im Lenbachhaus** Paintings by Lenbach, Kandinsky, Klee and members of the *Blaue Reiter* group.
268 **Neue Pinakothek** 19th-20th C paintings.
269 **Residenzmuseum** Applied art especially porcelain, silver and gold plate.
270 **Residenzschatzkammer** Jewelled *objets de vertu* and other valuable items.
271 **Schackgalerie** German late Romantic art.

MÜNNERSTADT, Bavaria
272 **Church** Veit Stoss paintings, Riemenschneider panels 1492.

MÜNSTER, Northern Rhineland-Westphalia

273 **Cathedral** 13th C transitional with later additions. 14th C cloisters. 13th C sculpture; 16th C painting and sculpture.
274 **Church of the Apostle** 13th-16th C. Gothic and early Renaissance frescoes.
275 **Überwasserkirche** 1340-46. Beautiful church with high Gothic piers.
276 **Rathaus** 1335. Excellent Gothic; exact reconstruction of original façade.
277 **Residenz** Good Baroque by Johann Konrad Schlaun. Now university.
278 **Provincial Fine Arts Museum** Westphalian art 15th-16th C; part of Liesborn altarpiece.

MURRHARDT, Baden-Württemberg
279 **St Walderich Chapel** Fine late Romanesque.

NENNIG, Rhineland-Palatinate
280 **Roman Villa** Mosaic floor.

NERESHEIM, Baden-Württemberg
281 **Abbey Church** Remodelled Baroque by Balthasar Neumann 1757-92; his last and one of his finest works.

NEUENSTEIN, Baden-Württemberg
282 **Castle** 16th-17th C Renaissance. Interesting contemporary furnishings and objets d'art.

NEUMAGEN, Rhineland-Palatinate
283 Large Roman burial grounds. 2nd-3rd C finds in Rheinisches Landesmuseum, Trier.

NEUÖTTING, Bavaria
284 **St Nicholas** Gothic by Stetthaimer; started 1410; nave 1484-1510 similar to St Martin, Landshut.

NEUSCHWANSTEIN, Bavaria
285 **Castle** Begun in 1869 for Ludwig II of Bavaria. Both castle and setting pure Wagnerian fantasy; interiors like opera sets.

NEUWERK, Lower Saxony
286 **Lighthouse** 14th C, oldest on German coast.

NÖRDLINGEN, Bavaria
287 **St George** Late 15th C hall church. Fan vaulting; 15th C pulpit; parts of carved altarpiece *c.* 1470 by Friedrich Herlin (rest in town museum); organ 1610.
288 **Rathaus** 13th C. Renaissance-style exterior staircase 1618.
289 **Reichsstadtmuseum** Swabian masters.

NUREMBERG, Bavaria
290 **Frauenkirche** Gothic hall church 1352-61. w porch and late 15th C altars by Adam Krafft notable.
291 **St Lawrence** Good Gothic; begun *c.* 1260; late Gothic choir by Konrad Roritzer; fine w façade with rose window; stained glass; early 15th C crucifix; Adam Krafft tabernacle 1493-96; Veit Stoss *Annunciation* 1517-18.
292 **St Sebald** Superb Romanesque to Gothic, 13th-14th C. Complex 14th C E chancel. 14th C sculptures; 15th C paintings; late 15th-early 16th C sculptures by Veit Stoss and Adam Krafft; St Sebald's tomb by Peter Vischer 1519.
293 **Castle** 12th-16th C. Pentagonal tower 11th-12th C (remains of burgrave's fortress); Romanesque chapel; imperial stables 1494-95.
294 **Albrecht Dürer-Haus** 15th C. Tracery of gable noteworthy. Dürer lived here 1509-28. Drawings.
295 **Heilig-Geist-Spital** *c.* 1350; enlarged 1487-1527.
296 **Schöner Brunnen** Gothic by Heinrich Parler 1385-96.
297 **Germanisches Nationalmuseum** Very large collection. History of German art and culture from prehistoric times to *c.* 1920; perhaps best on 14th-16th C.

OBERAMMERGAU, Bavaria
298 **Pfarrkirche** Stuccowork by Joseph Schmutzer.

OBERMARCHTAL, Baden-Württemberg
299 **Abbey Church** Baroque by Christian Thumb and Franz Beer; started 1686.

OBERSTENFELD, Baden-Württemberg
300 **Stiftskirche** Early Romanesque.

OCHSENFURT, Bavaria
301 **Pfarrkirche** 14th C. *St Nicholas* by Tilman Riemenschneider.
302 **Rathaus** Fine Gothic 1490.

OGGERSHEIM, Hesse

303 **Maria Himmelfahrt** Peter Verschaffelt 1774-77. Excellent example of Classical style.

OSNABRÜCK, Lower Saxony

304 **Cathedral** Mainly 13th c transitional; Romanesque towers and cloisters. 13th c crucifix; 16th c carved altarpiece.

305 **St John** Gothic hall church; choir 1256-92. Strong Romanesque elements evident in piers.

306 **St Mary** 14th c Gothic hall church. 16th c Passion altarpiece from Antwerp.

OSTERHOVEN, Bavaria

307 **Premonstratensian Monastery Church** 1726-40. By J M Fischer. Frescoes by C D Asam, altars and stuccowork by E Q Asam.

OTTOBEUREN, Bavaria

308 **Benedictine Abbey** Completely remodelled in Baroque style. Abbey buildings, 1711-31, with magnificent staircases; galleries; Kaisersaal; library; chapels (frescoes by Amigoni).

309 **Church** Enormous, magnificent Baroque and Rococo building by J M Fischer 1737-66. Beautiful, rich, luminous interior. 12th c *Christ*; choir stalls by Martin Herrmann 1764. Frescoes by J J and F A Zeiller; plasterwork by J M Feichtmayer; carvings by J Christian.

PADERBORN, Northern Rhineland-Westphalia

310 **Cathedral** Mainly 13th c transitional. Tower with fine Romanesque bays; 12th c atrium; 'Paradise Door' with late 12th- early 13th c panels; 13th c statues. Chapel of St Bartholomew, Romanesque 1017. Rather oriental-looking interior; dome and carved capitals.

311 **Diocesan Museum** Medieval ecclesiastical art.

PAPPENHEIM, Bavaria

312 **St Gallus** 8th c Carolingian church

PASSAU, Bavaria

313 **Cathedral** 14th c Flamboyant Gothic; rebuilt Baroque. Gothic chevet; octagonal dome over crossing. Ornate interior.

314 **Neue Residenz** 1712. Good interiors.

315 **Museum of Municipal and Cultural History** State collections.

PEISSENBERG, Bavaria

316 **Maria Aich Pilgrim Church** Ceiling by Grünewald.

PLÖN, Schleswig-Holstein

317 **Castle** 1635. English-style gardens among best in Germany.

POMMERSFELDEN, Bavaria

318 **Castle** Baroque. Notable 3-storey staircase by Welsch. Frescoes: paintings.

RASTATT, Baden-Württemberg

319 **Maria Einsiedeln Chapel** Beautiful Baroque 1711.

320 **Castle** Early Baroque by Rossi 1700; general plan Italian influenced.

RATZEBURG, Schleswig-Holstein

321 **Cathedral** Founded 1154 by Henry the Lion. Fine s doorway; high altar 1430.

322 **St Georgsberger** Romanesque 1150. May be oldest stone church in N Germany.

RECKLINGHAUSEN, Northern Rhineland-Westphalia

323 **Ikonenmuseum** Byzantine, Russian, Balkan icons, miniatures etc.; Coptic sculptures and textiles.

324 **Städtische Kunsthalle** Works by contemporary artists.

REGENSBURG, Bavaria

325 **Cathedral** 1275-1534; spires finished 1869. Among finest examples of Gothic ecclesiastical architecture in Germany. Shows s French influence. 3 E apses; w façade Flamboyant towers; statues. 11th c bronze doors; 14th c stained glass.

326 **St Emmeramus** Romanesque with Rococo decor. 12th c porch with Romanesque sculpture.

327 **St James** 12th c columnar basilica; no transept. N portal with fine Romanesque sculpture.

328 **Altes Rathaus** 1350; painted façade. Notable Gothic Reichssaal; tapestries.

329 **Castle** (former St Emmeramus abbey) Halls; library; Gothic cloisters, funerary chapel. Contains paintings.

330 **Golden Tower** Mid 13th c. Aristocratic residence like those in N Italy.

331 **Porta Praetoria** Roman gateway AD 179.

REICHENAU, Baden-Württemberg

332 **Marienmünster in Mittelzell** 724-819; additions 10th-11th c. Has basilican form. Mainly Romanesque with Gothic chancel.

333 **St George in Oberzell** Basically late 9th c Carolingian basilica; crypt 985; Gothic choir. Murals *c.* 1000.

334 **St Peter and St Paul in Niederzell** 10th c basilica.

REMAGEN, Rhineland-Palatinate

335 **Roman Gateway** Reliefs.

ROHR, Bavaria

336 **Church** Baroque by Asam brothers 1718-25. Contains Assumption of the Virgin Altar.

ROTHENBURG OB DER TAUBER, Bavaria

337 **Franciscan Church** Gothic. Creglingen Virgin 1400; 15th-16th c sculpture.

338 **St James** 14th c Gothic. Tilman Riemenschneider's *Altarpiece of the Holy Blood* 1504.

339 **Rathaus** Part 14th c with belfry; part Renaissance (balcony 1681).

ROTT AM INN, Bavaria

340 **Abbey Church** Remodelled Baroque by J M Fischer; stuccowork by Feichtmayr; frescoes by Matthäus Günther.

ROTTENBUCH, Bavaria

341 **Abbey Church** Romanesque; rebuilt late 15th c; remodelled in Baroque style 1737-42. Excellent Rococo interior by the Schmutzers and Matthäus Günther.

ROTTWEIL, Baden-Württemberg

342 **Kapellenkirche** Gothic. Elaborate Flamboyant tower with loggia. Sculptures.

343 **Städtische Kunstsammlung Lorenzkapelle** Gothic sculpture.

344 **Stadtmuseum** Allemanic and Roman exhibits including Orpheus Mosaic.

SAARBRÜCKEN, Saar

345 **St Arnual** Gothic 13th-14th c; Baroque tower. 15th c tombs.

346 **Ludwigskirche** Baroque by Stengel.

347 **Saarmuseum** 18th c applied and 19th-20th c fine art.

ST BLASIEN, Baden-Württemberg

348 **St Blaise** Rebuilt by d'Ixnard after fire in 1768. Rotunda in French style (rare in Germany). Enormous dome with inner false dome; unusual interior layout.

ST GOAR, Rhineland-Palatinate

349 **Abbey Church** Rebuilt 15th c. Gothic hall church; Romanesque crypt. 15th c frescoes.

350 **Burg Rheinfels** Important 13th c fortress; rebuilt Renaissance style 16th c.

ST WENDEL, Saar

351 **St Wendel** Gothic; 15th c towers. 14th c tomb.

SALEM, Baden-Württemberg

352 **Abbey Church** Gothic 1299-1414. Usual Cistercian plan with flat chevet; fine tracery and latticework. Baroque interior, plasterwork by local craftsmen.

353 **Castle** (former abbey buildings) Founded 1134; rebuilt Baroque. Fine Imperial Hall (plasterwork by F J Feuchtmayer 1708-10).

SCHÄFTLARN, Bavaria

354 **Abbey Church** Beautiful 18th c Baroque.

SCHLEISSHEIM, Bavaria

355 **Neues Schloss** Enormous fine Baroque building 1701-27. Notable staircase by Effner. Magnificent interiors with fine Rococo stuccowork; frescoes; paintings, especially 16th-17th c Dutch and Flemish.

SCHLESWIG, Schleswig-Holstein

356 **Cathedral** Brick Gothic hall church; parts date from the 11th c; 12th c sculptures on exterior; 14th c crypt. Bordesholm Altar, 392 figures carved by Hans Brüggeman 1521; tomb of Frederick I of Denmark by Cornelius Floris 1552; *Blue Madonna* by Jürgen Ovens.

357 **Gottorf Castle** *c.* 1150. Rebuilt 19th c. Renaissance chapel 1600. Castle houses two museums. Note especially Nydam Ship 4th c; discovered 1863.

SCHLIERSEE, Bavaria

358 **Pfarrkirche** Rebuilt Baroque 1712. Good interior. *Virgin in Mantle* by Polack 1494; 15th-16th c sculptures. Painting and stuccowork by J B Zimmermann.

SCHUSSENRIED, Baden-Württemberg

359 **Former Abbey** Includes Rococo library by Dominikus Zimmermann 1754-61. Church remodelled Baroque; good choir stalls 1717.

SCHWÄBISCH-GMÜND, Baden-Württemberg

360 **Cathedral** 14th c Gothic by Heinrich Parler; nave first half 14th c (vaulting *c.* 1500); choir begun 1351 (net vaulting 1491-1521). Fine decorated exterior. Interior conforms to Cistercian plan. Stained glass; 14th-15th c sculptures; Renaissance choir stalls.

SCHWÄBISCH HALL, Baden-Württemberg

361 **St Michael** Romanesque; rebuilt 15th c as Gothic hall church; 16th c chancel. 15th-16th c altarpieces.

362 **Keckburg Museum** Romanesque dwelling tower. Local history.

SCHWARZ-RHEINDORF, Northern Rhineland-Westphalia

363 **Church** Two-storey Romanesque 1151. Typical use of blind arcades, round-arch friezes, dwarf gallery. Important Romanesque frescoes *c.* 1156.

SEGEBERG (Bad), Schleswig-Holstein

364 **St Mary** 1160. Oldest brick church in N Germany.

SIEGEN, Northern Rhineland-Westphalia

365 **St Nicholas** 13th c late Romanesque; unusual hexagonal domed nave.

SIGMARINGEN, Baden-Württemberg

366 **Hohenzollern Castle** Enormous complex of buildings 12th c onwards; fire 1893; rebuilt. Surviving interiors mainly 16th c. Paintings; tapestries; arms and armour; carriages.

SOEST, Northern Rhineland-Westphalia

367 **Cathedral** 11th-12th c Romanesque. Very elegant tower. 12th-13th c murals (restored).

368 **St Nicholas Chapel** Konrad von Soest St Nicholas altarpiece *c.* 1400.

SOLITUDE, Baden-Württemberg

369 **Castle** By La Guépière 1763-67. Central arcaded rotunda with Neoclassical interior. Most other interiors French Rococo.

SPEYER, Rhineland-Palatinate

370 **Cathedral** Begun 1031; altered late 12th c; burned by French 1689; restored 19th c. Largest Romanesque church in Europe; apses, flanked by towers, at both ends; superb crypt 1031-61; nave vaulting begun 1082. Exterior decoration Lombardian in origin; very high nave (108 ft); absolute harmony of 'metrical' system in interior; 15th c sculpture.

371 **Historisches Museum der Pfalz** General historical collection. Frankenthal porcelain.

STADE, Lower Saxony

372 **St Cosmas** 13th-15th c. Typical medieval brick church; Baroque onion spire; good 17th c furnishings.

STAFFELSTEIN, Bavaria

373 **Pfarrkirche** 768-814. One of 14 'Slavenkirchen' of Charlemagne.

STEINBACH, Hesse

374 **Einhardsbasilika** 9th c Carolingian. Sanctuary and lateral chapels with apse.

STEINGADEN, Bavaria

375 **Premonstratensian Monastery** Founded 1147. Exterior of abbey church Romanesque, rest remodelled in Baroque style; rich Rococo interior.

STEINHAUSEN, Baden-Württemberg

376 **Pilgrim Church** Baroque by Dominikus Zimmermann 1727-33. Oval aisle and chancel. Excellent Rococo interior.

STRAUBING, Bavaria

377 **Carmelite Church** Hall church by Hans von Burghausen, begun 1378. Choir with no aisle.

378 **St Peter** 1180. Romanesque pillared basilica. Agnes-Bernauer Chapel 1436.

STUPPACH, Baden-Württemberg

379 **Church** Matthias Grünewald *The Virgin with the Infant Christ* 1519 (part of the *Stuppach Madonna*).

STUTTGART, Baden-Württemberg

380 **Stiftskirche** 12th c basilica; 14th c choir; rebuilt 15th c; badly damaged in war. Fine early 16th c belfry porch.

381 **Altes Schloss** 13th c; rebuilt 1553-78 by A Tretsch. Rectangular with usual corner towers; triple-galleried Renaissance courtyard. Contains **Württemberg Landesmuseum**. Prehistoric, Roman, medieval. Sculptures include Jörg Syrlin's *Stations of the Cross* 1515.

382 **Staatsgalerie** Good general collection, but possibly best on 14th-16th c. Swabian and late 18th-19th c paintings.

TIEFENBRONN, Baden-Württemberg
383 **Pfarrkirche** Gothic. Lucas Moser altarpiece 1431 and other 15th-16th c altarpieces.

TÖNNING, Schleswig-Holstein
384 **St Lawrence** 1493; Baroque tower 1706. Paintings by Jürgen Ovens, a pupil of Rembrandt.

TRIER, Rhineland-Palatinate
385 **Cathedral** Central part of building is Roman 4th c; w end 11th c; E end 12th c Romanesque. Baroque interior; some Romanesque carvings and Gothic funerary monuments. Gothic cloisters. 15th c Madonna by Nikolaus Gerhaert of Leyden.

386 **Liebfrauenkirche** Transitional style 1235-70. Unusual Greek-cross plan (based on Braisne Abbey Church); outstanding interior.

387 **Imperial Baths** *c.* 300; rebuilt late 4th c.

388 **Porta Nigra** 4th c. Roman fortified gate; became a church in 11th c; restored by Napoleon 1804.

389 **Roman Bridge** 4th c; rebuilt 17th c.

390 **Episcopal Museum** Ecclesiastical art, particularly medieval sculpture. Also 4th c frescoes from palace under cathedral.

391 **Stadtbibliothek** Ill. MSS, especially Ada MS and Egbert Codex.

392 **Städtisches Museum** (in 11th c Romanesque Simeonstift) Folk art; local history.

393 **Rheinisches Landesmuseum** Excellent Roman section. Also prehistoric and medieval collections.

TÜBINGEN, Baden-Württemberg
394 **St George** 15th c late Gothic. Late Gothic pulpit and roodscreen; late 15th-16th c tombs; windows by Peter Hemmel.

395 **Burgsteige** Renaissance-style building on 11th-12th c foundations.

ÜBERLINGEN, Baden-Württemberg
396 **Minster** Gothic 1353-1586. Fan vaulting; high altar by Jörg Zürn.

397 **Rathaus** Gothic. Ratssaal 1490; richly carved.

ULM, Baden-Württemberg
398 **Cathedral** Gothic. Started 1377; nave and porch 1392-1419; openwork tower 1420-92; cathedral finished 1890. Built by members of Parler and Ensingen families of master builders. Highest church tower in world (528 ft); 4 aisles; no transept; fan vaulting. Stained glass by Peter Hemmel; Passion figure by Hans Multscher 1429; outstanding choir stalls by Jörg Syrlin the Elder 1469-74.

399 **Fischkasten Fountain** Jörg Syrlin the Elder 1482.

400 **Rathaus** Gothic 1370; Renaissance additions. Frescoes 1540; 16th c astronomical clock.

401 **Ulmer Museum** Arts of Ulm and Swabia; 20th c graphics.

VEITSHÖCHHEIM, Bavaria
402 **Castle** 1680; rebuilt Baroque by Balthasar Neumann 1763-75. Furniture. Good Baroque gardens; sculptures by d'Auvera, J P Wagner and F Dietz.

VIERZEHNHEILIGEN, Bavaria
403 **Church** Outstanding Rococo by Balthasar Neumann 1743-72. Tall onion spires; triple oval plan; curved aisles. Beautiful interior.

WASSERBURG, Bavaria
404 **Pfarrkirche** Gothic by Hans von Burghausen and Krumauer 1410-83.

405 **Patrizierhaus** Outstanding Baroque façade by J B Zimmermann.

406 **Rathaus** Gothic 1450 with Renaissance additions. Some good carved and painted 16th c interiors.

WEIKERSHEIM, Bavaria
407 **Castle** Rebuilt Renaissance style 1580-1680. Medieval keep. Good interiors, especially French styled Knights' Hall 1603. Good collec-

tion of 16th-18th c furniture; tapestries; porcelain.

WEINGARTEN, Baden-Württemberg
408 **Abbey Church** Important Baroque by Kaspar Moosbrugger 1715-24. Restored 1952-53. Murals by C D Asam; stuccowork.

WEISSENBURG, Bavaria
409 **Biricanis** Roman fort.

410 **Museum** Prehistoric, Roman and local exhibits.

WELTENBURG, Bavaria
411 **Abbey Church** Baroque by C D Asam 1717-21. Double oval plan. Beautiful interior.

WESSOBRUNN, Bavaria
412 **Former abbey buildings** Notable late 17th c Prince's Gallery, with outstanding stuccowork.

WETZLAR, Hesse
413 **Collegiate Church** *c.* 800 to late Gothic. Façade 12th c Romanesque, and 14th c Gothic; church finally completed in 13th c Gothic style.

WIBLINGEN, Baden-Württemberg
414 **Abbey buildings** Superb Rococo library 1744. Late Baroque abbey church. Unusually simple exterior; ceiling by Januarius Zick.

WIES, Bavaria
415 **Wieskirche** (Die Wies) A masterpiece by D and J B Zimmermann 1746-54. Simple Baroque exterior; elaborate Rococo interior which represents a complete fusion of decorative and architectural elements.

WIESENTHEID, Bavaria
416 **Pfarrkirche** Baroque by Balthasar Neumann 1727. Murals by Franz Marchini 1728.

417 **Castle** Fuchsbau wing Renaissance style 1576; rest mainly Baroque; imposing 18th c façade.

WIMPFEN (Bad), Baden-Württemberg
418 **St Peter** Romanesque (most of the original façade still exists) and Gothic. Cloisters 15th-16th c Gothic.

419 **Imperial Palace** Occupied by the Hohenstaufen emperors from Barbarossa to Henry VII. Remains include the Romanesque Steinhaus (16th c façade), two towers and a fine Romanesque arcade.

WOLFENBÜTTEL, Lower Saxony
420 **St Mary** 1608-23. Gothic with Renaissance decorative elements.

421 **Castle** 12th c; Renaissance additions; rebuilt in Baroque style.

WORMS, Rhineland-Palatinate
422 **Cathedral** *c.* 1000; present building completed 1224. Apse, flanked by towers, at both ends; possibly purest Romanesque exterior in Germany. Fine Romanesque pillared basilican interior with rib-vaulted nave. Important Romanesque and Gothic sculpture.

423 **Museum der Stadt Worms** Ecclesiastical art and Roman and local exhibits.

WURZACH, Baden-Württemberg
424 **Pfarrkirche** 1777. Neoclassical with strong French influence.

425 **Castle** Baroque, with good mid-18th c staircase.

WÜRZBURG, Bavaria
426 **Cathedral** 1034. Romanesque with interior partly in Baroque style; badly damaged in war.

427 **Käppele** Rococo pilgrimage church by Balthasar Neumann 1748. Decoration by J M Feichtmayr.

428 **Marienburg** 13th c; enlarged 15th-16th c. 13th c keep; Renaissance well; circular chapel (706); interior with Baroque decor.

429 **Old University** 1582. Renaissance style inner court. Renaissance style church 1591; Baroque tower by Petrini 1700.

430 **Residenz** Important Baroque by Neumann, Maximilian von Welsch and L Von Hildebrandt 1719-44. Excellent staircase, Imperial Hall and church, all with frescoes by Tiepolo *c.* 1753. Stuccowork by Antonio Bossi.

431 **Mainfränkisches Museum** General collection including religious art, Tilman Riemenschneider sculptures.

XANTEN, Northern Rhineland-Westphalia
432 **Cathedral** Outstanding example of ecclesiastical Gothic architecture; badly damaged in war. 12th c Romanesque; rebuilt Gothic mid-

13th-16th c. Romanesque w façade. 16th c altarpieces and cloisters.

433 **Abbey Church** Interesting late Baroque by J M Fischer 1738-53. Rococo interior stuccowork by J M Feichtmayr.

East Germany
with East Berlin

ALTENBURG, Thuringia
434 **Castle** Begun 10th c. Rebuilt 15th-18th c.

435 **Lindenau Museum** Rich collection of Italian paintings of 14th-15th c; also collections of modern painting and sculpture, Greek and Etruscan pottery.

ALTENKIRCHEN, Pomerania
436 **Village Church** 12th c Romanesque building, oldest on Rügen island.

ANNABERG-BUCHOLZ, Saxony
437 **St Anne** 1499-1520. 3-aisled Gothic church. Splendid doors in N aisle and old vestry; choir balustrade panels; altar (1522).

AUE, Saxony
438 **Klosterlein-Zelle** Cistercian church built before 1235. Contains engravings of the Virgin and other saints in ancient layer of plaster.

AUGUSTUSBERG, Saxony
439 **Palace** Built 16th c by Hieronymus Lotter for Elector Augustus I. Now restored. Houses museum for local history.

BAUTZEN, Saxony
440 **Cathedral** Built 13th-16th c. Inside, Catholic and Protestant sections separated by wrought-iron trellis.

441 **Ortenburg** Castle founded before 1000. Rebuilt in Renaissance style.

442 **Stadtmuseum** Contains gallery of paintings, collections of Baroque art and folk art.

BERLIN, (East)
443 **St Mary** Flamboyant Gothic hall church. 15th c mural; Baroque pulpit by Schlüter.

444 **Altes Museum** Fine colonnaded building by Schinkel, 1828.

445 **Brandenburger Tor** By Langhans 1789; surmounted by quadriga by Schadow 1794.

446 **National Opera House** By Knobelsdorff 1743.

447 **Neue Wache** Schinkel 1818. Built like temple with Doric colonnades.

448 **Schauspielhaus** Rebuilt by Schinkel; now being restored.

449 **Zeughaus** Baroque 1695-1706. Decorative carvings by Schlüter.

450 **Staatliche Museen zu Berlin** (former Kaiser-Friedrich-Museum) General collection. Egyptian dept. the best. Includes **National Galerie** with 19th-20th c painting; sculpture by Schadow, Canova etc. **Pergamon Museum** with outstanding Greco-Roman and Near Eastern depts. Reconstruction of Bablyonian processional way (*c.* 600 BC); magnificent Pergamon Altar 180-160 BC.

BRANDENBURG AN DER HAVEL, Brandenburg
451 **Cathedral** 12th c Romanesque basilica, remodelled in Gothic style in 14th c.

452 **St Catherine** Rebuilt from 1401. Corpus Domini chapel (dedicated 1473) fine example of late Gothic brick architecture.

453 **Rathaus** 14th c. 17-ft figure of Roland, erected 1474, stands in front.

CHORIN, Brandenburg
454 **Cistercian monastery** Founded 1273. Church is one of best preserved Cistercian buildings in N Germany.

COTTBUS, Brandenburg
455 **Klosterkirche** 14th c abbey church.

456 **Oberkirche** Late Gothic brick church *c.* 1500.

457 **Schloss Branitz** Built 1772. Very beautiful music room in Rococo style. Houses museum and art gallery. Work of the 19th c painter Karl Blechen particularly featured. Exhibition of prehistory and early history.

DESSAU, Saxony-Anhalt
458 **Ducal Palace** Early German Renaissance palace, right wing completed 1530-49. Partially remodelled and completed 1748-51 by G von Knobelsdorff.

459 **Mosigkau palace** Houses collection of German and Dutch paintings.
DOBERAN (Bad), Mecklenburg
460 **Cathedral** 3-aisled brick building completed 1368. Most of original decoration extant.
461 **Cistercian monastery** Founded 1171, burned down 1291. Part of Romanesque archway and Gothic farm buildings remain.
DORNBURG, Thuringia
462 **Goethe Palace** Renaissance-style structure. Interior restored in style of Goethe's time.
DRESDEN, Saxony
463 **Katholische Hofkirche** Former court church, now cathedral. Built 1738-51 for Augustus the Strong by Gaetano Chiaveri. Baroque structure in Saxon sandstone. Large figures of saints on balustrades attributed to Lorenzo Matielli.
464 **Franciscan church** Sole surviving medieval church; built from 1272.
465 **Altstadter Hauptwache** Guardhouse built 1830-31 by Friederich Schinkel. Façade imitates Greek Ionic temple.
466 **Brühlsche Terrasse** Pleasure garden laid out by Count Brühl in 18th C on former fortress wall.
467 **Japanisches Palais** (or Augusteum) Built 1715 as summer residence for Augustus II. Houses **Museum für Vorgeschichte** and large public library.
468 **Opera House** Designed by Gottfried Semper 1837-41 in Italian Renaissance style. Remodelled after 1869. Severely damaged in Second World War, restored since.
469 **Zwinger** Dresden's most famous Baroque structure (1711-22). Consists of courtyard with pavilions (Stadtpavillon and Wallpavillon) in two corners, and a gateway (Kronentor) on one side. Fourth side closed by Gemäldegalerie. Whole badly damaged in 1945, but being restored. Contains collections of porcelain (**Museum Johanneum**), pewter (**Museum für Kunsthandwerk**) and scientific instruments (**Mathematisch-Physikalischer Salon**).
470 **Albertinum** Museum containing important collections, including sculpture (some antique pieces) and contemporary painting. **Grünes Gewölbe** houses collection of precious stones and jewellery, including regalia of Augustus II as king of Poland, and works of the goldsmith Melchior Dinglinger.
471 **Gemäldegalerie** Magnificent collection of old masters—Italian, German, Flemish, Dutch, French, Spanish. Famous works include Raphael's *Sistine Madonna, Venus* by Giorgione, *The Tribute Money* by Titian, Rubens's *Judgment of Paris,* Van Dyck's *Charles I, his Queen and their Children,* and Vermeer's *Girl reading a Letter.*
EISENACH, Thuringia
472 **Dominican monastery** Buildings well preserved. Church, built 1240, houses museum of medieval arts.
473 **St Nicholas** Late Romanesque church, renovated 1886-87. Once belonged to Benedictine monastery.
474 **Stadtschloss** Built 1742. Rococo façade.
EISENBERG, Thuringia
475 **Schlosskirche** Baroque church 1680-92. Contains many fine art treasures.
ERFURT, Thuringia
476 **Cathedral** Founded 752 by Boniface. Some remnants of Romanesque structure, but rebuilt 13th-15th C in Gothic style. 14th C gallery an exceptionally beautiful specimen of Gothic architecture. Treasures include reredos with portrayal of the Virgin; bronze candelabrum *c.* 1160.
477 **Barfüsserkirche** Early 14th C Franciscan church of Discalced Friars.
478 **Kaufmännerkirche** Early medieval church with 2 towers. Art objects of 16th C donated by Friedemann family.
479 **Packhof** Baroque-style house (1705-11), formerly the residence of a merchant. Contains **Anger Museum** with picture gallery and collections of glass and faïence.
480 **Museum für Thüringer Volkskunde** Folk art, including tinware, ceramics, glassware, faïence and porcelain.

FALKENSTEIN, Saxony-Anhalt
481 **Castle** 12th C. Museum for furniture, art objects and medieval documents.
FREIBERG, Saxony
482 **Cathedral** Founded 12th C. Rebuilt in late Gothic style after burned down in 1484. Romanesque doorway (Golden Gate) of 1230-40 survives. 13th C wooden group of Crucifixion, stone pulpit (*c.* 1510) by Hans Witten, tomb of prince elector Maurice of Saxony (d. 1553) by Italian, Dutch and German artists. Interior of Gothic choir remodelled in late Renaissance style of N Italy late 16th C.
483 **Rathaus** Rebuilt 1472-74. Contains treasures of town archives.
484 **Stadt- und Bergwerkmuseum** Collections of plastic art (including works of the 16th C sculptor Peter Breuer), craft-works and items of local history.
FREYBURG, Thuringia
485 **St Mary** First half of 13th C. Similar to Naumburg Cathedral, but smaller.
486 **Neuenburg** Castle built 1070 as border fortification. Has Romanesque chapel (*c.* 1220) and residential tower of same date.
GEISING, Saxony
487 **Church** Rebuilt 1689, with octagonal spire. Contains wooden figure of Christ on the Cross and remains of late 15th C altarpiece.
GERA, Thuringia
488 **Rathaus** Fine Renaissance and Baroque building.
489 **Samson Fountain** Unique piece of Baroque craftsmanship.
GERNRODE, Saxony-Anhalt
490 **St Cyriakus** Oldest fully preserved complex in N Germany. Built under Otto II (973-83) as church of Benedictine monastery. Basilica with gallery, flat ceiling, alternating supports, transept and 2 apses. Holy Sepulchre, *c.* 1025.
GÖRLITZ, Saxony
491 **St Nicholas** Probably built *c.* 1100. Enlarged in late Gothic style.
492 **St Peter** Originally in transitional Romanesque-Gothic style; enlarged and altered several times. Fine W portal.
493 **Rathaus** Renaissance style. Fine staircase with figure of Justice at foot. Late Gothic carved coat of arms of Hungarian king Matthias Corvinus.
GOTHA, Thuringia
494 **Frankenberg Garden House** Charming Rococo house.
495 **Friedenstein palace** Built by Duke Ernst the Pious 1643-54 in austere style. Houses museum with collections of porcelain, paintings, faïences and furniture. Important collection of chinoiserie.
496 **Lustschloss Friedrichstal** Late Baroque palace (1711).
497 **Rathaus** Renaissance style, 1567-74. 100-ft high tower; fine council chamber and spiral staircase.
GREIZ, Saxony
498 **Oberburg** Castle founded 9th-10th C. Only remnant of old buildings is tower. Other parts built 16th-17th C.
499 **Summer palace** Built 1779 by Italian architect. Houses collections of books and copperplate engravings (mainly English).
500 **Unterburg** Semi-classical building. Houses museum of local history.
GÜSTROW, Mecklenburg
501 **Cathedral** Brick church of *c.* 1230-15th C. *Hovering Angel,* sculpture by Ernst Barlach (1927); tomb of Günther von Passow with sculpture by C P Diessart.
502 **Ducal castle** Renaissance style (1559-89).
HALBERSTADT, Saxony-Anhalt
503 **Cathedral** 13th-17th C. Gothic with French influences. Towers show Romanesque features. Former chapter house contains cathedral treasures, including Romanesque triumphal group of Crucifixion (*c.* 1220).
504 **Liebfrauenkirche** Romanesque basilica of 12th-13th C, restored 1848, but 13th C vaults preserved in choir and transept. Wooden statue of the Virgin (first half 13th C); choir screen *c.* 1200; mural frescoes.

HALLE, Saxony-Anhalt
505 **Cathedral** Formerly Dominican church. Rebuilt 1520-23 by Cardinal Albert of Brandenburg. Pediment of façade in Renaissance style. Statues of Christ, Apostles and saints by pupil of Hans Bachofen.
506 **Giebichenstein** 10th C castle. Later addition, known as Unterburg, made in 15th C.
507 **Moritzburg** End of 15th C. Only one wing extant. Houses the **Staatliche Galerie,** which contains many works of 20th C.
HAMERSLEBEN, Saxony-Anhalt
508 **Monastery of Augustinian canons** Romanesque basilica; transept and 2 towers.
JENA, Thuringia
509 **Stadtkirche** 1438-1528.
510 **Johannistor** 14th C gate, only remnant of town fortifications.
511 **Vorgeschichtliches Museum** Prehistoric collections.
KARL-MARX STADT (formerly **CHEMNITZ**), Saxony
512 **Schlosskirche** Gothic church on foundations of Romanesque Benedictine monastery church. Contains huge whipping-post by Hans Witten.
513 **Altes Rathaus** Restored in Renaissance style. Fine late Gothic reticulated vaulting in former council chamber.
514 **Red Tower** Once one of 25 fortified towers in town wall. Restored.
515 **Schlossberg** Site of part of early Gothic cloister and Renaissance-style hall. Houses museum of local history.
516 **Museum am Theaterplatz** Works of Impressionists and Expressionists. Good collection of sculpture.
KYFFHAUSEN, Thuringia
517 **Palace** Built *c.* 1116 by King Henry V. Rebuilt 1152 by Emperor Frederick Barbarossa.
LEHNIN, Brandenburg
518 **Cistercian monastery** Founded 1180. Brick church with 3 aisles and Gothic vault.
LEIPZIG, Saxony
519 **St Paulinus** Built 1229-40; restored 1900. Has grooved cloister.
520 **St Thomas** Begun 13th C, rebuilt in late Gothic style. High-pitched roof of 1496.
521 **Auerbachs Hof** Inn, built *c.* 1530. Wine cellar contains 16th C murals depicting Faust legend.
522 **Gehli Palace** 1755-56. Minor Rococo building.
523 **Opera House** Inaugurated 1960. Modern theatre in wood and fine stone.
524 **Rathaus** Built 1558 by Hieronymus Lotter with Renaissance-style frontage. High central tower.
525 **Stock Exchange building** Elegant, richly decorated building of late 17th C. Restored.
526 **Kunstgewerbemuseum** Exhibitions of craft works; collections of etchings and woodcuts.
527 **Museum der Bildenden Künste** Particularly good collection of Baroque works.
LEUCHTENBURG, Thuringia
528 **Castle** First documented 1216. Towers and large belfry. Houses museum.
LÜBBEN, Brandenburg
529 **Paul-Gerhardt-Kirche** Late Gothic brick church. Noteworthy Renaissance altar.
530 **Palace** Begun 14th C. Renaissance-style E gable.
LÜBBENAU, Brandenburg
531 **Palace** Built 1817 in Neoclassical style on foundations of former Wasserburg.
532 **Spreewald Museum** Local history and folklore.
MAGDEBURG, Saxony-Anhalt
533 **Cathedral** Pure Gothic building built 1209-63 on site of an Ottonian church. Vaulted basilica on cruciform plan. 2 344-ft high towers. Completed 16th C; restored after war damage. Sculptures of Wise and Foolish Virgins; tomb monuments of medieval archbishops.
534 **Liebfrauenkirche** Romanesque church, founded 11th C, completed 13th C and restored 1890-91. Early Gothic arches, 1220.
535 **Statue of Otto I** Only medieval German

monument dedicated to an emperor. Stands in 13th C market place.

536 **Rathaus** Renaissance style, 1691. Enlarged 1866.

537 **Kulturhistorisches Museum** Art objects, handicrafts, local history, prehistory.

MEISSEN, Saxony

538 **Cathedral** Original Romanesque structure remodelled in 12th C. W towers begun in 10th C, completed in 13th-15th C. Restored 1903-08. 13th C statues modelled on Naumburg figures; tombs of house of Wettin in Princes' Chapel; marble high relief of *Deposition* by Adolf Dauher (*c.* 1520).

539 **Albrechtsburg** Completed *c.* 1525. Has late Gothic projecting arched windows and spiral staircase. 19th C history painting on walls. Houses museum of medieval sculpture.

540 **Rathaus** Built 1479. Restored 1875.

MERSEBURG, Saxony-Anhalt

541 **Cathedral** Founded 1015. Remodelled 13th and 16th C. Restored 1884-86. Bronze plaque of Rudolph of Swabia, important piece of 11th C German sculpture.

542 **Castle** Episcopal palace of 1480-89 transformed into ducal residential palace 17th C. Site of important Carolingian fortress.

NAUMBURG, Thuringia

543 **Cathedral** Romanesque-Gothic transitional church, rebuilt from 1220. Crypt of original building preserved. W choir with 12 overlifesize figures of founders attributed to Naumburg Master (active 1249-70). Sculptural group of Crucifixion; Passion scenes on choir screen. Restored in 19th C.

544 **Market Place** Well preserved 16th C buildings.

NEUBRANDENBURG, Mecklenburg

545 **Town wall** with tower and four Gothic gates; considered most beautiful in N Germany.

NORDHAUSEN, Saxony-Anhalt

546 **Cathedral** 12th C. Late Romanesque tower; late Gothic main aisle of 14th-15th C.

547 **St Blaise** 1234 2 sloping towers.

PAULINZELLA, Thuringia

548 **Church of Benedictine monastery** Begun 1112, now ruined. Paradise Portal preserved. Fine sculptural decoration.

PILLNITZ, Saxony

549 **Palace** Built 1720-24 by Pöppelmann for Augustus the Strong. Consists of Wasserpalais and Bergpalais, which face one another and are connected by formal gardens. Collection of pictures by 19th and 20th C artists (mainly German) in Bergpalais. Small collection of early German and Netherlandish masters in Wasserpalais, also some Italian paintings.

PIRNA, Saxony

550 **Stadtkirche** 1502-46. Stellate and reticular vault. Sandstone Renaissance altar of 16th C; late Gothic pulpit; 16th C baptismal font.

551 **Gabled houses** of medieval period with balconies and sandstone gateways.

POTSDAM, Brandenburg

552 **St Nicholas** Church by 19th C architect Schinkel.

553 **Charlottenhof** Palace by Schinkel (1826) in Neoclassical style.

554 **Chinese Tea House** 1754 by Büring. Clover-leaf plan with round roof supported by columns in form of palm-trees. Collection of E Asian porcelains of 16th-18th C.

555 **Einstein Tower** 1919-21 by Mendelsohn. Observatory.

556 **Neues Palais** 1763-66. By Büring, Manger and Gontard. Huge, rather ostentatious palace.

557 **Orangery** 1851-60. By Persius, Stüler and Hesse. In style of Italian Renaissance palaces.

558 **Sanssouci** 1744-47 Rococo-style palace by Knobelsdorff for Frederick the Great. Music Room contains paintings by the French painter Pesne; Voltaire room has painted woodcarvings. Park contains sculptures by 18th C French artists on mythological subjects.

559 **Bildergalerie** In Sanssouci Park. Collection of paintings, mainly of Flemish and Italian Baroque.

560 **Potsdam Rococo Museum** Housed in Neue Kammern.

QUEDLINBURG, Saxony-Anhalt

561 **Nunnery church** 1070-1129. Fine specimen of Salian architecture: 3-aisled basilica with flat roof, alternating piers, transept and gallery. Burial plaques of abbesses; Romanesque tapestries; portable altar with enamel decoration.

562 **Rathaus** Gothic with ornamental corner towers. Fine Renaissance portal.

REGENSTEIN, Saxony-Anhalt

563 **Castle** Most rooms carved out of sandstone rock on which castle stands. Watchtower and dungeons well preserved.

ROSTOCK, Mecklenburg

564 **St Mary** 13th-15th C. 2 Romanesque towers. Bronze font; astronomical clock.

565 **St Nicholas** Begun 1250. Restored *c.* 1450 and again 1890-94.

566 **Rathaus** 14th C structure with Renaissance-style façade.

RUDOLSTADT, Thuringia

567 **Heidecksburg** Rebuilt 1735 after fire destroyed original Gothic building. Rococo-style W wing particularly splendid. Houses **Staatliche Museen Heidecksburg**

SAALECK, Thuringia

568 **Castle** 12th C. 2 round towers. Houses museum.

SAALFELD, Thuringia

569 **St John** Late Gothic church.

570 **Hoher Schwarm** Remains of 13th C castle.

571 **Kitzerstein** 16th C castle.

572 **Rathaus** Fine early Renaissance building 1526-37.

SCHULPFORTE, Thuringia

573 **Cistercian monastery** Remains of 12th C monastery buildings and church. Nave (1137-50) and choir (1268-1310) good example of Romanesque-Gothic transitional architecture.

SCHWERIN, Mecklenburg

574 **Cathedral** Gothic brick basilica 1178-1416. Most of surviving building of 15th C.

575 **St Nicholas** Baroque brick church 1708-11.

576 **Ducal palace** Originally built 16th C. Largely rebuilt 1844-57 in French Renaissance style.

577 **Staatliches Museum** Important collection of 17th C Dutch masters; Flemish painting; portrait-busts by Parisian sculptor Jean-Antoine Houdon; 19th C painting; post-1945 art works of E Germany. Also exhibitions of porcelain, glass and faïence; graphics; medieval sculpture and painting.

STRALSUND, Pomerania

578 **St James** Begun 1303. Transformed into 3-aisled basilica later in 14th C.

579 **St Mary** Late 13th-15th C. Huge W end.

580 **St Nicholas** 1276. 3-aisled basilica. W end square towers built on after 1366. Mural paintings of the 14th and 15th C.

581 **Rathaus** Late Gothic brick building. Façade second half of 14th C.

582 **Kulturhistorisches Museum** Prehistory, ecclesiastical art, furniture, modern art.

TORGAU, Saxony-Anhalt

583 **Hartenfels** Castle dating to 15th C. Built around irregular courtyard. Has large winding staircase of 1535-36. Chapel 1470-*c.* 1540.

WARTBURG, Thuringia

584 **Castle** Oldest parts date from 11th C. Much restored after 1847. Connected with Tannhäuser legend. Elisabethgalerie has wall paintings (1855) by Moritz von Schwind. Castle houses museum with works by Lucas Cranach and Tilman Riemenschneider; 14th C Gothic treasure chest; minstrel's harp depicting competiton of troubadours held in Wartburg in 1207.

WECHSELBURG, Saxony

585 **Monastery church** Romanesque basilica (early 13th C). Important 13th C sculpture of Triumphal Cross; tomb of the founder, Dedo of Wettin, and his wife; 13th C choir screen.

WEIMAR, Thuringia

586 **Stadtkirche** (or Herderkirche). Gothic church with later classical alterations. Triptych with Crucifixion centrepiece showing Luther besides the cross.

587 **Belvedere palace** Built 1724-32 in light Baroque style as pleasure palace.

588 **Goethe House** Representative 19th C nobleman's house. Much of original furniture preserved.

589 **Grünes Schloss** 18th C palace containing collection of portraits.

590 **Residential palace** Built 1789-1803 under supervision of Goethe after former palace burned down. Main hall is fine Neoclassical piece of architecture.

591 **Schlossmuseum** Collection of German art from 18th to 20th C. Also collections of graphics, Rococo art and coins.

WERNIGERODE, Saxony-Anhalt

592 **St Silvester** 13th C Romanesque church, altered in later times. Some valuable art objects.

593 **Castle** Built 1680 in Baroque style, renovated 1861-83. Houses **Feudalmuseum** with medieval painting and sculpture, furniture, silver, glass, porcelain, also embroidered textiles of 13th-16th C.

594 **Rathaus** 1538. Framed building adapted from 15th C theatre. Richly decorated panelling of Renaissance; carved figures on timber-work.

WISMAR, Mecklenburg

595 **Fürstenhof** 1553-54. Renaissance structure on medieval foundations. One of finest Renaissance palaces in N Germany.

596 **Wasserkunst** Sandstone fountain by Dutch artist Brandin, 1580.

WITTENBERG, Saxony-Anhalt

597 **Collegiate church** 15th C. Restored after 1945. Altar by Lucas Cranach the Younger (1547); baptismal font by Hermann Vischer (1457).

598 **Schlosskirche** 1490-99. Where Luther nailed his 95 theses in 1517. Contains tombs of Luther and Melanchthon; good stained glass. Church rebuilt after fire of 1760.

599 **Augustinian monastery** 1502. Houses collection of paintings (some by Cranach), MSS and medallions.

600 **Melanchthon House** Fine example of private house of Renaissance period.

601 **Reformationsgeschichtliches Museum** Contains paintings, woodcuts, etchings, MSS etc. connected with Reformation.

WÖRLITZ, Saxony-Anhalt

602 **Gothic House** Late 18th C. Houses collections of Dutch and Italian 16th-17th C paintings, engravings etc. Also arms, Swiss glass-painting.

603 **Neues Schloss** Late 18th C palace in Neoclassical style. Houses large collection of Dutch, French, Italian, German 17th-18th C paintings, Chinese porcelain.

604 **The Monument** Contains portraits of princes of Anhalt.

605 **The Pantheon** Contains statues and busts, and copies of antique achitectural monuments.

ZITTAU, Saxony

606 **St John** 19th C church by Schinkel.

607 **Kreuzkirche** 17th C church, similar in style to Bohemian churches.

608 **Altes Gymnasium** 1586. Beautiful Renaissance portal.

609 **Christian-Weise Bibliothek** Library with fine collection of books and MSS, including about 200 incunabula, 15th C missals and 16th C rare editions.

ZWICKAU, Saxony

610 **St Catherine** Built 1212-19 as Benedictine convent. Some Romanesque features remain, though now largely late Gothic. Kunigunde Altar by Lucas Cranach the Elder; pulpit by Paul Speck (16th C).

611 **St Mary** Built late 12th C. Present structure mainly 15th-16th C, when interior enlarged. Great Altar by Michael Wolgemut (1479); remains of late Gothic choir stalls; Holy Tomb by Michael Heuffner, Pietà by Peter Breuer. Baroque roof added 1677.

612 **Oberstein** Renaissance castle of *c.* 1590.

613 **City and County Museum** Collections of graphic art, local history.

Index

The numbers in Roman type refer to text and captions, the heavy type to illustrations, the italics to the Museums and Monuments index.

Acknowledgments

Numbers in heavy type refer to colour illustrations. Photographs were provided by the following: H. Arnold, Füssen in Allgäu 212; L. Aufsberg, Sonthofen in Allgäu 1, **3**, 10, 14, 45, 83, 122, 124, 136, 184, **189**, **259**; Bauhaus Archiv, Darmstadt 235; Bavaria Verlag 123; Bayerische Staat. Gemäldesammlungen, Munich 159, 214; Bayerisches Nationalmuseum, Munich 173, 182; Joachim Blauel, Munich **86**, **99**, **101**, **106**, **166**, **175**, **176**, **191**, **192**, **193**, **194**, **196**, **219**, **231**, **232**; Joachim Blauel–Bavaria **130**; Wolfgang Braunfels **38**; F. Bruckmann Verlag 25, 49, 72, 81, 91, 102, 109, 140, 172, 198, 207, 211, 213, 216, 217, 224, 236, 240, 243; Deutsche Presse Agentur, Frankfurt on Main 239; Dyckerhoff & Widman, Munich 234; R. B. Fleming and Co., London Introduction; Hans Jürgen Hansen, Munich 141, 205, 206; Claus Hansmann, Munich 179; W. Hege–Bavaria 67; Hessisches Landesmuseum, Darmstadt 222, 223; M. Holford, London **200**; Jos. Jeiter, Hadamar 28, 32, 35, 46, 50; K. M. Kempter–Bavaria **149**; Walter Klein, Düsseldorf **249**; Kleinhempel, Hamburg **79**, **201**, **220**; Dagmar Korn, Düsseldorf 241; Krause–Willenberg–Bavaria 188; Photo Löbl, Bad Tolz 20, **39**, 92, 104, 105, 110, 125, **143**, 151, **164**, **255**; Walter Lüden, Hamburg 11, 15, 68, 69, 70, 127, 199; Bildarchiv Foto Marburg 13, 17, 26, 29, 31, 33, 36, 47, 53, 54, 55, 71, 89, 94, 112, 181, 197; Omnia–Bavaria **155**; Johannes Padelt–Bavaria 129; U. Pfistermeister, Artelshofen 51, 52, 56, 82, 88, 90, 126, 138, 152, 174, 180; Pinakothek, Munich 137; Preiss & Co., Munich **Frontispiece**, 75, **78**, 84, 85, **96**, **97**, **108**, **115**, **117**, **144**, **147**, **156**, **165**, **190**, **204**, **218**, **221**, **225**, **226**, **229**, **230**, **233**, **244**, **245**, **246**, **247**, **248**, **250**, **251**, **253**, **257**, **258**; Hans Rathschlag, Cologne 95; G. Reinhold, Leipzig-Molkau **132**, **195**, **202**; Hans Retzlaff–Bavaria 34, **57**, 170; Scala, Florence–**Front jacket**, **half title**, 2, 4, 5, 6, 7, 8, 9, 22, 23, 24, 40, 42, 43, 44, 58, 59, 61, 62, 63, **64**, 65, 66, 73, 74, 76, 77, 87, 98, 100, 107, **116**, 118, 119, 120, 121, **131**, 133, 145, 146, 148, 150, 154, **161**, **162**, **163**, 167, 168, 169, **171**, 177, **227**, **228**, 252, **256**; Toni Schneiders, Lindau 37, 128, 135, 153, 157, 178, 185, 186, **254**; Th. & H. Seeger, Egg 12, 19, 21; J. Slominsky, Essen **41**; Staatliche Kunsthalle, Karlsruhe 183, 210; Staatliche Museen, East Berlin **203**, 208, 215; Staatliche Museen, West Berlin 209; Staatliche Museen Gemäldegalerie, West Berlin 142; Staatliche Museen, Nationalgalerie, West Berlin, 242; Ullstein, Berlin Contents page, 16, 27, 80, 93, 103, 114, 134, 158, 160; Ullstein–Eckelt 18; Ullstein–Hans Retzlaff 30, 48, 111, 113, 187; Ullstein–W. Stangenberg 139; Verkehrsamt der Stadt–Köln **60**; Wilhelm-Lembruck Museum, Duisburg 237; Liselotte Witzel, Essen 238.

No **247** Rights Reserved ADAGP, Paris
Nos **244**, **250** © SPADEM, Paris 1969

Art Treasures in northern Germany

Cathedrals, Churches and Monasteries ✠
Roman Remains 🏛
Museums and Libraries ⌂
Civic and Public Buildings ⌂
Palaces and Castles ♜

The museums and monuments shown on this map
are listed on pages 164-172

NORTH SEA

Seebüll
Flensburg
Glücksbu
Schleswig
Tönning
Bordesho
SCHLESW

Neuwerk

Lüdingworth

Stade

Emden

Bremen

LOWER SAXONY

Cloppenburg

Osnabrück
Minden
Ha
Bückeburg
Hameln
Hilde
Hämelschenburg

Münster

NORTHERN RHINELAND-WESTPHALIA

Kalkar
Xanten
Recklinghausen
Detmold
Extern Stones
Corvey
Essen
Dortmund
Soest
Paderborn
Lippoldsbe
Duisburg
Essen-Werden
Hagen
Mönchen-
Gladbach
Düsseldorf
Arolsen
Kassel
Brauweiler
COLOGNE
Fritzlar
Aachen
Brühl
Siegen
Haina
Schwarz-Rheindorf
Bonn
Marburg
Remagen
Hersfeld
BELGIUM
HESSE
Andernach
Giessen
Laachersee
Koblenz
Wetzlar
Fulda
Bürresheim
Limburg an der Lahn
RHINELAND-
PALATINATE
Eltz
Gelnhausen
Cochem
St Goar
FRANKFURT AM MAIN
Karden
Kiedrich

THE NETHERLANDS